BIBLIOGRAPHY
OF THE
Continental Reformation

Materials Available in English

Second Edition
Revised and Enlarged

by
ROLAND H. BAINTON
and
ERIC W. GRITSCH

Archon Books
1972

Library of Congress Cataloging in Publication Data

Bainton, Roland Herbert, 1894–
  Bibliography of the continental reformation.

  1. Reformation--Bibliography. I. Gritsch, Eric
W. joint author. II. Title.
Z7830.B16 1972   016.2706   72-8216
ISBN 0-208-01219-0

First edition © 1935 by the American Society of Church History.
Second edition © 1972 by The Shoe String Press, Inc. Published
1972 as an Archon Book by The Shoe String Press, Inc., Hamden,
Connecticut 06514

CONTENTS

FOREWORD

This bibliography is designed to meet the needs of the student of the Reformation who is limited to the English language. His wants are not adequately served by the magnificent work of Karl Schottenloher, *Bibliographie zur deutschen Geschichte im Zeitalter der Glaubensspaltung 1517-1585* (Leipzig, 1933-), to which the advanced student will necessarily turn. English titles in this work are comparatively few and not easy to segregate. The English Reformation has been eliminated from our survey because material is abundant on this subject in English and we have the bibliography of Conyers Read, *Bibliography of British History,* Tudor Period, *1485-1603* (Oxford, 1933), and the section on the English Reformation in S. J. Case, *A Bibliographical Guide to the History of Christianity* (Chicago, 1931), consists almost entirely of material in English. The omission of the precursors and of the Counter-reformation in our survey is a matter of arbitrary delimitation. There is no pretense of completeness, but there has been less selection in the case of neglected folk like the Anabaptists than for the major figures on whom there are good modern biographies. Similarly with regard to translation, where there are modern editions the reader is referred to the bibliographies for the earlier and more inaccessible material.

Brackets indicate information supplied from a source outside the book. No distinction is made between a publication date on the title page and a copyright date on the reverse. The latest edition known to me is listed, not the latest impression.

I am indebted for help in checking to Mr. J. H. Melzer.

Roland H. Bainton

FOREWORD TO THE SECOND EDITION

I have been loyal to my "doctor father's" basic method used in the first edition. What he said then about the needs of the student of the Reformation is still true: his wants are not adequately served by other available bibliographies.

Meanwhile, the abundant materials on the English Reformation are available in the second edition of Conyers Read, *Bibliography of British History, Tudor Period, 1485-1603* (Oxford, 1959). This volume discloses the mass of recent English-language publications on the continental Reformation. I have listed the works I found and blended them into Professor Bainton's edition. To achieve perfection in such a collection of materials is well-nigh impossible. So I apologize in advance to unlisted authors, and I encourage them to provide me with the bibliographical data of their work—perhaps for a third edition!

The Roman Catholic reform, Erasmus and Arminius have been included in this edition. These inclusions are as arbitrary as the omissions. Here too I am following Professor Bainton's arbitrary delimitations.

As always, I am tremendously indebted to my wife Ruth, who has become my expert editor and typist. Mr. David P. Gleason, my student assistant, deserves special thanks for perusing a number of journals in search of material.

E. W. G.

ABBREVIATIONS OF JOURNALS

AB	*Art Bulletin,* New York, 1913+
ACQ	*American Catholic Quarterly Review,* Philadelphia, 1876-1960. Becomes *Church Theological Review,* N.Y. 1961+
AHAP	*American Historical Association Papers,* N.Y., & Washington, 1885-91.
AHR	*American Historical Review,* N.Y., 1895+
AJE	*American Journal of Education* (Ed. Barnard), Hartford, Conn., 1855-82
AJT	*American Journal of Theology,* Chicago, 1887-1920.
AQ	*Augustana Quarterly,* Rock Island, Ill., 1922-1948, continued by LQ
AR	*Andover Review,* Boston & N.Y., 1884-93.
ARG	*Archiv für Reformationsgeschichte,* Gütersloh, 1903+
ASCH	*American Society of Church History Papers,* N.Y., 1888-97, 2S 1906-1934.
BHR	*Bibliothèque d'Humanisme et Renaissance,* Paris, 1941+
BHS	*Baptist Historical Society, Transactions of,* Ld., 1909+
BJRL	*Bulletin of the John Rylands Library,* Manchester, 1903+
BLFRR	*Bulletin of the Library, Foundation for Reformation Research,* St. Louis, Mo., 1966+
BMC	*Burlington Magazine for Connoisseurs,* Ld., 1903+
BQ (Ld)	*Baptist Quarterly,* Ld., including the Transactions of the *Baptist Historical Society,* ns 1922+
BQ (Ph)	*Baptist Quarterly,* Philadelphia, 1867-77, continued by BR.
BQR	*Baptist Quarterly Review,* Cincinnati & N.Y., 1881-92, continuation of BR.
BR	*Baptist Review,* Cincinnati, 1879-81, continuation of BQ (Ph), continued by BQR.
BS	*Bibliotheca Sacra,* Andover, Mass., and Oberlin, O., 1844+
BSA	*Bibliographical Society of America, Papers of,* N.Y., 1904/06+

BW   *Biblical World,* Chicago, 1882-92, ns 1893-1920.
CBQ   *Catholic Biblical Quarterly,* Washington, D.C., 1939+
CC   *Christian Century,* Chicago, 1884+
CH   *Church History,* Chicago, 1932+
CHJ   *Cambridge Historical Journal,* Ld., 1923+
CHR   *Catholic Historical Review,* Washington, 1915-21, ns
          1921+
ConQ   *Constructive Quarterly,* N.Y., & Ld., 1913-22.
CQ   *Crozer Quarterly,* Philadelphia, 1924+
CR   *Contemporary Review,* Ld., 1866+
CTJ   *Calvin Theological Journal,* Grand Rapids, Mich., 1966+
CTM   *Concordia Theological Monthly,* St. Louis, 1930+
CW   *Catholic World,* N.Y., 1865+
D   *Dialog, a Journal of Theology,* Minneapolis, Minn.,
          1962+
EcHR   *Economic History Review,* Ld., 1927+
EHR   *English Historical Review,* Ld., 1886+
EQ   *Evangelical Quarterly,* London, 1929+
ER   *Edinburgh Review,* 1802+
ET   *Expository Times,* Aberdeen & Edinburgh, 1889+
GCR   *Goshen College Record,* Goshen, Ind.
GR   *Germanic Review* (Columbia, Univ.) N.Y., 1926+
H   *History,* London, 1912+
HCS   *Haverford College Studies,* Haverford, Pa., 1889-1922.
HSA   *Huguenot Society of America, Proceedings of,* N.Y.,
          1883+
HSL   *Huguenot Society of London, Proceedings of,* Ld.,
          1885+
HTR   *Harvard Theological Review,* Cambridge, Mass., 1908+
HTS   *Harvard Theological Studies,* Cambridge, Mass., 1916+
I   *Interpretation,* Richmond, Va., 1947+
JBR   *Journal of Bible and Religion,* Walcott, N.Y., 1933+
JEGP   *Journal of English and Germanic Philology,* Urbana,
          Ill., 1897+
JEH   *Journal of Ecclesiastical History,* London, 1950+
JES   *Journal of Ecumenical Studies,* Pittsburgh, 1964+
JHH   *Johns Hopkins Hospital Bulletin,* Baltimore, Md.,
          1890+

JHI   *Journal of the History of Ideas,* Lancaster, Pa. & N.Y.,
          1940+
JMH   *Journal of Modern History,* Chicago, 1929+
JPE   *Journal of Political Economy,* Chicago, 1892+
JPHS   *Journal of the Presbyterian Historical Society,* Phila-
          delphia, 1901+
JR   *Journal of Religion,* Chicago, 1921+
JRH   *Journal of Religious History,* Sidney, 1960+
JRT   *Journal of Religious Thought,* Washington, D.C.,
          1943+
JTS   *Journal of Theological Studies,* Ld., 1899+
LA   *Living Age,* Boston, 1844+
LCQ   *Lutheran Church Quarterly,* Gettysburg, Pa., 1928-
          1949.
LCR   *Lutheran Church Review,* Philadelphia, 1882+
LQ   *Lutheran Quarterly,* Gettysburg, Pa., ns 1871-1926,
          1949+
          Lutheran Theological Seminaries, Editorial Council,
          Gettysburg, Pa., 1949+
LW   *Lutheran World* (Lutheran World Federation) Ham-
          burg, 1954+
ML   *Mennonite Life,* Newton, Kansas, 1946+
MQR   *Mennonite Quarterly Review,* Goshen, Ind., 1927+
MdR   *Modern Review,* Ld., 1880-84.
MethR   *Methodist Review,* Louisville, Ky., 1847+
MR   *Mercersburg Review,* 1849-78, continued by RQR.
OC   *Open Court,* Chicago, 1887+
PRR   *Presbyterian and Reformed Review,* N.Y., & Philadel-
          phia, 1890-1902, continued by PTR.
PTR   *Princeton Theological Review,* Princeton, N.J., 1903+
QR   *Quarterly Review,* Ld., 1809+
RCR   *Reformed Church Review,* Lancaster, Pa., 1897-1926,
          continuation of RQR.
RL   *Religion in Life,* N.Y., 1932+
RQR   *Reformed Quarterly Review,* Philadelphia, 1879-96,
          continuation of MR, continued by RCR.
RfR   *Reformed Review,* Holland, Mich., 1947+, continuation
          of RCR

RR   *Review of Religion*, N.Y., 1936-1958.
RST   *Reformationsgeschichtliche Studien und Texte*, Münster,
          1906+
SAQ   *South Atlantic Quarterly*, Durham, N.C., 1902+
SCJ   *The Sixteenth Century Journal*, St. Louis, Mo., 1972+
          Continuation of *Sixteenth Century Essays and Studies*,
          St. Louis, 1970-71.
SJT   *Scottish Journal of Theology*, Edinburgh, 1948+
SR   *School Review*, Ithaca, N.Y., 1893+
SS   *School and Society*, N.Y., 1915+
SWJT   *Southwestern Journal of Theology*, Fort Worth, Tex.,
          1958+
TR   *Theological Review*, Ld., 1864-79.
TS   *Theological Studies*, N.Y., 1940+
TT   *Theology Today*, Philadelphia, 1944+
UR   *Unitarian Review*, Boston, 1874-91.
US   *Una Sancta*, Ridgefield Park, N.J., 1940+
ZKG   *Zeitschrift für Kirchengeschichte*, Gotha & Tübingen,
          1876+

Other Journals

Art Bulletin, N.Y., 1-6, -1907, supplement, 1944+
Atlantic Baptist, New Brunswick, 1827+
Auburn Seminary Record, Auburn, N.Y.
Bibliotheca Sacra, Andover, Mass., & Oberlin, O., 1844+
Brethren Life and Thought, Chicago, 1956+
Bulletin of the American Congregational Association, Boston,
          1949+
Bulletin of the History of Medicine, Baltimore, 1933+
Century Illustrated Magazine, N.Y., 1870+
Heythrop Journal, Oxford, 1960+
Hibbert Journal, London, Boston, 1902+
Huntington Library Quarterly, Cambridge, Mass., 1937+
The Interior, Chicago, 1870-1910, when it became *The Continent*.
Library Quarterly, Chicago, 1931+
Medievalia et Humanistica, Boulder, Colo., 1943+; Cleveland,
          1970+
North American Review, Boston, 1815+

Renaissance Quarterly, N.Y., 1967+
Review and Expositor, Louisville, Ky., 1904+
Studies in the Renaissance, N.Y., 1956+
Union Seminary Magazine=Union Seminary Review (Union
　　　　　　Theological Seminary) Richmond, Va., 1889+
Union Seminary Quarterly Review, N.Y., 1945+
Westminster Theological Journal, Philadelphia, 1938+

BIBLIOGRAPHIES

(See also individual reformers, countries and movements)

ADAMS, HERBERT M. (COMP.). *Catalogue of Books Printed on the Continent of Europe 1501-1600 in Cambridge Libraries.* 2 vols. London & Cambridge, 1967.

BAINTON, ROLAND H., (COMP.). *Survey of Periodical Literature in the United States, 1945-1951.* ARG XLIII (1952), 88-106.

BESTERMAN, THEODORE. *Early Printed Books to the End of the Sixteenth Century: a Bibliography of Bibliographies.* 2nd ed. Geneva, 1961. 2389 entries. Indices: authors, subjects, printers and booksellers, printing places, libraries. *A World Bibliography of Bibliographies.* 4th ed., 5 vols. Geneva, 1965.

CASE, SHIRLEY JACKSON, ED. *Bibliographical Guide to the History of Christianity.* Chicago, 1931. xi+265 pages.

COMITÉ INTERNATIONAL DES SCIENCES HISTORIQUES. *Bibliographie de la Réforme, 1450-1648.* Leiden, 1958-. This international bibliography contains works which appeared from 1940 to 1955. The fascicules cover various countries. English titles are listed in the alphabetical author list. Available fascicules are:
1. Germany and the Netherlands, edited by Günter Franz, 1958, 1961. 156 pages.
2. Belgium, Sweden, Norway, Denmark (Ireland and U.S.A.), edited by Léon E. Halkin and Raymond W. Albright, 1960. 156 pages.
3. Italy, Spain, Portugal, edited by Paolo Brezzi and Eugenio Dupré-Theseider, 1961. 138 pages.
4. France (England) and Switzerland, edited by J. Queguiner and others, 1963. 145 pages.
5. Poland, Hungary, Czechoslovakia and Finland, edited by Anna Kotarska, 1965. 108 pages.
6. Austria, edited by Gerhard Rill, 1967. 47 pages.

CORNELL UNIVERSITY LIBRARY OF. *Catalogue of the President White Library. 1. The Protestant Reformation and Its Forerunners.* Ithaca, N.Y., 1889. vi+93 pages. *Supplement: Portraits of the Reformers,* pp. 95-106. Compiled with excellent notes by George Lincoln Burr.

DICKENS, A. G. *Recent Books on Reformation and Counter-Reformation.* JEH XIX, 2 (1968), 219-226.

GRIMM, HAROLD J. *Reformation Research.* LQ III, 3 (1951), 313-314. *The Reformation Era, 1500-1650.* London and N.Y., 1954. *Bibliography,* pp. 617-684. Excellent guide.

A Guide to Historical Literature, edited by William Henry Allison and others. N.Y., 1931, xxxviii+1922 pages.

HINZ, JAMES A. *Toward the Control of Bibliography for the Study of the Sixteenth Century.* BLFRR VI (1971), 1-8. Helpful hints on how to use bibliographical aids. Lists a bibliography of bibliographies.

The Historical Association. Leaflet No. 55. *Bibliography of Church History* prepared by J. P. Whitney. Ld., May, 1923. 44 pages.

The Historical Association. Leaflet No. 66. *The History of the Church. A Select Bibliography.* 2nd ed., prepared by Owen Chadwick. London, 1966. 52 pages.

HUDSON, WINTHROP S. *Post-Reformation Church History. Studies published in the United States Since the War.* JEH I, 2 (1950), 225-231. Discusses Reformation materials.

KIEFFER, GEORGE LINN, ROCKWELL, WILLIAM WALKER and PANNKOKE, OTTO HERMANN. *List of References on the History of the Reformation in Germany.* White Plains, N.Y., 1917. 60 pages.

KRÜGER, GUSTAV, *Literature on Church History in Germany, Austria, Switzerland, Holland and the Scandinavian Countries, 1914-1920.* III. The Reformation and the Counter Reformation. HTR XVII (1924), 2-49.

MCGIFFERT, ARTHUR C. *Special Reading List. The Reformation.* Bulletin of the General Theological Library. IX, 2. Boston, Mass., Jan., 1917. 19 pages.

MCSHANE, E. D. *The History of the Church from 1300 to 1648: A Survey of Research, 1955-1960.* TS XXII, 1 (1961), 59-85.

PAUCK, WILHELM. *The Historiography of the German Reformation during the Past Twenty Years.* CH IX, 4 (1940), 305-340.

RICHARDSON, ERNEST CUSHING, *An Alphabetical Subject Index and Index Encyclopaedia to Periodical Articles on Religion, 1890-1899.* N.Y., 1907. xlii+1168 pages.

ROACH, JOHN (ED.) *A Bibliography of Modern History.* Cambridge, 1968. XXIV + 388 pages.
Lists international publications on the continental reformation. Contains the most significant English titles.

ROBINSON, JAMES HARVEY, *The Study of the Lutheran Revolt,* AHR VIII (1903), 205-216.

RYAN, M. *Recent Works on the Reformation.* ACQ XXXVI (1911), 691-711.

SMITH, GERALD BIRNEY, ED. *A Guide to the Study of the Christian Religion.* Chicago, 1916. x+759 pages.

SPITZ, LEWIS W., (ED). *Guide to Reformation Literature; Study Projects in Commemoration of the 450th Anniversary of the Reformation, 1517-1967.* With contributions by Heino O. Kadai. N.Y., 1967. 24 pages.
Limited. Useful for beginners.
Reformation and Humanism in Marxist Historical Research. LW XVI (1969), 1924-1939.

Successor to a Guide to Historical Literature, edited by George Frederick Howe and others. N.Y., 1961. xxxv + 962 pages.

SWIDLER, LEONARD. *Catholic Reformation Scholarship in Germany.* JES II, 2 (1965), 189-204.

WINCHELL, CONSTANCE M. *Guide to Reference Books.* VIIth enlarged edition of I. G. Mudge's book by same title. Chicago, 1951.
This is the basic source for all fields of research.
References to the continental Reformation are listed under "modern history" and names of countries.

Compare also the bibliographies in the *Cambridge Modern History* II, Cambridge, Eng., 1904, and Preserved Smith, *Age of the Reformation,* N.Y., 1920.

ENCYCLOPEDIA ARTICLES

The Catholic Encyclopedia, 17 vols. N.Y., 1907-1922.
Is valuable for the point of view.

The Cyclopedia of Biblical, Theological and Ecclesiastical Literature, by John McClintock and James Strong. 12 vols. N.Y., 1891. Has a large number of brief accurate articles by such men as Philip Schaff, G. P. Fisher and H. E. Jacobs.

A Cyclopedia of Education. Paul Monroe, 5 vols. N.Y., 1911-1913. Has in the index a subject entry "Reformation and Education" and a list of Reformation educators. Among the articles are: Reformation and Education, Arthur F. Leach; Calvin and Calvinism, Herbert D. Foster; Castellion, Catechisms and Luther, Foster Watson; Beza, Percival R. Cole; Ramus, Frank P. Graves; Brenz, Corderius, Melanchthon, John Sturm and Zwingli, unsigned.

The Encyclopedia Americana, IVth edition, 30 vols. N.Y., Chicago, Washington, 1957. This edition contains a number of articles equaling, and sometimes surpassing, those in the *Britannica.* Wilhelm Pauck heads a list of Reformation scholars who contributed to this edition. Some articles are unsigned.

The Encyclopaedia Britannica, XIth edition, 29 vols. Cambridge, Eng., 1910-1911; XIVth edition, 24 vols. Ld., and N.Y., 1929. There is a classified list of articles under the headings "Reformation subjects" and "Reformation biographies." The range is by no means so extensive as in the Schaff-Herzog. The articles are usually shorter and frequently unsigned. The fourteenth edition is a mutilation of the eleventh. In but very few cases has new work been introduced. In the eleventh the article Reformation was by James Harvey Robinson, in the fourteenth by G. G. Coulton, who draws heavily on his stores of medieval lore to illustrate the background. The article Luther in the eleventh was by T. M. Lindsay, in the fourteenth by James Mackinnon.
A revised edition, 23 vols. Chicago, Toronto, Geneva, Sydney, Tokyo, 1966. This edition introduces new work. The articles on Luther and the Reformation in general are by E. Gordon Rupp; on Calvin by Edward A. Dowey and on the Anabaptists by George H. Williams. Brief bibliographical sketches follow the articles.

The Encyclopedia of the Lutheran Church, edited by Julius Bodensieck. 3 vols. Philadelphia, 1965.

Contains materials relating to the Lutheran World Federation.
The articles on the Reformation are uneven. Roland H.
Bainton's *Luther* is a gem. The article on Thomas Müntzer
has been translated from another encyclopedia without
references to sources or author. Much of the material is
dated, since it is taken from older German reference works.

The Encyclopedia of Philosophy, edited by Paul Edwards. 8 vols.
London and N.Y., 1967.
Contains a general article on the Reformation by B. A. Gerrish and articles on less than 20 reformers, seemingly selected
at random. Zwingli, for example, is left out. The article on
Sebastian Franck is excellent and is followed by an almost
complete bibliography. The articles on *German, Hungarian,*
and *Polish Philosophy,* under the heading of *Reformation,*
are useful.

The Encyclopaedia of the Social Sciences, N.Y., 1930-.
This work is making a distinct contribution in the few articles
which touch the Reformation. The one by Gerhard Ritter
on Luther is a gem. Walter Köhler has done Castellio. Why
was Acontius omitted? Sebastian Franck is the work of Karl
Völker, and Thomas Münzer of Michael Freund.

The Encyclopaedia of Religion and Ethics, 13 vols., N.Y., 1908-
1927.
Has a detailed subject index. The major articles on the Reforma-
tion are few. Anabaptism receives a brief external survey by
W. J. McGlothlin. H. M. Gwatkin has done the article Reforma-
tion with a long discussion of the causes especially the economic
and moral abuses. Further articles are: Calvinism, James Orr;
Covenant Theology, William Adams Brown; Erastianism, J.
Y. Evans; Huguenots, W. T. Whitley; Luther, Henry E. Jacobs;
Mennonites, W. J. Kühler; Synergism, D. Mackenzie; Typology,
J. R. Darbyshire; Unitarianism, J. E. Carpenter.

An Encyclopedia of Religion, edited by Vergilius Ferm. N.Y., 1945.
xix + 844 pages.
Updates the *Encyclopedia of Religion and Ethics.* The articles
are very short, but informative. Most subjects related to the
Reformation are covered by competent scholars. Wilhelm
Pauck wrote on Luther, Reformation, and Matthew Spinka
and Gerald R. Cragg wrote articles. Articles on the "left wing"

of the Reformation are slightly outdated (Müntzer is still regarded as an "Anabaptist").

An Encyclopedia of World History, IVth edition by William L. Langer. Boston, 1968. XXXVII + 1504 pages.

Based on the German handbook *Ploetz,* this volume presents chronological sketches of the continental reformation in the various countries. Excellent index.

International Encyclopedia of the Social Sciences. 17 vols. N.Y., 1968.

Since all articles are limited to 5000 words, scholars had to cling to essentials. Articles by noted Reformation experts include Lewis W. Spitz on Luther and John T. McNeill on Calvin. But omissions such as "Reformation," "Müntzer," and a number of other men, movements and ideas, weaken this edition.

The Lutheran Encylopedia, one vol. N.Y., 1899, edited by Henry Eyster Jacobs.

Is concerned chiefly with American Lutheranism. There are treatments of Luther, the Augsburg Confession and the Schmalkald articles.

The Mennonite Encyclopedia. 4 vols. Hillsboro, Kan., 1955-1959. Vol. I reissued in 1969, slightly revised.

Comprehensive work on the Reformation, and excellent source on the "left wing." Signed articles by scholars from various traditions, supplemented by excellent bibliographical references.

The New Cambridge Modern History. 14 vols. Cambridge, 1957-1970. Vol. II, *The Reformation 1520-59,* contains very good summaries by Reformation scholars. E. G. Rupp and Ernst Bizer on Luther and Germany; E. A. Payne on Switzerland; N. K. Andersen on Scandinavia and the Baltic; Delio Contimori on Italy; F. C. Spooner on France; and R. R. Betts on Poland, Bohemia and Hungary.

Vol. III, *The Counter-Reformation and Price Revolution 1559-1610* contains a very good summary of Roman Catholic, Lutheran and Calvinist developments, written by T. M. Parker.

The New Catholic Encyclopedia. 15 vols, prepared by an editorial staff at the Catholic University of America. New York, St. Louis, San Francisco, Toronto, London, Sidney, 1967.

Reflects a new point of view. The signed articles are followed
by brief bibliographies reflecting ecumenical scholarship.
W. S. Barron's article on the continental Protestant Reformation is very useful. John P. Dolan did a revisionist article on
Luther.

New Schaff-Herzog Encyclopedia of Religious Knowledge, 12
vols. N.Y., 1908-1912. Vol. XIII, Index prepared by George
William Gilmore, c. 1914.
This encyclopedia is the best for the Reformation. Most of
the articles are by the German specialists whose work frequently is available in English in no other form. The index
volume appeared two years after the set and sometimes does
not accompany it, but the list of contributors serves much
the same purpose, if one is aware that for the Italian Reformation one should consult Benrath, for the French Bonet-
Maury, for doctrine R. Seeberg and Kattenbusch, for polity
and law Sehling, for Lutheranism Kawerau, Köstlin and Kolde,
for Württemberg G. Bossert, for Hesse Carl Mirbt, for Basel
R. Staehlin, for Montbeliard John Vienot, for some of the
heretics Lachenmann, for the Anabaptists and Spiritual Reformers Hegler, revised by Holl, and also A. H. Newman and
W. Köhler, for Calvinism Warfield, and for miscellaneous
topics Hermelink, Karl Müller, Paul Tschackert, Philip and
David Schaff.

The Oxford Dictionary of the Christian Church, edited by F. L.
Cross. London, N.Y., Toronto, 1957. xix+1942 pages.
Valuable because of its excellent bibliographical references.
Articles unsigned, but contributors listed.

Twentieth Century Encyclopedia of Religious Knowledge, edited
by Lefferts A. Loetscher, an extension of *The New Schaff-
Herzog Encyclopedia.* 2 vols. Grand Rapids, Mich., 1955.
Contains some very good brief essays on Luther by Ernest
G. Schwiebert, the Reformation by Albert Hyma, Calvin by
John T. McNeill, and related men, movements and ideas.
The bibliographical references are very useful, though in-
complete. A very good general reference work.

The Westminster Dictionary of Church History, edited by Jerald
C. Brauer. Philadelphia, 1971. VII + 887 pages.
Emphasis on the history of the institutional church. The brief

articles are unsigned, but contributors are listed. Some articles are uneven in quality. The article on Müntzer, for example, lack the insights of modern scholarship (he is labeled "anabaptist"), while the article on "radical Reformation" uses the latest research.

COLLECTED ESSAYS ON THE REFORMATION

BAINTON, ROLAND H. *Studies on the Reformation* (Collected Papers in Church History Series Two). Boston, 1963. 289 pages.
Illuminating essays, produced over the years, on Luther, the left wing, and post-Reformation struggles. Most of these essays have been published in books and journals.
The Bible and the Reformation. pp. 1-12.
Luther's Struggle for Faith. pp. 13-19.
Luther's Attitudes on Religious Liberty. pp. 20-45.
Luther and the Via Media at the Marburg Colloquy. pp. 46-50.
The Man of Sorrows in Dürer and Luther. pp. 51-61.
The Joachimite Prophecy: Osiander and Sachs. pp. 62-66.
Luther on Birds, Dogs and Babies. pp. 67-74.
Luther's Life in Review: Critiques of Heinrich Böhmer and Erik Erikson. pp. 75-103.
Interpretations of the Reformation. pp. 104-116.
The Left Wing of the Reformation. pp. 119-129.
New Documents on Early Protestant Rationalism. pp. 130-138.
Sebastian Castellio, Champion of Religious Liberty. pp. 139-181.
William Postell and the Netherlands. pp. 185-198.
Sebastion Castellio and the British-American Tradition. pp. 182-184.
The Anabaptist Contribution to History. pp. 199-207.
The Struggle for Religious Liberty. pp. 211-242.
St. Ignatius Loyola's Methods of Religious Teaching. pp. 243-247.
GERRISH, BRIAN A. (ED.) *Reformers in Profile.* Philadelphia, 1967. vii+264 pages.

Essays on reformers, with bibliographies.

SPITZ, LEWIS W. *Desiderius Erasmus.* pp. 60-83

CRANZ, EDWARD F. *Martin Luther.* pp. 86-114.

THOMPSON, BARD. *Ulrich Zwingli.* pp. 115-141.

GERRISH, BRIAN A. *John Calvin.* pp. 142-164.

WENGER, JOHN C. *Menno Simons.* pp. 194-212.

HILLERBRAND, HANS J. *Thomas Muentzer,* pp. 213-229.

McNALLY, ROBERT E. *Ignatius Loyola.* pp. 232-256.

HURSTFIELD, JOEL (ED.) *The Reformation Crisis.* New York, 1965. 2d ed. 1966. ix+126 pages.

Essays based on a BBC broadcast in 1962, with a brief bibliography.

HAY, DENIS. *The Background to the Reformation.* pp. 8-20.

RUPP, GORDON E. *Luther and the Reformation.* pp. 21-31.

POTTER, G. R. *Zwingli and Calvin.* pp. 32-43.

EVENNETT, H. O. *The Counter-Reformation.* pp. 58-71.

ELTON, G. R. *1555: A Political Retrospect.* pp. 72-82.

KOENIGSBERGER, H. G. *The Reformation and Social Revolution.* pp. 83-94.

HURSTFIELD, JOEL. *The Search for Compromise in England and France.* pp. 95-106.

MEYER, CARL S. (ED.) *Sixteenth Century Essays and Studies.* 2 vols. St. Louis, 1970.

Papers of the Sixteenth Century Studies Conferences. Vol. I. 125 pages.

PEACHEY, PAUL. *Marxist Historiography of the Radical Reformation: Causality or Covariation?* pp. 1-16.

FRIESEN, ABRAHAM. *The Marxist Interpretation of Anabaptism.* pp. 17-34.

GROSSMANN, MARIA. *Wittenberg Printing, Early Sixteenth Century.* pp. 53-74.

ANDERSON, MARVIN A.

Gregorio Cortese and Roman Catholic Reform. pp. 75-106.

LINDBERG, CARTER. *Luther and Feuerbach.* pp. 107-125.

Vol. II. 118 pages.

PAYNE, JOHN B. *Erasmus: Interpreter of Romans.* pp. 1-35.

REID, STANFORD W. *The Battle Hymns of the Lord. Cal-*

1950. Rev. and enlarged edition, Glencoe, Ill., 1961. London, Oxford, N.Y., 1968. x+399 pages.

A collection of classic essays on the Reformation and on Protestantism.

Luther and the Reformation. pp. 3-17.

Luther's Faith. pp. 19-28.

Luther's Conception of the Church. pp. 29-59.

Calvin's Institutes. pp. 61-72.

Luther and Butzer. pp. 73-83.

Calvin and Butzer. pp. 85-99.

The Ministry in the Time of the Reformation. pp. 101-142.

Protestant Reactions to the Council of Trent. pp. 145-161.

RUPP, E. GORDON. *Patterns of Reformation.* London, Philadelphia, 1969. xxiii+427 pages.

Excellent biographical essays.

Johannes Oecolompadius: The Reformer as Scholar. pp. 3-46.

Andrew Karlstadt: The Reformer as Puritan. pp. 49-153.

Thomas Müntzer: The Reformer as Rebel. pp. 157-353.

Vadianus and Johannes Kessler of St. Gall. pp. 357-399.

Includes a translation of *Of the Mystery of Baptism,* ascribed to Hans Hut.

STEINMETZ, DAVID C. *Reformers in the Wings.* Philadelphia, 1971. ix+240 pages.

Biographical essays with bibliographies.

Johannes Staupitz. pp. 18-29.

Gasparo Contarini. pp. 30-42.

Philip Melanchthon. pp. 69-81.

Johannes Bugenhagen. pp. 82-90.

Andreas Osiander. pp. 91-99.

Nikolaus von Amsdorf. pp. 100-108.

Johannes Brenz. pp. 109-118.

Martin Bucer. pp. 121-132.

Heinrich Bullinger. pp. 133-142.

Peter Martyr Vermigli. pp. 151-161.

Theodore Beza. pp. 162-171.

Andreas Bodenstein von Carlstadt. pp. 175-185.

Caspar Schwenckfeld. pp. 186-196.

Balthasar Hubmaier. pp. 197-208.

Hans Denck. pp. 209-218.

Pilgram Marbeck. pp. 219-230.

STRAND, KENNETH A. (ED.) *Essays on the Northern Renaissance.* Ann Arbor, Mich., 1968. 128 pages.

HOAR, GEORGE A. *Protestant Reformation—A Tragedy or Triumph for Christian Humanism?* pp. 67-91.

SOWARDS, J. K. *Erasmus and the Apologetic Textbook: a Study of the De Duplici Copia Verborum Ac Rerum.* pp. 92-106.

WHITNEY, JAMES P. *Reformation Essays.* London, 1939. 171 pages.

Pertinent topics included in this volume:

Continuity Throughout the Reformation.

Erasmus.

Luther Literature.

Lutheran Germany and the Episcopate.

SOURCES IN TRANSLATION

(See also individual reformers and countries)

ALDEN, JOHN (COMP.) *Early English Books in the Georgetown University Library; a checklist of the 1540-1640 period.* Washington, 1952.

Based on *A Short-Title Catalogue . . .* by Pollard and Redgrave.

BAINTON, ROLAND H. *The Age of Reformation.* New York, Princeton, Toronto, London, 1956. 192 pages.

Readings in Luther, Zwingli, Calvin, the radicals in Germany and Switzerland. Political documents such as edicts, confessions and court records are also included.

ELTON, GEOFFREY R. *Renaissance and Reformation, 1300-1648* (Ideas and Institutions in Western Civilization series, 3). New York, 1963. xii+305 pages.

Broad representative collection.

FOSDICK, HARRY E. *Great Voices of the Reformation, an Anthology.* N.Y., 1952. xxx+546 pages.

Contains excerpts from Luther's most popular treatises, as

well as from Melanchthon, Zwingli, Calvin and some Anabaptists. Not as useful as some more modern collections.

HAGEN, KENNETH. *An Addition to the Letters of John Lang.
Introduction and Translation.* ARG LX (1969), 27-32.
Addressed to George Spalatin, showing his friendly relation-
ship with Luther in 1516.

HILLERBRAND, HANS J. *The Reformation; a Narrative History
Related by Contemporary Observers and Participants* (Lon-
don edition entitled *The Reformation in Its Own Words*).
N.Y., 1964. 495 pages.
The strength of this collection is the translation of left wing
sources and political documents.
The Protestant Reformation (Documentary History of West-
ern Civilization series). New York, 1968. xxvii+290 pages.
Not as valuable as the earlier collection. Contains helpful
bibliographical notes emphasizing English works.

KIDD, B. J. *Documents Illustrative of the Continental Reformation.* Oxford Clarendon Press, 1911. xix+742 pages.
Documents in Latin and French are left in the original, but
documents in German are translated.
New editions: London, 1966; N.Y., 1966; Oxford, 1970.

KLARWILL, VICTOR VON. *Fugger News Letters, being a selection of unpublished letters from the correspondence of the
house of Fugger during the years 1568-1605,* tr. Pauline de
Chary, foreword by H. Gordon Selfridge. Ld., 1925. xlv+284
pages.
(The second series 1926 deals with England.)
New edition edited by George T. Matthews. N.Y., 1971.
256 pages.

The Library of Christian Classics. 26 vols., edited by John Baillie,
John T. McNeill and Henry P. van Dusen. Philadelphia, 1953-
1964.
XIV: *Advocates of Reform: from Wyclif to Erasmus,* edited
by Matthew Spinka. 1953. 399 pages.
XV: *Martin Luther: Lectures on Romans,* edited by Wilhelm
Pauck. 1961. lxvi+444 pages.
XVI: *Martin Luther: Early Theological Works,* edited by
James Atkinson. 1962. 380 pages.
XVII: *Luther and Erasmus: Free Will and Salvation,* edited

by E. Gordon Rupp in collaboration with A. N. Marlow.
1969. xiv+348 pages.
XVIII: *Martin Luther: Letters of Spiritual Counsel,* edited
by Theodore G. Tappert. 1955. 367 pages.
XIX: *Melanchthon and Bucer,* edited by Wilhelm Pauck.
1969. xx+406 pages.
XX-XXI: *John Calvin: Institutes of the Christian Religion,*
edited by John T. McNeill. 1960. lxxi+1734 pages.
XXII: *John Calvin: Theological Treatises,* edited by J. K. S.
Reid. 1954. 355 pages.
XXIII: *John Calvin: Commentaries,* edited by Joseph
Haroutunian, in collaboration with Louise P. Smith. 1958.
414 pages.
XXIV: *Zwingli and Bullinger,* edited by G. W. Bromiley.
1953. 364 pages.
XXV: *Spiritual and Anabaptist Writers,* edited by George H.
Williams. 1957. 421 pages.
A well-balanced collection of sources with critical introduc-
tions.

MANSCHRECK, CLYDE L. (COMP.). *Prayers of the Reformers.*
Philadelphia, 1958. 183 pages.
Prayers by Luther, Melanchthon, Calvin and some English
reformers. Arranged according to liturgical and spiritual
categories.

OBERMAN, HEIKO A. (ED.) *Forerunners of the Reformation.*
The Shape of Late Medieval Thought, tr. Paul L. Nyhus.
N.Y., Chicago, San Francisco, 1966. x+333 pages.
Valuable introduction. Selections from the writings of Biel,
Staupitz, Cajetan, Prierias, Hoen and Erasmus.

POLLARD, A. W., and REDGRAVE, G. R. *A Short-Title Catalogue*
of Books Printed in England, Scotland and Ireland and of
English Books printed Abroad 1475-1640. Ld., 1926, xvi+
609 pages.
Available in University Microfilms, Ann Arbor, Mich., 1956.

Portable Renaissance Reader, edited by James B. Ross and Mary
M. McLaughlin, 2nd ed. rev. N.Y., 1953. 756 pages.
Contains a great variety of readings, emphasizing philosophy,
the arts, and Italian culture in general. Part V offers theological readings, beginning with Jerome of Prague and conclud-

ing with St. John of the Cross.

REICH, EMIL. *Select Documents Illustrating Medieval and Modern History*. Ld., 1905. xvi+794 pages.
Contains a few documents on the Reformation. Only those in German and Dutch are translated.

RHEGIUS, URBANUS. *To the Young Preachers of the Gospel in the Principality of Lünebert*, tr. C. M. Jacobs. LCQ I (1928), 350-353.

ROBINSON, JAMES HARVEY. *Readings in European History*. Vol. II. From the opening of the Protestant Revolt to the Present Day. Boston, 1906. xxxii+629 pages.

SASTROW, BARTHOLOMEW. *Social Germany in Luther's Time Being the Memoirs of Bartholomew Sastrow*, tr. Albert D. Vandam, Ld., 1905. xxv+349 pages.

SLEIDANUS, JOHANNES. *The General History of the Reformation of the Church*, Ld., 1689. 16+638+100+31 pages.

SMITH, PRESERVED. *Some Old Unpublished Letters*. HTR XII (1919), 201-218.
Unpublished Letters of the Reformers. LCR XLI (1922) 293-316.

SPITZ, LEWIS W. *The Protestant Reformation* (Sources of Civilization in the West series). Englewood Cliffs, N.J., 1966. viii+178 pages.
Selections from Erasmus, Luther, Zwingli, Calvin, and Swiss Anabaptists.

STOKES, FRANCIS G. (ED. & TR.) *Epistolae Obscurorum Virorum (Letters of Obscure Men): The Latin Text with an English Rendering, Notes and an Historical Introduction*. New Haven, 1925. lxxiii+560 pages.
New edition with an introduction by Hajo Holborn. N.Y., 1964. xiv+262 pages.
A classic source collection of underground Humanist writings by Hutten *et al.*

STRAUSS, GERALD (COMP.) *Manifestations of Discontent in Germany on the Eve of the Reformation. A Collection of Documents*. Bloomington, Ind., 1971. xxiii+247 pages.
A fine selection and translation of material from the "Grievances of the German Nation," economic and political protests, the peasant rebellion, and some popular pamphlets.

University of Pennsylvania. Department of History, *Translation and Reprints from the Original Sources of European History.* Reformation Number, Philadelphia, 1897. Gathers up separate numbers as follows:

1 (series III, 6) *The Pre-Reformation Period,* ed. James Harvey Robinson, 34 pages.

2 (series 1, 1) *The Early Reformation Period in England,* ed. Edward P. Cheyney. 20 pages.

3 (series II, 6) *The Period of the Early Reformation in Germany,* ed. James Harvey Robinson and Merrick Whitcomb. 39 pages.

4 (series III, 3) *The Period of the Later Reformation,* ed. Merrick Whitcomb. 32 pages.

5 (series III, 4) *The Witch Persecutions,* ed. George L. Burr, 36 pages.

WEBSTER, DAVID, and GREEN, LOUIS (EDS.) *Documents in Renaissance and Reformation History.* North Melbourne, 1969. xi+226 pages. Broad selection of sources.

ZIEGLER, DONALD J. *Great Debates of the Reformation.* N.Y., 1969. vii+358 pages.

Contains selections from the Leipzig Debate (1519), the Second Zürich Disputation (1523), the Marburg Colloquy (1529), the Münster Colloquy (1523), the Regensburg Colloquy (1541), the Council of Trent (1545), the Poissy Colloquy (1561), the Diet of Prague (1575), and the Emden Disputation (1578).

GENERAL HISTORIES OF THE REFORMATION

BABINGTON, JOHN A. *The Reformation. A Religious and Historical Sketch.* Port Washington, N.Y., 1971. x + 362 pages.

BAINTON, ROLAND H. *The Reformation of the Sixteenth Century.* Boston, 1952. xi + 276 pages.

Probably the best survey in English. Contains useful bibliography. Available in subsequent paperback editions.

BELLOC, HILAIRE. *How the Reformation Happened.* London, 1950. 293 pages.

Fair.

BLAYNEY, IDA W. *The Age of Luther. The Spirit of Renaissance–Humanism and the Age of Reformation.* N.Y., 1957. xi + 499 pages.
Average.

BRINTON, HENRY. *The Context of the Reformation.* London, 1968. 188 pages.

The Cambridge Modern History planned by the late Lord Acton. Vol. II. *The Reformation.* Cambridge, Eng., 1904. A series of essays with excellent bibliographies.

CHADWICK, OWEN. *The Reformation* (The Pelican History of the Church series). Baltimore, Md., 1964. 463 pages.
A very useful survey, weak on individual reformers. Contains bibliography.

COWIE, LEONARD. *The Reformation* (Young Historian Books series). N.Y., 1968. 112 pages.

CRISTIANI, LEON. *The Revolt Against the Church.* Vol. 78 of *The Twentieth Century Encyclopedia of Catholicism.* Translated from the French by R. F. Trevett. N.Y., 1962. viii + 143 pages.
A survey from the "golden year" 1450 to the beginnings of the modern Roman Catholic foreign mission in the 17th century.

DANIEL-ROPS, HENRY. *The Protestant Reformation.* (History of the Church of Christ series), translated by Audrey Butler. London, N.Y., 1961. 560 pages. Also in paperback.
A relatively fair view by a Roman Catholic scholar.

DANNENFELDT, KARL H. *The Church of the Renaissance and Reformation. Decline and Reform from 1300-1600* (Church in History series). St. Louis, 1970. 145 pages.

DICKENS, ARTHUR G. *Martin Luther and the Reformation* (Teach Yourself History Library series). London, 1967. vii + 186 pages.
Useful for laymen. Emphasis on Luther and Lutheranism.

DOLAN, JOHN P. *History of the Reformation. A Conciliatory Assessment of Opposite Views.* Introd. by Jaroslav Pelikan. N.Y., Tournai, Paris, Rome, 1965. xvii + 417 pages.
Traces the roots of the Reformation and analyzes Roman Catholic thought through the Council of Trent.

DURANT, WILL. *The Reformation. A History of European Civilization from Wyclif to Calvin: 1300-1564* (The Story of

Civilization series). N.Y., 1957. xviii+1025 pages.
A general survey, weak on the left wing. Stresses the compet-
itive aspects of the Reformation as a prelude to the modern era.

ELTON, GEOFFREY R. *Reformation Europe, 1517-1559*
(Meridian Histories of Modern Europe series). Cleveland,
1963. 349 pages. Paperback.
Excellent, with bibliography.

FISHER, GEORGE PARK. *The Reformation.* N.Y., rev. ed., 1906.
xxx+525 pages. An outline.

GRANT, ARTHUR J. *A History of Europe from 1494-1610*
(History of Medieval and Modern Europe series). London,
N.Y., 1931. Revised bibliography, 1957. 5th edition, 1964.
xiii+572 pages.
A good survey of events in the various countries. Stresses
political developments. Weak on left wing.

GRIMM, HAROLD J. *The Reformation Era, 1500-1650.* London,
N.Y., 1954. xiii+675 pages. With a revised and expanded
bibliography, 1965. xiii+703 pages. New edition, 1972.
The best survey of the Reformation.

HAGENBACH, K. R. *A History of the Reformation in Germany
and Switzerland chiefly,* tr. Evelina Moore. 2 vols. (Clark's
Foreign Theological Library, ns LIX and LXII). Edinburgh,
1878-79. Valuable especially for Switzerland.

HARBISON, ELMORE H. *The Age of Reformation* (The Development of Western Civilization series). Ithaca, N.Y., 1955. 145
pages.
A good textbook.

HARDWICK, CHARLES. *A History of the Christian Church During the Reformation.* New ed. rev. by W. Stubbs, Ld. 1880.
xi+424 pages.
An outline, opprobrious toward the Anabaptists and Socinians.

HÄUSSER, LUDWIG. *The Period of the Reformation 1517 to 1648,*
ed. Wilhelm Oncken, tr. Mrs. G. Sturge, 2 vols. Ld., 1873.
Serviceable survey chiefly of political events. The Anabaptists
are not so much as mentioned.

HILLERBRAND, HANS. *Men and Ideas in the 16th Century.*
Chicago, 1971. 130 pages.
Outlines basic events, from Luther's 95 theses to the Edict
of Nantes in 1598.

Christendom Divided. The Protestant Reformation (Theological Resources series). New York, Philadelphia, London, 1971. xiii+344 pages.

A good survey, emphasizing Luther's influence and political implications.

HOLBORN, HAJO. *A History of Modern Germany.* 3 vols. London, N.Y., 1959.

Vol. I. *The Reformation.* xvi+374 pages.

Excellent. Stresses political history, ending in 1648.

HUGHES, PHILIP. *The Revolt Against the Church. Aquinas to Luther* (History of the Church series). N.Y., 1947. xvi+556 pages.

Rather traditional Roman Catholic treatment, stressing late Middle Ages. Luther is dealt with in the final chapter.

A Popular History of the Reformation. Garden City, N.Y., 1957. 343 pages.

Traditional Roman Catholic interpretation. Stresses English Reformation.

HULME, EDWARD MASLIN, *The Renaissance, the Protestant Revolution and the Catholic Reformation in Continental Europe.* rev. ed., N.Y., 1923. 629 pages.

Cordial to that in the Reformation which was making for rationalism and bourgeois democracy. Contains material not generally included on the toleration controversy.

HYMA, ALBERT. *Renaissance to Reformation.* Grand Rapids, Mich., 1951. 591 pages.

A fine survey of the mainstream of the Reformation. Weak on the left wing.

JANSSEN, JOHANNES, *History of the German People at the Close of the Middle Ages,* tr. M. A. Mitchell and A. M. Christie. 14 volumes. St. Louis, 1896-1909.

The first two volumes cover social conditions on the eve of the Reformation. The third takes Luther down to 1524. The fourth deals with the Peasants' War. The remainder through the tenth cover the history to 1618. The last four volumes deal with philosophy, education, art, literature, etc. The point of view is that the German church was in many respects flourishing during the 15th century, but the new Humanists of the type of Erasmus and Hutten poured undeserved con-

tempt upon all things medieval. Luther completed the dis-
integration.
New edition, 16 vols. N.Y., 1966.
Vols. 15 and 16 have title: *History of the German People
After the Close of the Middle Ages.* Index vol. 434 pages.
Representative of an enlightened traditional Roman Catholic
interpretation.

KIDD, B. J., *The Continental Reformation,* 3d ed., N.Y., 1913.
142 pages.
A little handbook.

LATOURETTE, KENNETH S. *A History of Christianity.* Vol.
III. *Three Centuries of Advance. A.D. 1500-1800.* N.Y., 1939.
ix+503 pages.
Covers very little of the history of the continental reformation. Focuses on missionary expansion.

LAU, FRANZ, and BIZER, ERNST. *A History of the Reformation in Germany to 1555.* Tr. by Brian A. Hardy. (A History
of the Christian Church series.) London, 1969. xii+249 pages.
Excellent summary of events, and bibliography.

LÉONARD, ÉMILE G. *A History of Protestantism,* edited by H. H.
Rowley, translated by Joyce M. H. Reid. London, 1965.
xiv+461 pages.
A classic French study, covering only Luther, Lutheranism,
Calvin and the Counter Reformation. Extensive bibliography.

LINDSAY, THOMAS M. *A History of the Reformation.* (Inter-
national Theological Library)
Vol. I. *The Reformation in Germany from Its Beginning to
the religious Peace of Augsburg.* N.Y., 1916. xvi+527 pages.
There is a good section on social conditions on the eve of the
Reformation. The treatment of Luther is warm hearted rather
than penetrating.
Vol. II. *The Reformation in Switzerland, France, the Netherlands, Scotland and England, the Anabaptist and Socinian
Movements, the Counter-Reformation.* N.Y., 1917. xvii+631
pages.
The usual description of the second volume as inferior to the
first does not seem to me warranted, though the treatment
of the Anabaptists is unsatisfactory.
2d ed. Edinburg, 1956.

LORTZ, JOSEPH. *The Reformation in Germany,* translated by
Ronald Walls. 2 vols. London, N.Y., 1968.
Vol. I: covers the period to 1525. viii+488 pages.
Vol. II: from 1525-1548. 414 pages.
The first major Roman Catholic revisionist history. Lortz's
work created a school of German Roman Catholic Reforma-
tion scholars interested in ecumenical revisions of Reforma-
tion history.
LUCAS, HENRY S. *The Renaissance and the Reformation.* N.Y.,
& Ld., 1934. xviii+765 pages.
Competent and well balanced. The prime interest is in social,
political and cultural history. Theology and philosophy do
not fare so well. The chapter on the Anabaptists makes use
of recent Dutch scholarship. 2d ed. N.Y., 1960.
MAJOR, RUSSEL J. *The Age of Renaissance and Reformation.*
A Short History. Philadelphia, 1970. xvii+385 pages.
Stresses the Renaissance. The final chapter deals with the
Reformation as such. Contains a bibliography.
MERLE D'AUBIGNÉ, J. H. *A History of the Reformation of the*
Sixteenth Century. 6 vols. Translated by H. White. N.Y., 1835.
Still worth consulting for the excerpts from sources.
MÖLLER, WILHELM. *History of the Christian Church,* ed. G.
Kawerau, tr. J. H. Freese.
Vol. III. *Reformation and Counter-Reformation.* Ld. and
N.Y., 1900. xi+476 pages.
An excellent compendium. There are good sketches of Sebastian
Franck and Caspar Schwenckfeld.
MOSSE, GEORGE L. *The Reformation* (Berkshire Studies in Euro-
pean History series). N.Y., Chicago, San Francisco, Toronto,
London, 1963. 136 pages.
An introduction for laymen.
The New Cambridge Modern History. 14 vols. Cambridge, 1957-
1970.
Vol. II: *The Reformation, 1520-1559,* edited by G. R. Elton.
1958. xvi+685 pages.
Covers all countries and movements. Stresses political thought,
education and warfare.
Vol. III: *The Counter-Reformation and Price Revolution,*
1559-1610, edited by R. B. Wernham. 1968. xvi+598 pages.

On economy, social and political thought, education, science and colonization. Weak on counter-reformation and Trent.

NEW, JOHN F. *The Renaissance and Reformation. A Short History.* N.Y., 1969. 189 pages.

PHILIPPSON, MARTIN. *The Age of the Reformation,* tr. under the supervision of John Henry Wright. (A History of All Nations XI.) Philadelphia and N.Y., 1905. xiv+482 pages. Many illustrations from contemporary woodcuts. Sad on the Anabaptists.

PLUMMER, ALFRED. *The Continental Reformation in Germany, France and Switzerland from the birth of Luther to the Death of Calvin.* Ld., 1912. xiii+217 pages. Slight.

RANKE, LEOPOLD VON. *History of the Reformation in Germany,* 2d ed. tr. Sarah Austin. 2 vols. Ld., 1845-47. Deals largely with the political aspects. New edition, edited by Robert A. Johnson. N.Y., 1966.

RICE, EUGENE F. *The Foundation of Early Modern Europe, 1460-1559* (Norton History of Modern Europe series). N.Y., 1970. x+182 pages. Useful textbook.

ROBERTSON, ARCHIBALD. *The Reformation.* London, 1960. vii+232 pages. Textbook. Weak on Luther and the left wing.

SCHAFF, PHILIP. *History of the Christian Church.*
Vol. VI. *The German Reformation.* N.Y., 1888. xvii+755 pages.
Vol. VII. *The Swiss Reformation.* N.Y., 1892. xvii+890 pages.
Schaff followed in the main the best secondary works of his day with a limited use of sources. The work is always careful, accurate and in good temper.
New edition. Grand Rapids, Mich., 1962.
Vol. VII: *The German Reformation.*
Vol. VIII: *The Swiss Reformation.*

SEEBOHM, F. *The Era of the Prostestant Revolution.* (Epochs of History.) 2d ed. N.Y., 1914. xv+250 pages. A convenient outline. New edition, 1971.

SIMON, EDITH. *The Reformation.* N.Y., 1966. 191 pages.
An essay with pictures.
SMELLIE, ALEXANDER. *The Reformation in Its Literature.*
Ld., N.Y., 1925. 320 pages.
Popular reviews of some of the works of Luther, Calvin, etc.
SMITH, PRESERVED. *The Age of the Reformation* (American
Historical Series.) N.Y., 1920. xii+861 pages.
The first half of the book is devoted to a sketch of the
Reformation by countries, the second to a discussion of
social and cultural conditions, interpretations of the Reforma-
tion and an excellent bibliography.
New edition in 2 vols. N.Y., 1962. paperback.
SPALDING, H. J. *A History of the Protestant Reformation.*
7th ed. 2 vols. in one. Baltimore, 1876.
The less reputable type of Catholic polemic against the
Reformation.
SPITZ, LEWIS. *The Renaissance and Reformation Movements.*
Chicago, 1971. xv+614 pages.
A fine textbook with illustrations, maps, and a bibliography.
STEVENSON, WILLIAM. *The Story of the Reformation.* Rich-
mond, 1959. 206 pages.
A fair textbook, includes bibliography.
STONE, J. M. *Reformation and Renaissance.* Ld., 1904. xi+470
pages.
Catholic, gives a vivid picture of Bucer's violence against the
nuns of Strassburg.
STUBBS, WILLIAM. *Lectures on European History.* ed. A. Hassall.
Ld., N.Y., 1904. viii+424 pages.
The author says, "I intend in this course to steer clear of
the religious part of the Reformation history: as clear as
I can."
SYKES, NORMAN. *The Crisis of the Reformation,* (Christian
Challenge series.) London, 1938. 122 pages.
A dated textbook.
TORBET, ROBERT G. *The Protestant Reformation. A Cooper-
ative Text,* (Faith for Life series). Philadelphia, Chicago, Los
Angeles, 1961. 96 pages.
A useful text, with an appendix containing suggestions for
group meetings.

VEDDER, H. C. *The Reformation in Germany.* N.Y., 1914. xlix+466 pages.
His sympathies lie with the Peasants and the Anabaptists.

WALKER, WILLISTON. *The Reformation,* (Ten Epochs of Church History). N.Y., 1901. vii+478 pages.
An outline.

WHITNEY, JAMES POUNDER. *The Reformation* (The Church Universal Series VI) 1907. N.Y., viii+501 pages.
The council of Trent receives disproportionate attention. The Italian Reformation is omitted. The Anabaptists receive scant treatment.
The History of the Reformation. London, 1958. xv+526 pages.
Good textbook.

SPECIAL PHASES OF REFORMATION HISTORY

EXPLANATION OF THE REFORMATION

BELLOC, HILAIRE. *What Was the Reformation?* CW XCIV (1911), 26-35, 359-371.
How the Reformation Happened. N.Y., 1928. 290 pages.

FAULKNER, JOHN ALFRED. *Was There Need of a Reformation?* LQ XLVII (1917), 471-490.

HAYES, CARLTON, J. H. *Significance of the Reformation in the light of contemporary scholarship.* CHR XVII (1932), 395-420.

LORTZ, JOSEPH. *How the Reformation Came,* translated by Otto M. Knab. N.Y., 1964. 115 pages.
Suggestions for a new ecumenical approach to the Reformation, by the best-known German Roman Catholic historian.

REID, WILLIAM J. (ED.) *The Reformation: Revival or Revolution?* (European Problem Studies series.) N.Y., 1968. 122 pages.

RITTER, GERHARD. *Lutheranism, Catholicism, and the Humanistic View of Life.* ARG XLIV (1953), 145-159.
Shows how the German understanding of Luther's Reformation has changed.

Why the Reformation Occurred in Germany. CH XXVII 2 (1958), 99-106. Reprinted in CTM XXX (1959), 723-732.

ROPE, H. E. G. *What Led to the Reformation?* CW CXXIII (1926), 811-818.

ROTH, ERICH. *Martin Luther and the Continental Reformation.* CQ CLIII (1952), 12-27, 171-185.
Stresses the religious character of the Reformation.

SCHAFF, DAVID S. *The origin and purpose of the Protestant Reformation.* LQ XLVIII (1918), 1-18.

SMITH, PRESERVED. *The Reformation 1517-1917.* BS LXXV (1918), 1-21.

SPITZ, LEWIS W. (ED.) *The Reformation: Material or Spiritual?* (Problems in European Civilization series.) Boston, 1962. 104 pages.
Pinpoints interpretations and contains a bibliographical essay.

STANGE, DOUGLAS C. *A Marxist De-Lutheranization of the German Reformation.* CTM XXXVIII 9, (1967), 596-600.

THURSTON, H. *Lea on the Causes of the Reformation.* ACQ XXVIII (1903), 417-434.

WRIGHT, C. J. *The Abiding Significance of the Reformation.* *Hibbert Journal* XXXVI (1938) 199-211.

INTELLECTUAL AND CULTURAL

BAINTON, ROLAND H. *Changing Ideas and Ideals in the Sixteenth Century.* JMH VIII (1936), 417-443.
New Documents on Early Protestant Rationalism. CH VII (1938), 179-187. Reprinted in the author's *Studies on the Reformation.*
A review of an Italian edition of works by Castellio, Renato, Socinus, Blandrata and others.

BEARD, CHARLES. *The Reformation of the Sixteenth Century in Its Relation to Modern Thought and Knowledge.* (Hibbert Lectures). Ld., 1883. x+451 pages.
The Reformation interpreted as a "revolt against finality." New edition, with a foreword by Joseph Dorfman and introduction by Ernest Barker. Ann Arbor, 1962. 450 pages. Paperback.

CANTOR, NORMAN F. (ED.) *Perspectives on the European Past. Conversations with Historians.* London, N.Y., 1971.

DICKENS, A. G. *The Reformation.* pp. 252-274.

CLARK, GEORGE N. *Early Modern Europe from About 1450 to 1720.* Cambridge, N.Y., 1957. Paperback ed., 1970. 270 pages.

DAWSON, CHRISTOPHER H. *The Dividing of Christendom,* with foreword by Douglas Horton. N.Y., 1965. x+304 pages. An essay covering the period from the Reformation to the French Revolution by a classic Roman Catholic scholar.

FERGUSON, WALLACE K. *The Church in a Changing World: a Contribution to the Interpretation of the Renaissance.* AHR LIX 1 (1953), 1-18.

FOSTER, CLAUDE R. JR. *The Wartburg: Symbol of a Synthesis?* CC LXXXIV 43 (1967), 1358-1366.
A report on travel to, and history of, the Wartburg.

GELDER, HERMAN AREND E. VANN. *The Two Reformations in the 16th Century. A Study of the Religious Aspects and Consequences of Renaissance and Humanism,* translated by Jan F. Finlay and Alison Hanham. The Hague, 1961. x+406 pages.
An interesting but debatable thesis on the interrelationships of Renaissance, Humanism and Reformation.

GILMORE, MYRON D. *The World of Humanism, 1453-1517* (The Rise of Modern Europe series) N.Y., 1952. xv+326 pages. Paperback.
Good background readings touching on the Reformation, with a bibliography.

HILLERBRAND, HANS J. *The Spread of the Protestant Reformation of the Sixteenth Century: a Case Study in the Transfer of Ideas.* SAQ LXVII (1968), 265-286.

HOLBORN, HAJO. *Ulrich von Hutten and the German Reformation,* translated by Roland H. Bainton (Yale Historical Publications series). London, Oxford, New Haven, 1937. viii+ 214 pages.
Very useful treatment of the relationship between Humanism and Reformation.

HOLBORN, LOUISE W. *Printing and the Growth of a Protestant Movement in Germany* from 1517 to 1524. CH XI 2 (1942), 123-137.

HOLL, KARL. *The Cultural Significance of the Reformation*

(Living Age Books series), with an introduction by Wilhelm
Pauck, translated by Karl and Barbara Hertz and John H.
Lichtblau. N.Y., 1959. 191 pages.
A classic essay, written in 1911.

LAU, FRANZ. *Germany, Western Culture, and the Gospel of
the Glory and Grace of God.* LQ XIX 3 (1967), 257-273.

RAMSEY, PAUL. *A Theory of Virtue According to the Principles
of the Reformation.* JR XXVII 3 (1947), 178-196.
Emphasizes Augustine, the classical traditions and the modern
scene in contrast to Luther.

RICE, EUGENE F. JR. *The Humanist Idea of Christian Antiquity:
Lefèvre d'Étaples and His Circle. Studies in the Renaissance,*
IX (1962), 126-160.

SCHWIEBERT, ERNEST G. *The Electoral Town of Wittenberg.
Medievalia et Humanistica* III (1945), pp.?

SMITH, LACEY BALDWIN. *The Reformation and the Decay of
Medieval Ideals.* CH XXIV 3 (1955), 212-220.

SPITZ, LEWIS W. *The Religious Renaissance of the German Humanists.* Cambridge, Mass., 1963. 369 pages.
Excellent expositions of important figures such as Agricola,
Reuchlin, Hutten, Pirkheimer, Erasmus and Luther, with
bibliographies.

STRAUSS, GERALD. *The Image of Germany in the 16th Century.*
GR XXXIV (1959), 232–234.
Nuremberg in the Sixteenth Century (New Dimensions in
History series). N.Y., 1966. vi+305 pages.
Emphasizes the role of the city council.

TAYLOR, HENRY OSBORN. *Thought and Expression in the Six-
teenth Century,* 2 vols., N.Y., 1920.
2d rev. ed. N.Y., 1959.
Book I: *The Humanism of Italy.*
Book II: *Erasmus and Luther,* appendix on Melanchthon and
Zwingli.
Book III: *The French Mind,* with a chapter on Calvin.
Book V: *Philosophy and Science,* on Greek classical thought,
Cusa, Da Vinci, medicine, the natural sciences and a summary
on the 16th Century.

TILLMANNS, W. G. *The Lotthers: Forgotten Printers of the Reformation.* CTM XXII 4 (1951), 260-264.

WOLF, JOHN B. *Early Modern Europe 1500-1789 A.D.* (World
    Civilization series). Glenview, Ill., Palo Alto, Cal., Tucker,
    Ga., Oakland, N.J., Dallas, Tx., 1971. 224 pages.
    Emphasizes the political, economic and intellectual history
    of the Reformation. Widely used at the College level.
YULE, GEORGE. *Continental Patterns and the Reformation in
    England and Scotland.* SJT XXII 3 (1969), 305-323.

BIBLICAL SCHOLARSHIP

The Cambridge History of the Bible. Vol. II, *The West from the
    Reformation to the Present Day,* edited by S. L. Greenslade.
    Cambridge, 1963. x+590 pages.
    Chapt. I: BAINTON, ROLAND H. *The Bible in the Reforma-
    tion.* 1-37.
    Chapt. II: HALL, BASIL. *Biblical Scholarship: Editions and
    Commentaries.* 38-93.
    Chapt. III: *Continental Versions to c. 1600.* 94-140.
    Covers German, Italian, French, Dutch, Spanish, East-Central
    Europe and Scandinavian versions. Each section is written by
    a different scholar.
    Chapt. V: SYKES, NORMAN. *The Religion of Protestants.*
    175-198.
    Chapt. VI: GEHAN, F. J. *The Bible in the Roman Church
    from Trent to the Present Day.* 199-237.
COULTON, GEORGE G. *The Bible and the Reformation.* London,
    1938. 46 pages.
    A brief, popular essay by a well-known medievalist.
FULLERTON, KEMPER. *The Reformation Principle of Exegesis
    and the Interpretation of Prophecy.* AJT XII (1908), 422-442.
GERRISH, B. A. *Biblical Authority and the Continental Reforma-
    tion.* SJT X 4 (1957), 337-360.
HOWORTH, HENRY H. *The Origin and Authority of the Biblical
    Canon According to the Continental Reformers.* JHS VIII
    (1907), 321-365; IX (1908), 188-230.
LEHMANN, PAUL L. *The Reformers' Use of the Bible.* TT III 3
    (1946), 328-344.
LENHARDT, J. M. *Protestant Latin Bibles of the Reformation.*
    CBQ VIII (1946), 23-28; 416-432.

LOCKWOOD, DEAN P. and BAINTON, ROLAND H. *Classical and Biblical Scholarship in the Age of the Renaissance and Reformation.* CH X 2 (1941), 125-143.

MAYER, F. E. *Romanism, Calvinism, and Lutheranism on the Authority of Scripture.* CTM VIII 4 (1937), 260-272.

METZGER, BRUCE M. *The Geneva Bible of 1560.* TT XVII 3 (1960), 339-352.

MONTGOMERY, JOHN W. *Sixtus of Siena and Roman Catholic Biblical Scholarship in the Reformation.* ARG LIV (1963), 214-233.

An evaluation of the most influential biblical scholar in Italy, with a survey of the work *Bibliotheca Sancta.*

PREUS, JAMES SAMUEL. *From Shadow to Promise; Old Testament Interpretation from Augustine to the Young Luther.* Cambridge, Mass., 1969. viii+301 pages.

Explores a rare field of medieval and Reformation studies.

REID, JOHN K. S. *The Authority of Scripture; a Study of the Reformation and Post-Reformation Understanding of the Bible.* London, 1957. 286 pages.

A useful summary of the teachings of the major reformers on the subject, with emphasis on Luther and Calvin.

SCHWARZ, WERNER. *Principles and Problems of Biblical Translation. Some Reformation Controversies and Their Background.* Cambridge, 1955. xiv+224 pages.

Analyzes Reuchlin, Erasmus and Luther.

SMITH, PRESERVED. *Methods of Reformation Interpreters of the Bible.* BW XXXVIII (1911), 235-245.

TILLICH, PAUL. *The Recovery of the Prophetic Tradition in the Reformation. Three lectures delivered at the Washington Cathedral Library, Washington, D.C., Nov-Dec. 1950.* Washington, 1950. 30 pages.

A limited edition of a transcript. The lecture *The New Community* on ecclesiology is valuable.

VAN DEN BRINK, J. N. BAKHUIZEN. *Bible and Biblical Theology in the Early Reformation.* SJT XIV 4 (1961), 337-352.
Bible and Biblical Theology in the Early Reformation. SJT XV 1 (1962), 50-65.

THEOLOGY

(See also individual reformers)

ADAM, KARL. *One and Holy,* tr. by Cecily Hastings. N.Y., 1951. xi+130 pages. Reprinted 1969.

A classic work on Luther and the Reformation as sources for Christian unity.

The Roots of the Reformation, tr. by Cecily Hastings. N.Y., 1951. 95 pages.

A Roman Catholic view, with an analysis of Luther and an ecumenical outlook, by a German irenicist.

AULEN, GUSTAF E. H. *Reformation and Catholicity,* tr. by Eric H. Wahlstrom. Philadelphia, 1961. 203 pages.

An attempt to ascertain the ecumenical significance of the Reformation.

BAINTON, ROLAND H. *Man, God, and the Church in the Age of the Renaissance.* JRT XI 2 (1954) 119-133.

Contrasts Renaissance and Reformation.

BARCLAY, ALEXANDER. *The Protestant Doctrine of the Lord's Supper.* Glasgow, 1927. xiv+302 pages.

Solid, finds three periods in Zwingli's development.

BORNKAMM, HEINRICH. *The Heart of Reformation Faith. The Fundamental Axioms of Evangelical Belief,* tr. by John W. Doberstein. London, Evanston, New York, 1965. 126 pages.

A useful outline of Lutheran theology.

BROWN, ROBERT MCAFEE. *Tradition as a Protestant Problem.* TT XVII 4 (1961), 430-454.

COATES, THOMAS. *Were the Reformers Mission-Minded?* CTM XL 9 (1969), 600-611.

On Luther, Zwingli and Calvin.

CLARK, FRANCIS. *Eucharistic Sacrifice and the Reformation.* London, Westminster, Md., 1960. x+582 pages.

A Roman Catholic explanation of the Reformation in view of medieval and ecumenical eucharistic teachings.

CLASEN, CLAUS-PETER. *Medieval Heresies in the Reformation.* CH XXXII 4 (1963), 392-414.

CUNNINGHAM, WILLIAM. *The Reformers and the Theology of the Reformation.* Edinburgh, 1862. vi+616 pages. (Vol. I of his collected works.) 2nd ed., 1866.

New edition edited by James Buchanan and James Bannerman (The Students' Reformed Theological Library series). London, 1967. vi+616 pages.

DAVIES, RUPERT ERIC. *The Problem of Authority in the Continental Reformers; a Study in Luther, Zwingli, and Calvin.* London, 1946. 158 pages.
A critical analysis, arguing that the reformers' solutions do not settle the modern problem of authority.

GERHART, E. V. *Reformation Theology.* AR III (1885), 97-107, 210-227, 397-423.

GERRISH, BRIAN A. *Atonement and "Saving Faith."* TT XVII 2 (1960), 181-191.
Substantially on Luther and other reformers.

HOLBROOK, CLYDE A. *The Heart of the Reformation.* CC LXVII 42 (1950), 1237-1238.

JUNGKUNTZ, THEODORE. *Private Confession: a 20th Century Issue Seen from a 16th Century Perspective.* CTM XXXIX 2 (1968), 106-115.

MCNEILL, JOHN T. *Natural Law in the Teaching of the Reformers.* JR XXVI 3 (1946), 168-182.

NUGENT, DONALD. *The Historical Dimension in Reformation Theology.* JES V 3 (1968), 555-571.

OUTLER, ALBERT C. *The Problem of Religious Community in Protestantism.* JRT I 2 (1944), 117-127.
Summarizes the major reformers in the light of modern ecumenism.

PELIKAN, JAROSLAV. *From Luther to Kierkegaard: a Study in the History of Theology.* St. Louis, 1950. 2d ed. 1963. vii+171 pages.
Useful on Luther, Melanchthon and 16th century confessions.

RICHARD, J. W. *Two Reformation Theologies* (Lutheran and Calvinist). LQ XXXIII (1903), 171-207, 316-355, 505-554.

ROBINSON, WILLIAM C. *The Reformation. A Rediscovery of Grace.* Grand Rapids, Mich., 1962. xx+189 pages.
Develops theme in grace, God, gospel, justification, theology, word and church.

ROUSE, RUTH and NEILL, STEPHEN (EDS.). *A History of the Ecumenical Movement, 1517-1948.* London, 1954.
MCNEILL, JOHN T. *The Ecumenical Idea and Efforts to*

Realize It, 1517-1618. pp. 25-69.

RUPP, E. GORDON. *Word and Spirit in the First Years of the Reformation.* ARG XLIX (1958), 13-36.

Patterns of Salvation in the First Age of the Reformation. ARG LVII (1966), 52-66.

Shows the relation of early reformation theologies to Luther.

SCHAFF, PHILIP. *The Principle of Protestantism,* translated by John W. Nevin (Lancaster Series on the Mercersburg theology). Philadelphia, 1964. 268 pages.

A reprint of a classic essay.

TRINKAUS, C. *The Problem of Free Will in the Renaissance and the Reformation.* JHI X (1949), 51-62.

WHALE, JOHN S. *The Protestant Tradition. An Essay in Interpretation.* Cambridge, 1955. xv+360 pages. New edition, 1959.

Perceptive on Luther, Calvin and the left wing as types.

ART AND ILLUSTRATIONS

BAINTON, ROLAND H. *Eyn Wunderliche Weyssagung, Osiander-Sachs-Luther.* GR XXI (1946), 161-164. Reprinted as *The Joachimite Prophecy: Osiander and Sachs* in the author's *Studies on the Reformation.*

The story of an illustrated booklet published in Nürnberg in 1527.

Dürer and Luther as the Man of Sorrows. The Art Bulletin XXIX (1947), 269-272. Reprinted in the author's *Studies on the Reformation.*

CHRISTENSEN, CARL C. *Municipal Patronage and the Crisis of the Arts in Reformation Nuernberg.* CH XXXVI 2 (1967), 140-150.

Iconoclasm and the Preservation of Ecclesiastical Art in Reformation Nuernberg. ARG LXI (1970), 205-220.

COULTON, G. G. *Art and the Reformation.* Oxford, 1928. xxii+622 pages. New edition, Cambridge, 1953.

Encyclopaedia of the Arts, edited by Geoffrey Hindley *et al.* London, N.Y., 1966. 966 pages.

Useful on 16th century artists. Illustrated.

KIBISH, C. G. *Lucas Cranach's Christ Blessing the Children. A Problem of Lutheran Iconography. Art Bulletin* XXXVII (1950), 196-203.

MEINHOLD, PETER. *The Reformation in Pictures*. Berlin, Hamburg, 1967. 73 pages.
An international edition, with text in English, German and Swedish.

PANOFSKY, ERWIN. *The Life and Art of Albrecht Dürer*. Princeton, 1955. xxxii+317 pages.
A standard work.

THULIN, OSKAR (ED.) *Illustrated History of the Reformation*, translated by Jalo E. Nopola *et al*. St. Louis, 1967. 327 pages.
Contains excellent pictorial material.

ATLASES AND TOPOGRAPHY

ANDERSON, CHARLES S. *Augsburg Historical Atlas of Christianity in the Middle Ages and Reformation*. Minneapolis, 1967. 61 pages.
A very handy tool.

DARBY, H. C. and FULLARD, HAROLD (EDS.) *Atlas* (The New Cambridge Modern History series). Cambridge, 1970. xxiv+319 pages.
Excellent. Contains maps on the Peasants' War, 16th century explorations, and treaty settlements.

STRAUSS, GERALD. *Topographical-Historical Method in Sixteenth-Century German Scholarship. Studies in the Renaissance* V (1958), 87-101.
Sixteenth-Century Germany: Its Topography and Topographers. Madison, Wis., 1959. viii+197 pages.
Excellent; includes bibliography.

MODERN ASPECTS

ANDERSON, CHARLES S. *The Reformation . . . Then and Now*. (Tower Book series). Minneapolis, Minn., 1966. 119 pages.

ATKINSON, JAMES. *Rome and Reformation: a Stubborn Problem Re-Examined* (Christian Foundations series). London, 1966. 94 pages.

BAINTON, ROLAND H. *Let's Agree on the Reformation*. CC LXIV (1947), 237-239.
Interpretations of the Reformation. AHR LXVI 1 (1960), 74-84. Reprinted in the author's *Studies on the Reformation*.

BROWN, ROBERT MCAFEE. *The Reformation Then and Now—a Reformed Perspective.* LW XIV 3 (1967), 33-42.

CLEBSCH, WILLIAM A. *New Perspectives on the Reformation.* RL XXXV (1965-1966), 8-19.

GRIMM, HAROLD J. *The Reformation in Recent Historical Thought* (Service Center for Teachers of History series). N.Y., 1964. 28 pages.

HODGES, JOSEPH P. *The Influence and Implications of the Reformation.* London, 1938. xvi+211 pages.

HYMA, ALBERT. *The Reformation and Present Problems.* RL V 4 (1936), 564-575.

KRONER, RICHARD. *The Meaning of the Reformation Today.* LQ III 4 (1951), 340-352.

LOHSE, BERNHARD. *The Significance of the Reformation Today.* LQ XIX 3 (1967), 231-248.

LORTZ, JOSEPH. *The Reformation: a Problem for Today,* translated by John C. Dwyer. Westminster, Md., 1964. 261 pages.

MANSCHRECK, CLYDE L. *The Reformation and Protestantism Today.* (Association Reflection series.) N.Y., 1960. 128 pages.

MARSHALL, R. P. *Wesley and the Reformation.* RL XXXIX 3 (1970), 426-433.

MCLELLAND, JOSEPH C. *The Reformation and Its Significance Today.* Philadelphia, 1962. 238 pages.
Fair.

PELIKAN, JAROSLAV. *The Tragic Necessity of the Reformation.* CC LXXVI 36 (1959), 1017-1020.

PERSSON, PER ERIK. *The Reformation in Recent Roman Catholic Theology.* D II 1 (1963), 24-31.

RUPP, E. GORDON. *The Old Reformation and the New* (The Cato Lecture 1966). Philadelphia, 1967. 68 pages.

SCHWIEBERT, ERNEST G. *The Reformation from a New Perspective.* CH XVII 1 (1948), 3-31.

SKYDSGAARD, KIRSTEN E. *The Papal Council and the Gospel.* Minneapolis, Minn., 1961.
DIETZFELBINGER, HERMAN. *The Ecumenical Responsibility of the Reformation.* pp. 1-11.

ZEMAN, J. K. *Reformation: Relevant? The Atlantic Baptist* V (1969)

THE REFORMATION AND EDUCATION
(See also individual reformers)

EBY, FREDERICK. *Early Protestant Educators, the Educational Writings of Martin Luther, John Calvin and Other Leaders of Protestant Thought.* N.Y., 1931. xiii+312 pages. Includes translations of excerpts.
The Development of Modern Education. Its Theory, Organization and Practice. N.Y., 1952. x+719 pages.
A standard work. Chapters 2-7 deal with education in the 16th century to Comenius.

HARBISON, ELMORE H. *The Christian Scholar in the Age of the Reformation.* N.Y., 1956. ix+177 pages.
Surveys humanism, and contains sketches of Erasmus, Luther, and Calvin.

JORDAN, DAVIS STARR. *The Influence of the Reformation upon Education.* SS VI (1917), 151-155.

MONROE, PAUL. *Thomas Platter and the Educational Renaissance of the Sixteenth Century* (International Education Series). N.Y., 1904. xxii+227 pages.
Translation of the autobiography with introduction.

[RAUMER, KARL G. VON] *German Educational Reformers,* rev. ed. Hartford. Conn., 1878. 724 pages. (Reprinted from the translation of his *Geschichte der Pädagogik* in AJE IV, 1858, 167-182, 401-415, 421-449, 714-728, 729-740, 741-764.)

REU, M. *Religious Instruction of the Young in the Sixteenth Century.* LCR XXXIV (1915), 566-585.
Religious Instruction during the Sixteenth Century, LCR XXXV (1916), 234-250.

SCHWIEBERT, ERNEST G. *Remnants of a Reformation Library. Library Quarterly* X (1940), 494-531.
Discusses the library of Wittenberg University.
New Groups and Ideas at the University of Wittenberg. ARG XLIX (1958), 60-78.
Shows the transformation of the University between 1512-1536 from a medieval to a Protestant institution.

WATSON, FOSTER. *Maturinus Corderius: Schoolmaster at Paris, Bordeaux, and Geneva in the Sixteenth Century.* SR XII (1904), 281-298.

WOODWARD, WILLIAM HARRISON. *Studies in Education During the Age of the Renaissance.* Cambridge, Eng., 1906. xx+ 336 pages.
Includes Sadoleto, Cordier, Melanchthon.
New edition, N.Y., 1965.

LITURGY

(See also individual reformers)

ARKIN, IRVIN. *Rome and the Lutheran Liturgy.* CTM XXII 8 (1951), 578-591.

BOMBERGER, J. H. A. *The Old Palatinate Liturgy of 1563.* MR II (1850), 81-96; III (1851), 97-128.

DUBBS, J. H. *Early Reformed Hymnology.* RQR XXVII (1880), 504-524.

HORN, EDWARD T. *The Reformation of Worship in the City of Nuernberg.* LCR XI (1892), 123-145.

NICHOLS, JAMES H. *The Liturgical Tradition of the Reformed Churches.* TT XI 2 (1954), 210-224.

REED, LUTHER D. *The Lutheran Liturgy. Philadelphia,* 1947. xx+692 pages. Revised edition, 1959. xxiii+824 pages.
Contains chapters (3-5) on the liturgical reformations in Germany, Switzerland and Sweden, with bibliography.

REIM, E. *Miscellanea: the Liturgical Crisis in Wittenberg, 1524.* CTM XX 4 (1949), 284-292.

RIEDEL, J. (ED.) *Cantors at the Crossroads. Essays on Church Music in Honor of Walter E. Buszin.* St. Louis, 1967.
JENNY, MARKUS. *The Hymns of Zwingli and Luther: a Comparison.* pp. 45-63.

THOMPSON, BARD (ED.) *Liturgies of the Western Church.* Cleveland, N.Y., 1961. xiv+434 pages.
Translations of the liturgical writings of Luther, Zwingli, Bucer, Calvin, Oecolampadius, and Farel.

POLITICAL THOUGHT AND RELATIONS

ALLEN, J. W. *A History of Political Thought in the Sixteenth Century.* N.Y., 1928, xxii+525 pages. Penetrating comments on Lutheranism and Calvinism. The section on the Anabaptists is the weakest.

New editions, London & N.Y., 1957, 1960. xii+527 pages.
Paperback.

ANDERSON, WILLIAM K. *Luther and Calvin: a Contrast in Politics.* RL IX 2 (1940), 256-267.

BARON, HANS. *Religion and Politics in the German Imperial Cities During the Reformation.* EHR LII (1937), 405-427, 614-633.
Excellent.
Imperial Reform and the Hapsburgs, 1486-1504. AHR XLIV (1938-39), pp.?

BERGENDOFF, CONRAD. *Church and State in the Reformation Period.* LCQ III (1930), 36-62.

CANTOR, NORMAN F. (ED.) *Perspectives on the European Past. Conversations with Historians.* London, N.Y., 1971.
ELTON, G. R. *Government and Society in Renaissance and Reformation Europe.* pp. 228-251.

COATES, THOMAS. *The Reformation and Nationalism.* CTM XV 9 (1944), 577-595.

COLE, RICHARD G. *Propaganda as a Source of Reformation History.* LQ XXII (1970), 166-171.

DORWART, REINHOLD A. *Church Organization in Brandenburg— Prussia from the Reformation to 1740.* HTR XXXI 4 (1938), 251-262.

DUNN, RICHARD S. *The Age of Religious Wars, 1559-1689* (Norton History of Modern Europe series). N.Y., 1970. 258 pages.
A good survey.

DUNNING, WILLIAM ARCHIBALD. *A History of Political Theories from Luther to Montesquieu.* N.Y., Ld., 1905. x+459 pages.

FIGGIS, JOHN NEVILLE. *Studies of Political Thought from Gerson to Grotius, 1414-1625.* Cambridge, Eng., 1923. vii+224 pages.
New edition, 1956.

GILBERT, FELIX. *Political Thought of the Renaissance and Reformation. Huntington Library Quarterly* IV (1941), 443-468.

HALL, T. C. *Politics and the Reformation.* BW XLI (1913), 229-235.

HEARNSHAW, FOSSEY J. C. (ED.) *The Social and Political Ideas*

of Some Great Thinkers of the Renaissance and Reforma-
tion. N.Y., 1949. 215 pages. Facs. repr., 1967.
Good analyses of Luther, Calvin, Erasmus, Machiavelli.
KIRCHNER, WALTHER. *Russia and Europe in the Age of the*
Reformation. ARG XLIII (1952), 172-186.
KRIEBEL, E. WILBUR. *The Political Results of the Reformation.*
RCR 4S XXI (1917), 510-531.
LANG, A. *The Reformation and Natural Law.* tr. J. Gresham
Machen. PTR VII (1909), 177-218.
MEYER, CARL S. *Fifteen Fifty-Nine Anno Domini.* CTM XXX
5 (1959), 323-339.
MOELLERING, RALPH L. *Attitudes Toward the Use of Force*
and Violence in Thomas Muentzer, Menno Simons, and
Martin Luther. CTM XXXI 7 (1960), 405-427.
MURRAY, R. H. *The Political Consequences of the Reformation.*
Boston, 1926. xxii+301 pages.
OMAN, CHARLES W. *History of the Art of War in the Sixteenth*
Century. N.Y., 1937. xv+784 pages.
A dated but classic work.
PIEPKORN, ARTHUR CARL. *Anglo-Lutheran Relations During*
the First Two Years of the Reign of Edward VI. CTM VI 9
(1935), 670-686.
SHERMAN, FRANKLIN. *The Christian in Secular Society: In-*
sights from the Reformation. US XXV 2 (1968), 96-106.
Draws conclusions from Luther and the Lutheran Confessions.
SPITZ, LEWIS W. *Particularism and Peace. Augsburg 1555.* CH
XXV 2 (1956), 110-126.
SWANSON, GUY E. *Religion and Regime. A Sociological Account*
of the Reformation. Ann Arbor, Mich., 1967. x+295 pages.
An excellent study of political change, well documented.
TONKIN, JOHN. *The Church and the Secular Order in Reforma-*
tion Thought. New York, London, 1971. xiv+219 pages.
On Luther, Calvin and Menno Simons. With bibliography.
WILLIAMSON, RENÉ DE VISME. *The Reformation and Political*
Life. CC LXXXIV 43 (1967), 1343-1345.

THE REFORMATION AND LIBERTY

(See also under Luther and Left Wing)

ACTON, JOHN EMERICH EDWARD DALBERG. *The History of Freedom and Other Essays.* Ld., 1907 and 1922. xxxix+ 638 pages.

BAINTON, ROLAND H. *The Parables of the Tares as the Proof Text for Religious Liberty to the End of the Sixteenth Century.* CH (1932), 2-24.

The Struggle for Religious Liberty. CH X 2 (1941), 95-124. Reprinted in the author's *Studies on the Reformation.* Includes a bibliography.

The Travail of Religious Liberty. Nine Biographical Studies. Philadelphia, 1951. 272 pages.

Pertinent to the Reformation: Calvin, Servetus, Castellio, Joris, Ochino.

BATES, SEARLE M. *Religious Liberty: an Inquiry.* London, N.Y., 1945. xviii+604 pages.

pp. 148-186 are concerned with the Reformation. Includes a bibliography.

BAUSLIN, DAVID H. *The Reformation and Civil Liberty.* LQ XXII (1892), 547-62.

BURR, GEORGE LINCOLN. *The Literature of Witchcraft.* AHAP IV (1890), 37-66.

The Fate of Diedrich Flade. AHAP V (1891), 3-57.

Anent the Middle Ages. AHR XVIII (1913), 710-726.

BURY, JOHN BAGNELL. *A History of Freedom of Thought* (Home University Library). N.Y., 1913. 256 pages.

DANNENFELDT, KARL H. *Leonhard Rauwolf, a Lutheran Pilgrim in Jerusalem, 1575.* ARG LV (1964), 18-36.

The story of a travelling scientist who was tolerant of other religions.

FAULKNER, JOHN ALFRED. *The Reformers and Toleration.* ASCH 2S V (1915), 1-22.

HOBHOUSE, WALTER. *The Church and the World in Idea and History* (Bampton Lectures 1909). Ld., 1910. xxv+411 pages.

LEA, HENRY C. (ED.) *Materials Toward a History of Witchcraft.* 3 vols. Philadelphia, 1939. New edition edited by Arthur C. Howland. London & N.Y., 1957.

A classic collection of sources. Contains material from the
16th century.

LECLER, JOSEPH. *Toleration and Reformation,* translated by
T. L. Westow. 2 vols. N.Y., London, 1960.
Vol. I: xv+432 pages. A survey of general practice in the
Middle Ages and a sketch of toleration controversies in
Switzerland and Poland.
Vol. II: ix+544 pages. Toleration in France, the Low Coun-
tries and England.

MACKINNON, JAMES. *A History of Modern Liberty.* Vol. II.
The Age of the Reformation. Ld., N.Y., 1906. xi+490 pages.

MIDELFORD, ERIK H. *Witchcraft and Religion in Sixteenth
Century Germany: the Formation and Consequences of an
Orthodoxy.* ARG LXII (1972), 266-278.

NORWOOD, FREDERICK A. *Strangers and Exiles.* 2 vols. Nashville, 1969. Vol. I, 496 pages; Vol. II, 478 pages.
Chapters 8, 9, and 16 deal with the problem of religious
liberty in the continental Reformation.

POPKIN, RICHARD H. *The History of Scepticism from Erasmus
to Descartes.* Assen, N.Y., 1960. xvii+236 pages.

RUFFINI, FRANCESCO. *Religious Liberty,* tr. J. Parker Heyes
(Theological Translation Library XXXII). Ld., N.Y., 1912.
xxiv+536 pages.

SCHAFF, PHILIP. *The Progress of Religious Freedom as Shown in
the History of Toleration Acts.* ASCH I (1888), 1-125.

SCHWAB, PAUL JOSIAH. *The Attitude of Wolfgang Musculus
toward Religious Tolerance* (Yale Studies in Religion VI).
Scottdale, Pa., 1933. 63 pages.

SHAW, DUNCAN (ED.) *Reformation and Revolution. Essays
Presented to Hugh Watt.* Edinburgh, 1967. 322 pages.
SIMPSON, M. A. *On the Troubles Begun at Frankfurt, 1556.*
HENDERSON, IAN. *Reassessment of the Reformers.*
The rest of the collection is devoted to Scotland.

STUDER, GERALD C. *A History of the Martyr's Mirror.* MQR
XXII (1948), 163-179.
Analyzes various martyrologies of the 16th century.

TRESSLER, V. G. A. *The Censor as a Factor in Civilization.* LQ
XL (1910), 229-252.

POLITICAL FIGURES OF THE REFORMATION

ARMSTRONG, E. *The Emperor Charles V.* 2d ed., 2 vols. Ld., 1910.

BELLOC, HILAIRE. *Characters of the Reformation.* N.Y., 1936. v+342 pages. New edition (Essays Index Report series). N.Y., 1970.

On Henry IV of France, Ferdinand II, and Gustavus Adolphus.

The others are English.

BRANDI, KARL. *The Emperor Charles V. The Growth and Destiny of a Man and of a World Empire,* translated by C. V. Wedgewood. London, 1939. N.Y., 1965. 655 pages. Paperback.

The most authoritative study.

EKMAN, ERNST. *Albrecht of Prussia and the Counts' War (1533-1536).* ARG LI (1960), 19-36.

Shows Albrecht's influence on Danish, Prussian and Swedish relations.

HANCOCK, ALTON O. *Philipp of Hesse's View of the Relationship of Prince and Church.* CH XXXV 2 (1966), 157-169.

HENDERSON, ERNEST F. *Two Lives of the Emperor Charles V.* AHR IX (1903), 23-35.

HILLERBRAND, HANS J. *Landgrave Philipp of Hesse, 1504-1567. Religion and Politics in the Reformation* (Reformation Essays series). St. Louis, 1967. 40 pages.

Valuable.

KÖSTLIN, JULIUS. *Frederick the Wise and the Castle Church at Wittenberg,* tr. George F. Behringer. LQ XXIII (1893), 211-228.

MCELWEE, WILLIAM L. *The Reign of Charles V, 1516-1558.* London, 1936. ix+253 pages.

Good summary, with bibliography.

RICHARD, J. W. *The Elector of Saxony's Confession of Faith.* LQ XXXI (1901), 301-336.

SCHWARZENFELD, GERTRUDE VON. *Charles V, Father of Europe,* translated by Ruth M. Bethell. Chicago, 1937. 306 pages.

Not as valuable as Brandi.

STRAUSS, DAVID FRIEDRICH. *Ulrich von Hutten.* tr. Mrs. G.
Sturge (from 2d German) Ld., 1874. xiv+386 pages.
STRAUSS, GERALD. *The Religious Policies of Dukes Wilhelm
and Ludwig of Bavaria in the First Decade of the Protestant
Era.* CH XXVIII 4 (1959), 350-373.
TYLER, ROYALL. *The Emperor Charles the Fifth.* Fairlawn, N.J.,
1956. 375 pages.
Good bibliography including original sources.

THE REFORMATION IN RELATION TO SOCIAL
QUESTIONS

GENERAL TREATMENTS

BAINTON, ROLAND H. *Women of the Reformation in Germany
and Italy.* Minneapolis, 1971. 279 pages.
A delightful and well researched book on 8 German and 6
Italian women, including such notables as Katherine von Bora,
Anna Zwingli and containing a sketch of Anabaptist women.
BAX, E. BELFORT. *German Society at the Close of the Middle
Ages.* Ld., 1894. xi+276 pages. New edition, N.Y., 1967.
CHATTERTON-HILL, GEORGE. *The Sociological Value of
Christianity.* Ld., 1912. xxii+285 pages.
Protestantism has always "served as a ferment of social dis-
organization and disruption."
COLE, RICHARD G. *The Pamphlet and Social Forces in the Re-
formation.* LQ XVII (1965), 195-205.
DICKENS, ARTHUR G. *Reformation and Society in Sixteenth
Century Europe* (History of European Civilization series).
N.Y., 1966. 216 pages.
Good.
GRIMM, HAROLD J. *Social Forces in the German Reformation.*
CH XXXI (1962), 3-13.
HEARNSHAW, FOSSEY JOHN COBB (ED.) *The Social and Po-
litical Ideas of Some Great Thinkers of the Renaissance and
Reformation.* Ld.[1925]. 215 pages. New edition, N.Y., 1967.
HENDERSON, R. W. *Sixteenth Century Community Benevo-
lence: an Attempt to Resocialize the Secular.* CH XXXVIII

4 (1969), 421-428.

HOLBORN, HAJO. *The Social Basis of the German Reformation.*
CH V (1936), 330-339.

MARTIN, ALFRED W. VON. *Sociology of the Renaissance,* tr.
W. L. Luethers. London, N.Y., 1944. x+100 pages.
A classic German study, originally presented in 1932.

PASCAL, ROY. *The Class Basis of Luther's Reformation.* HJ
XXIX (1930/31), 641-654.
The social basis of the German Reformation. Ld., 1933. ix+
246 pages.
New edition (Reprints of Economic Classics series). N.Y.,
1971.

PIEPKORN, ARTHUR CARL. *The Doctrine of Marriage in the
Theologians of Lutheran Orthodoxy.* CTM XXIV 7 (1953),
465-489.
*The Theologians of Lutheran Orthodoxy on Polygamy,
Celibacy, and Divorce.* CTM XXV 4 (1954), 276-283.

SHAPIRO, JACOB SELWYN. *Social Reform and the Reformation*
(Studies in History, Economics and Public Law, Columbia
University, XXXIV, No. 2). N.Y., 1909. 160 pages.
Also separate as a thesis, 1909.
Deals with social conditions, the Peasants' War, Luther's
attitude to various schemes of reform.
New edition, 1970.

SMITH, PRESERVED. *German Opinion on the Divorce of Henry
VIII.* EHR XXVII (1912), 671-681.

WALSH, J. J. *What Happened at the Reformation?* ACQ XXXIV
(1909), 193-206.
Contends that nursing suffered a setback.

THE PEASANTS' WAR

BAX, E. BELFORT. *The Peasants' War in Germany,* Ld., 1899.
xi+367 pages.

DAVIES, J. C. (ED.) *Studies Presented to Sir Hilary Jenkinson.*
Oxford, 1957.
HOLLAENDER, ALBERT E. *Articles of Almayne.* pp. 164-
177.
A translation of the *Twelve Articles.*

DIRRIM, ALLEN W. *Recent Marxist Historiography of the German*

Peasants Revolt—a Critique. BLFRR IV L (1969), 3-8.
ENGELS, FRIEDRICH. *The Peasant War in Germany,* tr. Moissaye
J. Olgin, Ld., 1926. 190 pages.
Stresses the middle class character of the Lutheran movement.
*The German Revolutions. The Peasant War in Germany and
Germany: Revolution and Counter-Revolution.* ed. Leonard
Krieger. (Classic European Historians series.) Chicago, 1967.
xlvii+246 pages.
A classic Marxist interpretation of the 1525 uprising.
GRIMM, HAROLD J. *Luther's Critics and the Peasant Revolt.*
LQ XIX (1946), 115-132.
HEYMANN, FREDERICK G. *The Hussite Revolution and the Ger-
man Peasants' War. Medievalia et Humanistica* new series
(1970), 141-159.
JANZOW, W. THEOPHIL. *Background for the Peasants' Revolt of
1524.* CTM XXII 9 (1951), 644-664.
NEWMAN, ALBERT H. *The Peasants' War.* BQR XI (1889), 48-
65.
OMAN, CHARLES W. C. *The German Peasant War of 1525.* EHR
V (1890), 65-94.
SESSIONS, KYLE C. (ED.) *Reformation and Authority. The Mean-
ing of the Peasants' Revolt* (Problems in European Civilization series). Lexington, Mass., 1968. xviii+107 pages.
Contains excerpts from Luther and modern interpreters, and
a bibliography.
STAYER, JAMES M. *Terrorism, the Peasant's War, and the "Wiedertäufer."* ARG LVI (1965), 227-229.
Relates the Krug confession of 1533 in Fulda to the question
of Anabaptism and the war.

KNIGHTS' REVOLT

HITCHCOCK, WILLIAM R. *The Background of the Knights' Revolt* (Univ. of California Publications in History series).
Berkeley & Los Angeles, 1958. vi+128 pages.

JEWS

BEN-SASSON, HAIM HILLEL. *Jewish-Christian Disputation in the
Setting of Humanism and Reformation in the German Empire.*
HTR LIX 4 (1966), 369-390.

HOLMIO, ARMAS K. E. *The Lutheran Reformation and the Jews. The Birth of the Protestant Jewish Missions.* Hancock, Mich., 1949. 218 pages.
Originally a Ph.D. dissertation. Dated, but well documented.
Martin Luther, Friend or Foe of the Jews. Chicago, 1949. 31 pages.
Analyzes Luther's most offensive treatise on the Jews in its historical context.

MEYER, CARL S. *Luther's Alleged Anti-Semitism.* CTM XXXII, 11 (1961), 692-696.

MOELLERING, RALPH. *Miscellanea: Luther's Attitude Toward the Jews.* CTM XIX 12 (1948), 920-934; XX 1 (1949), 45-59; XX 3 (1949), 194-215, 579.

SIIRALA, AARNE. *Luther and the Jews.* LW XI 3 (1964), 337-358.

TURKS

BOHNSTEDT, JOHN W. *The Infidel Scourge of God. The Turkish Menace as Seen by German Pamphleteers of the Reformation Era.*
(Transactions of the American Philosophical Society new series). 1968. 58 pages.
Contains bibliography.

BUCHANAN, HARVEY. *Luther and the Turks.* ARG XLVII (1956), 145-159.

BUSBECQ, OGIER GHISELIN DE. *The Turkish Letters of Ogier Ghiselin de Busbecq Imperial Ambassador at Constantinople 1554-1562,* tr. Edward Seymour Forster. Oxford 1927. xvi+265 pages.

FISCHER-GALATI, STEPHEN A. *Ottoman Imperialism and the Lutheran Struggle for Recognition in Germany, 1520-1529.* CH XXIII 1 (1954), 46-67.
Ottoman Imperialism and the Religious Peace of Nürnberg. ARG XLVII (1956), 160-179.
How the Turkish threat influenced negotiations with Protestants in 1532.
Ottoman Imperialism and German Protestantism 1521-1555. (Harvard Historical Monographs series.) Cambridge, 1959. viii+142 pages.

Includes a bibliography.

FORELL, GEORGE W. *Luther and the War Against the Turks.*
    CH XIV 4 (1945), 256-271.
    Luther and the War Against the Turks. CTM XVII 9 (1946),
    676-692.

MOORE, SIDNEY. *The Turkish Menace in the 16th Century.*
    Modern Language Review XL (1945), 30-36.

ROVILLARD, CLARENCE D. *The Turk in French History,*
    Thought and Literature, 1500-1660. Paris, 1949. 700 pages.
    Originally a Harvard dissertation, 1936.
    Contains bibliography of pamphlets relating to the Turks.

THE REFORMATION AND ECONOMIC QUESTIONS

GENERAL TREATMENTS

The Cambridge Economic History. 6 vols. Cambridge, 1941-1967.
    Vol. I: *The Agricultural Life in the Middle Ages,* ed. J. H.
    Clapham and Eileen Power. xvii+650 pages.
    Vol. II: *Trade & Industry in the Middle Ages,* ed. M. Postan
    and E. E. Rich. xv+604 pages.
    Vol. III: *Economic Organization and Policies in the Middle*
    Ages, ed. M. Postan *et al.* xiii+696 pages.
    These volumes describe various aspects of economics in the
    16th century.

DAY, CLIVE. *A History of Commerce.* N.Y., 1907. xiv+447 pages.
    Various new editions; rev. ed. N.Y., 1942. xxii+746 pages.
    Standard work. Chapters 15-17 describe commerce in the
    16th century, emphasizing the Fugger enterprise.

EHRENBERG, RICHARD. *Capital and Finance in the Age of the*
    Renaissance; a Study of the Fuggers and Their Connections.
    tr. H. M. Lucas. Ld., [1928]. 390 pages. (The Bedford series
    of Economic Handbooks II).

EELLS, EARNEST E. *Protestantism and Property.* PTR XXI
    (1923), 267-290, 430-457.

HARVEY, A. E. *Economic Self-Interest in the German Anti-Clerical-*
    ism of the 15th and 16th Centuries. AJT XIX (1915), 509-528.

HEATON, HERBERT. *Economic History of Europe.* London,
N.Y., 1936. xiv+775 pages. Rev. ed. N.Y., 1948. xiv+792
pages.
Standard survey, with bibliography.

JACOBS, CHARLES M. *The Economic Background of the Reformation,* LCR XLI (1922), 97-112.

MCARTHUR, ELLEN A. *The Regulation of Wages in the 16th
Century,* EHR XV (1900), 445-455.

NEF, JOHN U. *Industrial Europe at the Time of the Reformation.* JPE XLIX (1941), 1-40; 183-224.

NORWOOD, FREDERICK A. *The Reformation Refugees as an
Economic Force* (Studies in Church History series). Chicago,
1942. ix+206 pages.
A thorough study of the problem in England, Germany,
Switzerland and the Netherlands.

UNWIN, GEORGE. *Industrial Organization in the Sixteenth
and Seventeenth Centuries.* Oxford, 1904. 2d edition, with
introduction by T. S. Ashton, London, 1963. 277 pages.
Still useful. Contains bibliography.

WOOD, H. G. *The Influence of the Reformation on Ideas Concerning Wealth and Property.* In *Property: Its Duties and
Rights,* Ld., 1914 (2nd ed., 1915). pp., 133-167.

PROTESTANTISM AND THE RISE OF CAPITALISM

BIBLIOGRAPHY

PARSONS, TALCOTT. *"Capitalism" in Recent German Literature:
Sombart and Weber.* JPE XXXVI (1928), 641-661: XXXVII
(1929), 31-51.

POSTAN, M. *Studies in Bibliography. 1. Medieval capitalism.*
EcHR IV (1933), 212-227.

TAWNEY, RICHARD HENRY. *Studies in Bibliography,* II.
Modern Capitalism, EcHR IV (1933), 336-356.

DISCUSSION

BURRELL, SIDNEY A. *Calvinism, Capitalism, and the Middle Class: Some Afterthoughts on an Old Problem.* JMH XXXII (1960), 129-141.

CUNNINGHAM, WILLIAM. *Christianity and Economic Science.* Ld., 1914, viii+111 pages.
Devotes a chapter to Calvinism and capital; follows Weber.

DOBB, MAURICE H. *Studies in the Development of Capitalism.* London, 1946; N.Y., 1947. ix+396 pages.
A Marxist interpretation.

EISENSTADT, SAMUEL N. (ED.) *The Protestant Ethic and Modernization. A Comparative View.* London, N.Y., 1968. viii+407 pages.
A thorough discussion of the Weber thesis and its implications by a variety of scholars. Pertinent essays:
EISENSTADT, SAMUEL N. *The Protestant Ethic Thesis in an Analytical and Comparative Framework.* 3-45.
ANDRESKI, STANISLAV. *Method and Substantive Theory in Max Weber.* 46-63.
FISCHOFF, EPHRAIM. *The Protestant Ethic and the Spirit of Capitalism: the History of a Controversy.* 67-86.
LÜTHY, HERBERT. *Once Again: Calvinism and Capitalism.* 87-108.
BURRELL, SIDNEY A. *Calvinism, Capitalism and the Middle Classes: Some Afterthoughts on an Old Problem.* 135-154.
LITTLE, DAVID. *Calvinism and Law.* 177-183.
HOOYKAAS, R. *Science and Reformation.* 211-239.
Bibliographies are included.

FANFANI, AMINTORE. *Catholicism, Protestantism, and Capitalism.* London, 1935. v+224 pages.
Distinguishes between doctrinal and organizational influences.

FULLERTON, KEMPER. *Calvinism and Capitalism.* HTR XXI (1928), 163-195.
Summarizes Weber.

GREEN, ROBERT (ED.) *Protestantism and Capitalism* (Problems in European Civilization series). Boston, 1952. xii+116 pages.
Contains excerpts from Weber and other scholars involved in the controversy. With a bibliographical essay by the editor.

HUDSON, WINTHROP S. *Calvinism and the Spirit of Capitalism.*

CH XVIII (1950), 3-17.

HYMA, ALBERT. *Christianity, Capitalism and Communism: a Historical Analysis.* Ann Arbor, Mich., 1937. 303 pages. Chapters 3-6 deal with Calvinism.
Calvinism and Capitalism in the Dutch Netherlands 1555-1700. JMH X (1938), 321-343.

KITCH, M. J. (COMP.) *Capitalism and the Reformation* (Problems and Perspectives in History series). N.Y., 1967. Paperback, 1970. xx+218 pages.
Selection of discussion documents.

NELSON, N. *The Idea of Usury.* Princeton, 1949. pp.?.
Contains complete bibliography of the Weber debate.

O'BRIEN, GEORGE. *An Essay on the Economic Effects of the Reformation.* Ld., 1923. x+194 pages.
"The insistence of the capitalist on the removal of all restraints by the state is strictly analagous to the insistence of the Protestant on the removal of all restraints by the church. It is private judgment translated into the realm of industry."
New edition, Westminster, Md. 1944. Reprint, N.Y., 1970.

ROBERTSON, H. M. *Aspects of the Rise of Economic Individualism, a Criticism of Max Weber and His School.* Cambridge, Eng., 1933. xvi+223 pages.
"The doctrine of the 'calling' did not breed a spirit of capitalism. The spirit of capitalism was responsible for the gradual modification and attrition of the Puritan doctrine." "The same change of emphasis took place among the Catholics."

ROBINSON, CHALFANT. *Some Economic Results of the Protestant Reformation Doctrines.* PTR XV (1917), 623-644.
Discusses Weber.

SOMBART, WERNER. *The Jews and Modern Capitalism,* tr. M. Epstein. Ld., 1913. xvi+402 pages.

TAWNEY, RICHARD HENRY. *Religion and the Rise of Capitalism.* (Holland Memorial Lectures, 1922). Ld., 1926. xiii+339 pages.
Follows the lead of Weber.
Various new editions. Since 1947 available in paperback.

TROELTSCH, ERNEST. *The Social Teaching of the Christian Churches,* tr. Olive Wyon. 2 vols. Ld. 1931.
Follows Weber.
Various new editions.

WALKER, GORDON P. C. *Capitalism and the Reformation.*
EHR (1937), p.?
Argues against Weber and asserts that the Reformation was
a result of the price revolution.

WEBER, MAX. *The Protestant Ethic and the Spirit of Capitalism,*
tr. Talcott Parsons, Ld., 1930. xi+292 pages.
Traces a connection between the Puritan doctrines of the
calling, innerworldly asceticism and predestination, and the
rise of capitalism.
Various new editions. Since 1958 available in paperback.

POPULAR SATIRE

The Satirists of the Reformation. Unsigned article in LA XCV
(1867), 707-719.

WRIGHT, THOMAS. *The Satirical Literature of the Reformation.*
(*Essays on Archaeological Subjects.* II). Ld., 1861. pp. 272-
319.

CARTOONS

BETTEN, FRANCIS S. *The Cartoon in Luther's Warfare Against
the Church.* CHR ns V (1925-26), 252-264.

GEISBERG, MAX. *Cranach's Illustrations to the Lord's Prayer
and the Editions of Luther's Catechism.* BMC XLIII (1923),
85-87.
Reproduces 8 woodcuts.
The reader unfamiliar with German can learn much from the
following reproductions by Max Geisberg:
*Die deutsche Buchillustration in der ersten Hälfte des 16.
Jahrhunderts,* München, 1930–(6 vols. to date).
*Die Reformation in den Kampfbildern der Einblatt-Holz-
schnitte aus der ersten Hälfte des 16. Jahrhunderts.* München
1929. x pages+53 plates.
*Das Wiedertäuferreich in den gleichzeitigen Einblatt-Holz-
schnitten,* 16 Faksimile-Wiedergaben, München, 1929.

HAMMERTON, JOHN ALEXANDER. *Universal History of the
World.* 8 vols., Ld. 1928-29.
Vol. VI, *From the Reformation to the Age of Louis XIV.*
The chapter on the Reformation by R. H. Murray reproduces
some contemporary cartoons.

ROMAN CATHOLIC REFORM
(Counter Reformation)

SOURCES

GILBERT, FELIX. *Contarini on Savonarola: an Unknown Document of 1516.* ARG LIX (1968), 145-149.
> The first theological work of Contarini, reflecting his tolerance later exhibited in 16th century Roman Catholic Reform. With the Italian text.

LOYOLA, IGNATIUS. *Spiritual Exercises.* Various editions and translations since 1850. Standard translation by Anthony Mottola. N.Y., 1964. 200 pages.

O'LEARY, D. F. (TR.), and GOODIER, ALBAN (ED.) *Letters and Instructions of St. Ignatius.* St. Louis, 1914. pp.?

OLIN, JOHN C. (TR.) *The Catholic Reformation: Savonarola to Ignatius Loyola. Reform in the Church 1495-1540.* N.Y., 1969. xxvi+220 pages.
> Contains translations of documents with background material and bibliography.

PEERS, E. A. (ED. & TR.) *The Letters of Saint Teresa of Jesus.* 2 vols. London, 1950, 1951. xii+1006 pages.
> The work of one of the founders of the Carmelites.
> *The Complete Works of St. Teresa of Jesus.* 3 vols. London, 1946.

RAHNER, HUGO (COMP.) *Letters to Women,* tr. Kathleen Pond and S. A. H. Weetman. N.Y., 1960. xxiii+564 pages.
> From Ignatius.

SCHROEDER, H. J. (ED.) *Canons and Decrees of the Council of Trent. Original Text With English Translation.* London, St. Louis, 1941. xxxiii+608 pages.
> The standard Roman Catholic edition.

YOUNG, WILLIAM J. (TR.) *St. Ignatius' Own Story.* Chicago, 1956. 138 pages.
> Also contains a sampling of letters.
> *Letters of Ignatius of Loyola.* Chicago, 1959. xiii+450 pages.
> A fair selection of letters, with bibliography.

GENERAL TREATMENTS

BOTSTEIN, LEON, and KARNOFSKY, ELLEN (EDS.) *Essays in Western Civilization in Honor of Christian Mackauer.* Chicago, 1970. pp.?

COCHRANE, ERIC. *The Counter Reformation: a Survey.*

BURNS, EDWARD M. *The Counter Reformation.* Princeton, Toronto, London, N.Y., 1964. 186 pages.
A popular account by a political scientist, with selected readings from sources.

DANIEL-ROPS, HENRY. *The Catholic Reformation,* tr. J. Warrington. London, N.Y., 1961. 435 pages.
A classic Roman Catholic French study.

EVENNETT, HENRY O. *The Spirit of the Counter Reformation,* ed. John Bossy. Cambridge, London, 1968. xiii+159 pages.
The Birkbeck Lectures in Ecclesiastical History of 1951 at the University of Cambridge.

GARSTEIN, OSKAR. *Rome and the Counter-Reformation in Scandinavia, Until the Establishment of the S. Congregatio De Propaganda Fide in 1662* (Scandinavian University Books series). N.Y., 1964. xii+1113 pages.
The first volume of an incomplete series covering 1539-1583.

JANELLE, PIERRE. *The Catholic Reformation.* Milwaukee, 1949. xiv+397 pages.
A Roman Catholic study arguing that the Roman Catholic reformation was a continuation of 15th century humanist revival.

JOURDAN, GEORGE V. *The Movement Towards Catholic Reform in the Early XVIth Century.* N.Y., 1914; London, 1919. xxxi+336 pages.
Traces the relationship between humanism and early Reformation. Still useful, with appendices on Erasmus and other humanist reformers.

LUCAS, HENRY S. *Survival of Catholic Faith in the Sixteenth Century.* CHR XXIX (1943-44), 25-52.

KIDD, BERESFORD J. *The Counter Reformation, 1550-1600.* London, 1933, 1958, 1963. 270 pages.
Deals with all of Europe.

MCNALLY, ROBERT E. *Reform of the Church. Crisis and Criticism in Historical Perspective.* N.Y., 1963. 140 pages.

A Roman Catholic survey of reform attempts from the 13th through the 16th centuries, and an argument for continuing reformation. Contains an interesting account of Luther and Trent.

TAVARD, GEORGE H. *The Catholic Reform in the Sixteenth Century.* CH XXVI 3 (1957), 275-288.

Discusses recent research.

TRENT

ANDERSON, MARVIN W. *Trent and Justification (1546): a Protestant Reflection.* SJT XXI (1968), 385-406.

BAEPLER, RICHARD. *Scripture and Tradition in the Council of Trent.* CTM XXXI 6 (1960), 341-362.

CASTEEL, THEODORE W. *Calvin and Trent: Calvin's Reaction to the Council of Trent in the Context of His Conciliar Thought.* HTR LXIII 1 (1970), 91-118.

EVENNETT, HENRY O. *The Cardinal of Lorraine and the Council of Trent. A Study in the Counter-Reformation.* Cambridge, 1940. xvii+536 pages.

Includes a bibliography.

JEDIN, HUBERT. *A History of the Council of Trent.* 5 vols. Tr. Ernest Graf. London, N.Y., 1957-.

Vol. II. *The First Sessions at Trent, 1545-1547.* xi+562 pages. Translation of the rest to follow later. This is the authoritative work on Trent by a German Roman Catholic scholar. *Crisis and Closure of the Council of Trent. A Retrospective View from the Second Vatican Council,* tr. N. D. Smith. London, Melbourne, 1967. vi+189 pages.

JOEST, WILFRIED. *The Doctrine of Justification of the Council of Trent.* LW IX 3 (1962), 204-218.

KALB, ROBERT. *A Conversation Between Pasquil and German: Theological Mood and Method, 1537.* CTM XLI 3 (1970), 131-145.

On an anonymous pamphlet dealing with the preparations for the Council of Trent.

MCCUE, JAMES F. *The Doctrine of Transubstantiation from Berengar Through Trent: the Point at Issue.* HTR LXI 3 (1968), 385-430.

MCNALLY, ROBERT E. *The Council of Trent and the German Protestants.* TS XXV 1 (1964), 1-22.
The Council of Trent, the Spiritual Exercises, and the Catholic Reform (Facet Book series). Philadelphia, 1970. vii+24 pages.
The Council of Trent and the Spiritual Doctrine of the Counter Reformation. CH XXXIV 1 (1965), 36-49.
The Council of Trent and Vernacular Bibles. TS XXVII 2 (1966), 204-227.

O'DONOHOE, JAMES A. *Tridentine Seminary Legislation: Its Sources and Its Formation.* Louvain, 1957. vi+187 pages. Contains bibliography.

OLSEN, ARTHUR L. *Martin Chemnitz and the Council of Trent.* D II 1 (1963), 60-67.

PASCOE, LOUIS B. *The Council of Trent and Bible Study.* CHR LII (1966), 18-38.

PIEPKORN, ARTHUR CARL. *Martin Chemnitz' Views on Trent: the Genesis and the Genius of the Examen Concilii Tridentini.* CTM XXXVII 1 (1966), 5-37.

SPYKMAN, GORDON J. *Attrition and Contrition at the Council of Trent.* Kampen, 1955. ix+270 pages.
A study of the doctrine of repentance. With bibliography.

STRAUSS, FELIX F. *The Effect of the Council of Trent on the Episcopal Tenure of Duke Ernst of Bavaria, Archbishop-Confirmed of Salzburg, in 1554.* JMH XXXII (1960), 119-128.

TAVARD, GEORGE H. *Tradition in Early Post-Tridentine Theology.* TS XXIII (1962), 377-405.

THEISEN, REINOLD. *Mass Liturgy and the Council of Trent.* Collegeville, Minn., 1965. x+169 pages.

INDIVIDUAL FIGURES

BRODRICK, JAMES. *Saint Peter Canisius, S. J., 1521-1597.* London, 1935. xv+589 pages.

DOUGLAS, RICHARD M. *Jacobo Sadoleto, 1477-1547: Humanist and Reformer.* Cambridge, Mass., 1959. xvi+307 pages.
The biography of a reform cardinal. Includes bibliography.

JEDIN, HUBERT. *Papal Legate at the Council of Trent, Cardinal Seripando,* tr. Frederick Eckhoff. London, St. Louis, 1947. viii+720 pages.

NYHUS, PAUL L. *Caspar Schatzgeyer and Conrad Pellican: the Triumph of Dissension in the Early Sixteenth Century.* ARG LXI (1970), 179-204.
   The story of two Franciscans, one siding with Zwingli and the other with the Counter Reformation.
PEERS, E. A. *St. John of the Cross, and Other Lectures and Addresses, 1920-1945.* London, 1946. 231 pages.
   On mystics. The lecture on St. John was given at Cambridge, 1932.
   Mother of Carmel. A Portrait of St. Teresa of Jesus. 2d ed. London, 1946. 163 pages.
   Standard biography of one of the founders of the Carmelite reform order.

JESUITS

BOEHMER, HEINRICH. *The Jesuits. An Historical Study,* tr. Paul Z. Strodack. 4th ed. Philadelphia, 1928. 192 pages.
   A classic study by a Protestant Luther scholar.
BRODRICK, JAMES P. *The Economic Morals of the Jesuits. An Answer to Dr. H.M. Robertson.* London, 1934. 158 pages.
   Defends Jesuit economic behavior. See also the work of Robertson.
   The Origin of the Jesuits. Garden City, N.Y., 1940. 233 pages. Reprinted in 1960 as an Image Book.
   A standard reference work.
   The Progress of the Jesuits, 1556-1579. London, N.Y., 1947. vii+337 pages.
   The sequel to the author's *The Origins of the Jesuits.*
   Saint Ignatius Loyola. The Pilgrim Years, 1491-1538. London, N.Y., 1956. 372 pages.
DUDON, PAUL. *St. Ignatius of Loyola.* tr. William J. Young. (Science and Culture series.) Milwaukee, 1949. xiv+484 pages.
   A French Roman Catholic biography, includes bibliography.
FARRELL, ALLAN P. *The Jesuit Code of Liberal Education: Development and Scope of the Ratio Studiorum.* Milwaukee, 1938. xviii+478 pages.
   Includes bibliography.
GUIBERT, JOSEPH DE. *The Jesuits. Their Spiritual Doctrine*

and Practice. tr. William J. Young, ed. George E. Ganss.
Chicago, 1953. 2d ed. 1964. xxv+692 pages.
The most comprehensive work on the subject; contains
a bibliography.

HARNEY, MARTIN P. *The Jesuits in History. The Society of
Jesus through Four Centuries.* N.Y., 1941. xvi+513 pages.
The first nine chapters cover the Reformation period.

TOPICS

ANDERSON, MARVIN W. *Biblical Humanism and Roman
Catholic Reform: (1501-1542) Contarini, Pole, and Giberti.*
CTM XXXIX (1968), 686-707.

BETTEN, FRANCIS S. *The Roman Index of Forbidden Books,
Briefly Explained for Catholic Booklovers and Students.* St.
Louis, 1909. 69 pages. New editions: 1925, 1927, 1932.
A Jesuit explanation.

COCHRANE, ERIC. *New Light on Post-Tridentine Italy: a Note
on Recent Counter Reformation Scholarship.* CHR LVI
(1970), 291-319.

CUMING, G. J., and BAKER, DEREK (EDS.) *Councils and
Assemblies* (Studies in Church History series). Cambridge,
1971.
HALL, BASIL. *The Colloquies Between Catholics and
Protestants, 1539-41.* pp. 235-266.

HANSEN, KLAUS. *Petrus Canisius's Stand on Usury: an Example
of Jesuit Tactics in the German Counter Reformation.* ARG
LV (1964), 192-203.

HOAR, GEORGE A. *Early Evidences of Catholic Reform in the
Thought and Actions of Bartholomeus Arnoldi von Usingen.*
ARG LVI (1965), 155-163.
Analyzes Luther's friend and the sermon reprinted by Ken-
neth A. Strand in ARG LVI (1965), 145-155.

MACKENSEN, HEINZ. *The Diplomatic Role of Gasparo Cardinal
Contarini at the Colloquy of Ratisbon of 1541.* CH XXVII 4
(1958), 312-337.
*The Debate Between Eck and Melanchthon on Original Sin
at the Colloquy of Worms.* LQ XI 1 (1959), 42-56.
Describes a feature of Lutheran and Roman Catholic negotiations in 1541.

Contarini's Theological Role at Ratisbon in 1541. ARG LI
(1960), 36-56.
Describes his stand on sin and grace at the last negotiation
between Protestants and Catholics.
OAKLEY, FRANCIS. *Almain and Major: Conciliar Theory on
the Eve of the Reformation.* AHR LXX 3 (1965), 673-690.
POPKIN, RICHARD H. *Skepticism and the Counter-Reformation
in France.* ARG LI (1960), 58-86.
Shows the relationship between Roman Catholic apologists
and Montaigne.
ROSS, J. B. *Casparo Contarini and His Friends. Studies in the
Renaissance* XVII (1970), 192-232.
STRAND, KENNETH A. *Arnoldi von Usingen's Sermo de
Matrimonio Sacerdotum et Monachorum: the Text of a
Rare Edition.* ARG LVI (1965), 145-155.
Introduces and reprints the Latin text. See also the essay
by George A. Hoar.

MARTIN LUTHER

BIBLIOGRAPHY

CARLSON, EDGAR. *The Interpretation of Luther in Modern
Swedish Theology.* AQ XXIII (1944), 195-220.
The Reinterpretation of Luther. Philadelphia, 1948. 256 pages.
A critical evaluation of Swedish Luther research, spearheaded
by Aulen and Nygren.
DILLENBERGER, JOHN. *Survey: Literature in Luther Studies,
1950-1955.* CH XXV 2 (1956), 160-177.
*Major Volumes and Selected Periodical Literature in Luther
Studies, 1956-1959.* CH XXX 1 (1961), 61-87.
EDMANDS, JOHN. *Reading Notes on Luther.* Bulletin of the Mer-
cantile Library of Philadelphia. I, No. 5 (Oct. 1, 1883), 94-
98. Also separate, Philadelphia, 1883. 18 pages.
Excellent list of the older literature especially of the periodical articles in English.
EMERTON, EPHRAIM. *Martin Luther in the Light of Recent Criticism.* HTR VII (1914), 203-229, reprinted in LQ XLIV (1914),
370-392.

FOSTER, WILLIAM EMERSON. *Some Recent Views of Martin Luther*. Providence Public Library Monthly Reference Lists. III, No. II (Nov. 1883).

FRICK, W. K. *Luther Literature*. LCR XVI (1897), 588-611.
Covers not only English and German, but also Swedish and Norwegian.

GANSS, H. G. *Luther and his Protestant Biographers*. ACQ XXVI (1901), 582-601.

GRIMM, HAROLD J. *Luther Research Since 1920*. JMH XXXII (1960), 105-118.

HAIKOLA, LAURI. *Contributions in Finnish to Luther Research Since the Second World War*. LW XIII 3 (1966), 288-290.

HALL, GEORGE F. *Our Knowledge of Luther*. AQ XXV (1946), 35-45.
Surveys Luther literature.

HAMMER, E. W. *Index, 1,286 pages: the Altenburg Luther*. LQ I 2 (1949), 213-224.
On the edition of Luther's works published 1660-64.

JACOBS, H. E. *Biographies of Luther*. LCR XVI (1897), 558-563.

JAUERNIG, R. *Notes and Studies: the Weimar Edition of Luther's Works*. LQ III 1 (1951), 70-78.

KANTZENBACH, FRIEDRICH WILHELM. *Luther Research as a Problem in Comparative Theology*. LW XIII 3 (1966), 257-271.

LAMBERT, W. A. *Luther's Writings*. LCR XVI (1897), 564-587.

LINDBERG, CARTER. *Luther Research in America, 1945-1965*. LW XIII 3 (1966), 291-302.

PESCH, OTTO H. *Twenty Years of Catholic Luther Research*. LW XIII 3 (1966), 303-316.

PRENTER, REGIN. *Luther Research in Scandinavia Since 1945*. LW XIII 3 (1966), 272-287.

REU, JOHANN M. *Thirty-Five Years of Luther Research*. N.Y., 1970. 155 pages.

SAARNIVAARA, UURAS. *Some Questions Concerning Recent Luther Research*. LQ I 1 (1949), 91-96.
On the problem of dating the "tower experience."

SMITH, PRESERVED. *Recent Progress in the Study of Luther*. AJT XIII (1909), 259-268.

A Decade of Luther Study. HTR XIV (1921), 107-135.
WENTZ, ABDEL ROSS. *Recent German Research Concerning
   Luther.* LQ XXXIX (1909), 241-257.
   Martin Luther in the Changing Light of Four Centuries. LQ
   XLVII (1914), 20-31.
WILLIAMS, MELVIN G. *Martin Luther: Portraits in Prose.* CC
   LXXXIV 43 (1967), 1366-1372.
   Surveys historiographical fiction.

TRANSLATIONS

Bibliography

CLEBSCH, WILLIAM A. *The Earliest Translations of Luther into
   English.* HTR LVI 1 (1963), 75-86.
MORRIS, JOHN G. *The Translated Portions of Luther's Writings.*
   LQ XII (1882), 189-207.
ROBBERT, GEORGE S. *A Checklist of Luther's Writings in English.*
   CTM XXXVI 11 (1965), 772-792; XLI 4 (1970), 214-220.
SMITH, PRESERVED. *Complete List of Works of Luther in English.*
   LQ XLVIII (1918), 490-508.
   In view of the adequacy of this list I have merely analyzed
   the two major collections and called attention to a few
   works available only in separate form.
SPITZ, LEWIS W. *Luther Speaks English.* CTM XXVII 3 (1956),
   197-204.

Works

ALAND, KURT (ED.) *Martin Luther's 95 Theses. With the Per-
   tinent Documents from the History of the Reformation.*
   Tr. P. J. Schroeder. London and St. Louis, 1967. 116 pages.
ANDERSON, CHARLES S. (ED.) *Readings in Luther for Laymen.*
   Minneapolis, 1967. vii+304 pages.
   Chronological selections from various works under the
   categories "reformer" and "pastor," with useful introductions
   by the editor.
BAINTON, ROLAND H. (TR.) *The Martin Luther Christmas Book.*
   Philadelphia, 1948. 74 pages.
   Delightfully arranged, with 16th century woodcuts.

Luther's Meditations on the Gospels. Philadelphia, 1962.
115 pages.
Arranged in terms of a life of Christ.
Luther and Spalatin Letters Recovered in Boston. ARG
LIII (1962), 197.
Luther's letter (partly reproduced in the *Weimar Edition*
No. 96) appeared at an auction, and is reprinted here.
The Bondage of the Will by Martin Luther the Celebrated Re-
former Being His Reply to Erasmus translated by Henry Cole
M.A., with slight alteration from Edward Thomas Vaughan,
M.A., corrected by Henry Atherton, Grand Rapids, Michigan,
1931. 419 pages.
BROKERING, HERBERT F. (ED.) *Luther's Prayers*. Minneapolis,
1967. 120 pages.
Commentary on St. Paul's Epistle to the Galatians by Martin
Luther, a new edition, following the corrected and revised
English text of Rev. Erasmus Middleton printed from new
type with a foreword by Prof. Leander S. Keyser. Grand
Rapids, Michigan, 1930. 537 pages.
First Principles of the Reformation or the Ninety-Five Theses and
the Three Primary Works of Dr. Martin Luther, tr. ed. Henry
Wace and C. A. Buchheim. Philadelphia, 1885. lxxxviii+245
pages.
The Ninety-five Theses, Address to the Nobility, on Chris-
tian Liberty, Of Babylonish Captivity. Introductory essays
by Wace, *On the Primary Principles of Luther's Life and*
Teaching, and Buchheim, *The Political Course of the Ref-*
ormation in Germany 1517-46.
HALL, GEORGE I. *Luther's Preface to the Old Testament Apoc-*
ryphical Books. AQ (July 1934), 195-207.
KEPLER, SAMUEL T. (ED.) *Martin Luther: Table Talk*. Cleveland, 1952. xxiii+345 pages. New edition, ed. David L. Scheidt,
1970.
KERR, HUGH T. (ED.) *Compend of Luther's Theology*. Westminster, 1943. xix+253 pages.
Selections from Luther's works in terms of major dogmatic
loci.
LENKER, JOHN NICHOLAS. *The Precious and Sacred Writings of*
Martin Luther. At head of title: *Standard edition of Luther's*
works.

Each volume has separate title-page and several volumes are
printed without the general title-page. Minneapolis, Minn.,
1903-1910. Without series number. *Commentary on Genesis:*
Vol. I. *Luther on Creation.* 1904.
Vol. II. *Luther on Sin and Blood.* 1910.
  Luther's Commentary on the First Twenty-two Psalms.
    1903.
  Commentary on St. Peter and St. Jude. 1904.
  *Luther on Christian Education: Luther's catechetical
    writings.* 1907.
With series number.
  VII. *Luther's Epistle Sermons.* vol. 1, 1908.
  VIII. *Luther's Epistle Sermons.* vol. II, 1909.
   IX. *Luther's Epistle Sermons.* vol. III, 1909.
    X. *Luther's Church Postil Gospels.* vol. I, 1905.
   XI. *Luther's Church Postil Gospels.* vol. II, 1906.
  XII. *Luther's Church Postil Gospels.* vol. III, 1907.
  XIII. *Luther's Church Postil Gospels.* vol. IV, 1904.
  XIV. *Luther's Church Postil Gospels.* vol. V, 1905.
*Luther's Primary Works Together with His Shorter and Larger
    Catechisms,* tr. ed. Henry Wace and C. A. Buchheim, Ld.,
    1896, xvi+492 pages.
Luther's Works. American Edition. 55 vols. Philadelphia, 1955-.
    This edition is nearly complete. For individual listings, see
    ROBBERTS, GEORGE S. *A Checklist of Luther's Writings
    in English.*
PACKER, J. I. and JOHNSTON, O. R. (TR.)*Martin Luther on the
    Bondage of the Will. A New Translation of De Servo Arbitrio
    (1525).*Westwood, N.J., 1957. 312 pages.
PLASS, EWALD M. (ED.) *What Luther Says.* 3 vols. St. Louis,
    1959. xxvi+1667 pages.
    Alphabetically arranged. Very useful.
RUPP, E. GORDON, and DREWERY, BENJAMIN. *Martin Luther*
    (Documents of Modern History series). N.Y., 1970. xii+180
    pages.
    An anthology of Luther's life. Some documents are trans-
    lated for the first time.
SMITH, PRESERVED and GALLINGER, HERBERT PERCIVAL.
    Conversations with Luther, Boston, 1915. xxvii+260 pages.
    Classified excerpts from the Table Talk.

SMITH, PRESERVED. *Luther's Table Talk.* (Studies in History,
Economics and Public Law, Columbia Univ. XXVI, No. 2)
N.Y., 1907. 135 pages.
A discussion.

SMITH, PRESERVED. *Luther's Correspondence and Other Con-
temporary Letters,* tr., ed. Preserved Smith.
Vol. I, 1507-1521. Philadelphia, Pa., 1913. 583 pages.
Vol. II, 1521-1530, tr., ed. Preserved Smith and Charles M.
Jacobs, 1918. 568 pages.

TAPPERT, THEODORE E. (ED.) *Selected Writings of Martin
Luther.* 4 vols. Philadelphia, 1967.
A paperback edition of selections from *Luther's Works,* with
additions from other English editions.

WINTER, ERNST (ED. & TR.) *Discourse on Free Will by Erasmus
and Luther* (Milestones of Thought in the History of Ideas
series). N.Y., 1961. xiii+138 pages.

WOOLF, BERTRAM L. (ED. & TR.) *The Reformation Writings
of Martin Luther.* 2 vols. London, N.Y., 1952-1953.
Chiefly the early works; a useful collection for beginners in
Luther studies.

Works of Martin Luther with Introductions and Notes. Preface
signed by Henry Eyster Jacobs. 6 vols. 1915-1932. A. J.
Holman Co., Philadelphia, Pa.
Vol. I, 1915. x+412 pages. *Luther's Prefaces, Disputation on
Indulgences* (1517), *Treatise on Baptism* (1519), *Discussion
of Confession* (1520), *The Fourteen of Consolation* (1520),
Treatise on Good Works (1520), *Treatise on the New Testa-
ment* (1520), *The Papacy at Rome* (1520).
Vol. II, 1916. 476 pages. *Treatise concerning the Blessed
Sacrament and concerning the Brotherhoods* (1519), *A
Treatise concerning the Ban* (1520), *An Open Letter to the
Christian Nobility* (1520), *The Babylonian Captivity of the
Church* (1520), *A Treatise on Christian Liberty* (1520), *A
brief exposition of the Ten Commandments, the Creed, and
the Lord's Prayer* (1520), *The Eight Wittenberg Sermons*
(1522), *That Doctrines of Men Are to Be Rejected* (1522).
Vol. III, 1930. 464 pages. *An Argument in Defense of All the
Articles of Dr. Martin Luther Wrongly Condemned in the
Roman Bull* (1521), *The Magnificat* (1520-1), *An Earnest*

Exhortation for All Christians, Warning Them Against Insurrection and Rebellion (1522), *Secular Authority: to What Extent It Should Be Obeyed* (1523). *To the Leipzig Goat* (1521), *Reply to the Answer of the Leipzig Goat* (1521), *Answer to the Super-Christian, Super-Spiritual, and Super-Learned Book of the Goat Emser* (1521), *To the Knights of the Teutonic Order* (1523).
Vol. IV, 1931. 411 pages. *On Trading and Usury* (1524) *and A Treatise on Usury* (1520), *The Right and the Power of a Christian Congregation . . . to Call, Appoint, and Dismiss Teachers . . .* (1523), *Preface to an Ordinance of a Common Chest* (1523), *To the Councilmen of All the Cities in Germany that They Establish and Maintain Christian Schools* (1524), *A Sermon on Keeping Children in School* (1530), *The Burning of Friar Henry* (1525), *Admonition to Peace: a Reply to the Twelve Articles on the Peasants in Swabia* (1525), *Against the Robbing and Murdering Hordes of Peasants* (1525), *An Open Letter Concerning the Hard Book Against the Peasants* (1525), *An Exposition of the Eighty-Second Psalm* (1530), *An Exhortation to the Clergy Assembled at the Diet at Augsburg* (1530).
Vol. V, 1931. 330 pages. *On Translating* (1530), *Whether Soldiers, Too, Can Be Saved* (1526), *On War Against the Turk* (1529), *On the Councils and the Churches* (1539).
Vol. VI, 1932. viii+521 pages. *Luther's Liturgical Writings, Hymn Book Prefaces, Prefaces to the Books of the Bible.*

COLLECTED ESSAYS

ASHEIM, IVAR (ED.) *The Church, Mysticism, Sanctification and the Natural in Luther's Thought.* Philadelphia, 1967. 211 pages.
Lectures of the Third International Congress for Luther Research, held in Järvenpää, Finland, August 11-16, 1966. English lectures:
RUPP, E. GORDON. *Luther: the Contemporary Image.* 9-19.
PELIKAN, JAROSLAV. *Continuity and Order in Luther's View of Church and Ministry.* 143-155.
LAZARETH, WILLIAM H. *Luther on Civil Righteousness and Natural Law.* 180-188.

WILLIAMS, GEORGE H. *Sanctification in the Testimony
of So-Called "Schwärmer."* 194-211.
BAINTON, ROLAND H. *et al. Martin Luther Lectures.* 5 vols.
Decorah, Iowa, 1957-1961.
A major reassessment of Luther by international scholars.
Vol. I. BAINTON, ROLAND H., QUANBECK, WARREN A.,
and RUPP, E. GORDON. *Luther Today.* Decorah, 1957.
x+164 pages.

> BAINTON, ROLAND H. *Luther on Birds, Dogs, and
> Babies.* 3-12.
> *Luther's Use of Direct Discourse.* 13-25.
> *The Aarhus Conference.* 26-33.
> QUANBECK, WARREN A. *Experience Transforms Exegesis.*
> 37-59.
> *The Search for a New Method.* 60-81.
> *The Authority and Power of the Word of God.* 82-103.
> RUPP, E. GORDON. *Luther and Carlstadt.* 107-128.
> *Luther and Thomas Müntzer.* 129-146.
> *Luther and Zwingli.* 147-164.

Vol. II. PELIKAN, JAROSLAV, PRENTER, REGIN, and
PREUS, HERMAN A. *More About Luther.* 1958. 214 pages.

> PELIKAN, JAROSLAV. *Catholic Substance.* 3-22.
> *Protestant Principle.* 23-42.
> *Catholic Substance and Protestant Principle.* 43-62.
> PRENTER, REGIN. *The Living Word.* 65-80.
> *Holy Baptism.* 81-99.
> *The Lord's Supper.* 100-122.
> PREUS, HERMAN A. *In the Body of Christ.* 125-159.
> *In the Search for Truth.* 160-187.
> *On the Life of Worship.* 188-214.

Vol. III. TAPPERT, THEODORE, KOOIMAN, WILLEM J.,
and GREEN, LOWELL C. *The Mature Luther.* 1959. 179
pages.

> TAPPERT, THEODORE. *The Professor and His Students.*
> 3-20.
> *The Theologian and the Study of History.* 21-38.
> *The Professor of Theology.* 39-55.
> KOOIMAN, WILLEM J. *Luther at Home.* 59-75.
> *Luther as He Saw Himself.* 76-93.

The Picture of Nature. 176-194.

God and History. 195-217

The Nation (Das Volk). 218-236.

The State. 237-257.

The Gospel and the Social World. 258-272.

Luther's Translation of the New Testament. 273-283.

Luther's Death and Legacy. 284-303.

KADAI, HEINO O. (ED.) *Accents in Luther's Theology. Essays in Commemoration of the 450th Anniversary of the Reformation.* London, St. Louis, 1967. 272 pages.

TIETJEN, JOHN H. *The Abiding Validity of the Reformation.* 13-46.

SASSE, HERMANN. *Luther and the Word of God.* 47-97;

KOENKER, ERNEST B. *Man: Simul Justus et Peccator.* 98-123.

PELIKAN, JAROSLAV. *The Theology of the Means of Grace.* 124-147.

HOYER, GEORGE. *Christianhood, Priesthood and Brotherhood.* 148-198.

MARTY, MARTIN E. *Luther on Ethics: Man Free and Slave.* 199-229.

KADAI, HEINO O. *Luther's Theology of the Cross.* 230-272.

Luther Speaks. London, 1947. 192 pages.

"Essays for the fourth centenary of Martin Luther's death, written by a group of Lutheran ministers from North and Central Europe at present in Great Britain, with a foreword by the bishop of Oslo."

EHRENBERG, HANS P. *Luther and Private Prayer.* 41-46.

HARJUMPÄÄ, TOIVE. *Luther and Public Worship.* 47-54.

JENSEN, VIGGO. *Luther as Preacher.* 55-67.

BÜSING, WOLFGANG. *Luther as Teacher.* 68-88.

ABRAHAMSSON, ANDREAS. *The Eucharist in Luther's Teaching.* 89-95.

EHRENBERG, HANS P. *Luther as Theologian.* 96-114.

KRAMM, HANS HERBERT. *The Shaping of the Lutheran Church in Germany.* 117-133.

SÖDERBERG, CARL. *The Outline of the Lutheran Reformation in Scandinavia.* 134-140.

SCHWEITZER, CARL GUNTER. *The Inner Mission.* 141-152.

RUNDBLOM, A. *The Foreign Mission.* 153-160.

LAUN, T. F. *The Bible in Germany.* 161-169.

DAHMEN, GUNNAR. *The Lund School of Theology.* 170-177.

EHRENBERG, HANS P. *Postscript—At Martin Luther's Grave, 1946.* 178-189.

MEUSER, FRED W. (ED.) *Interpreting Luther's Legacy.* Minneapolis, 1969. 175 pages.

HALS, RONALD M. *Luther and the First Commandment.* 2-13.

DOERMANN, RALPH W. *Luther's Principles of Biblical Interpretation.* 14-25.

LIEFELD, THEODORE S. *Scripture and Tradition, in Luther and in Our Day.* 26-38.

MEUSER, FRED W. *The Changing Catholic View of Luther.* 40-54.

ELHARD, LELAND. *A Positive Response to Erik Erikson's "Young Man Luther."* 55-66.

SCHAAF, JAMES L. *The Smalcald Articles and Their Significance.* 68-82.

SCHWARZ, HANS. *Luther's Understanding of Heaven and Heil.* 83-94.

ZIETLOW, HAROLD H. *Concern for the Person in the Reformation.* 95-106.

BRAND, EUGENE L. *Luther's Liturgical Surgery.* 108-119.

SCHNEIDER, STANLEY D. *Luther, Preaching, and the Reformation.* 120-135.

BECKER, ARTHUR H. *Luther as "Seelsorger."* 136-150.

DOERMANN, GERHARD H. *Martin Luther—Parish Educator.* 151-161.

LUDWIG, LEONHARD. *Luther, Man of Prayers.* 162-175.

MEYER, CARL (ED.) *Luther for an Ecumenical Age. Essays in Commemoration of the 450th Anniversary of the Reformation.* St. Louis, 1967. 311 pages.

SPITZ, LEWIS W. *Man on This Isthmus.* 23-66.

RUPP, E. GORDON. *Luther's Ninety-Five Theses and the Theology of the Cross.* 67-81.

MEYER, CARL S. *A Dialog or Conversation Between a Father and His Son About Martin Luther's Doctrine (1523).* 82-107.

GRIMM, HAROLD J. *Lazarus Spengler, the Nürnberg Council, and the Reformation.* 108-119.

SCHWIEBERT, ERNEST G. *The Theses and Wittenberg.* 120-143.

BLUHM, HEINZ. *The Sources of Luther's Septembertestament: Galatians.* 144-171.

NAGEL, NORMAN. *Sacramentum et Exemplum In Luther's Understanding.* 172-199.

PELIKAN, JAROSLAV. *Luther's Defense of Infant Baptism.* 200-218.

BERTRAM, ROBERT. *The Radical Dialectic Between Faith and Works in Luther's Lectures on Galatians (1535).* 219-241.

PIEPKORN, ARTHUR CARL. *The Lutheran Symbolical Book. and Luther.* 242-270.

ATKINSON, JAMES. *Ecclesia Reformata Semper Reformanda.* 271-290.

LITTELL, FRANKLIN H. *Reformation, Restitution, and the Dialog.* 291-302.

OLIN, JOHN C., SMART, JAMES, and MCNALLY, ROBERT E. (EDS.) *Luther, Erasmus and the Reformation. A Catholic-Protestant Reappraisal.* N.Y., 1969. 150 pages.
Ecumenical addresses by Reformation scholars, read at the 1967 Union-Fordham Conference on the 450th Anniversary of Luther's reformation.

BAINTON, ROLAND H. *The Problem of Authority in the Age of the Reformation.* 14-25.

MCNALLY, ROBERT E. *The Reformation: a Catholic Reappraisal.* 26-47.

PAUCK, WILHELM. *The "Catholic" Luther.* 48-58.

MCDONOUGH, JOHN T. *The Essential Luther.* 59-66.

HOLBORN, HAJO. *Luther and the Princes.* 67-74.

GRIMM, HAROLD J. *The Reformation and the Urban Social Classes in Germany.* 75-86.

PHILLIPS, MARGARET MANN. *Some Last Words of Erasmus.* 87-113.

OLIN, JOHN C. *Erasmus and St. Ignatius Loyola.* 114-133.

SPITZ, LEWIS W. *Bibliographical Appendix: Recent Studies of Luther and the Reformation.* 134-150.

PELIKAN, JAROSLAV (ED.) *Interpreters of Luther: Essays in*

Honor of Wilhelm Pauck. Philadelphia, 1968. viii+374 pages.

HOLL, KARL. *Martin Luther on Luther*. 9-34.

ANDERSON, CHARLES S. *Robert Barnes on Luther*. 35-66.

GERRISH, B. A. *John Calvin on Luther*. 67-96.

CLEBSCH, WILLIAM A. *The Elizabethans on Luther*. 97-120.

WILLIAMS, GEORGE H. *Joseph Priestly on Luther*. 121-158.

NIELSEN, ERNEST D. *N.F.S. Grundtwig on Luther*. 159-186.

BACHMANN, E. THEODORE. *Walther, Schaff, and Krauth on Luther*. 187-230.

KOENKER, ERNEST B. *Søren Kierkegaard on Luther*. 231-252.

PELIKAN, JAROSLAV. *Adolf von Harnack on Luther*. 253-274.

PENZEL, KLAUS. *Ernst Troeltsch on Luther*. 275-303.

ADAMS, JAMES LUTHER. *Paul Tillich on Luther*. 304-334.

RUPP, E. GORDON. *The Righteousness of God. Luther Studies*. London, 1953. xiii+375 pages.

Essays on various developments of Luther's theology.

The Luther of Myth and the Luther of History. 3-36.

Luther in England. 37-55.

Captain Henry Bell and "Martin Luther's Divine Discourses." 56-77;

A Crisis of Vocabulary. 81-101.

The Bruised Conscience. 102-120.

The Righteousness of God. 121-137.

Luther's "Dictata Super Psalterium." (1513-15). 138-157.

Luther's Lectures on the Epistle to the Romans (1515-16). 158-191.

Luther's Lectures on the Epistles to the Galatians (1516-17), and Hebrews (1517-18). 192-216.

The Heidelberg Disputation (1518), the "Operationes in Psalmos" (1518-21), and the "Rationis Latomianae Confutation," (1521). 217-246.

Comment. 247-256.

Luther and Erasmus, 1525. 259-285.

Luther and Government (Regiment). 286-309.

Luther's Doctrine of the Church. 310-328.

Luther on the True and the False Church. 329-343.

Luther, a Man. 344-355.

STRAND, KENNETH ALBERT (ED.) *Essays on Luther.* Ann Arbor, 1969. 112 pages.

HYMA, ALBERT. *Introduction: New Light on Luther.* 9-27.

CROSSLEY, ROBERT N. *Luther and the Peasants War: a Brief Summary.* 31-44.

LANDEEN, WILLIAM M. *Martin Luther and the "Devotio Moderna" in Herford.* 45-64.

STRAND, KENNETH A. *Luther's Condemnation of the Rostock New Testament.* 65-74.

VERDUIN, LEONARD. *Luther's Dilemma: Restitution or Reformation?* 75-96.

CROSSLEY, ROBERT N. *The Peasants' War in Germany: Some Observations on Recent Historiography.* 98-105.

STRAND, KENNETH A. *Luther's Schooling in Magdeburg: a Note on Recent Views.* 106-112.

VAJTA, VILMOS (ED.) *Luther and Melanchthon in the History and Theology of the Reformation.* Philadelphia, 1961. 198 pages.

Lectures of the Second International Congress for Luther Research held August 8-13, 1960, in Münster, Germany. English lectures:

PAUCK, WILHELM. *Luther and Melanchthon.* 13-31.

GRIMM, HAROLD J. *The Relations of Luther and Melanchthon with the Townsmen.* 32-48.

QUANBECK, WARREN A. *Luther and Apocalyptic.* 119-128.

FRAENKEL, PETER. *Ten Questions Concerning Melanchthon, the Fathers, and the Eucharist.* 146-164.

TAPPERT, THEODORE G. *Melanchthon in America.* 189-198.

WICKS, JARED (ED.) *Catholic Scholars Dialogue With Luther.* Chicago, 1970. ix+228 pages.

LORTZ, JOSEPH. *The Basic Elements of Luther's Intellectual Style.* 3-33.

ISERLOH, ERWIN. *Luther's Christ-Mysticism.* 37-58.

PESCH, OTTO H. *Existential and Sapiential Theology—The Theological Confrontation between Luther and Thomas Aquinas.* 61-81.

HACKER, PAUL. *Martin Luther's Notion of Faith.* 85-105.

MCSORLY, HARRY J. *Erasmus versus Luther—Compounding the Reformation Tragedy.* 107-117.

MANNS, PETER. *Absolute and Incarnate Faith—Luther on Justification in the Galatians' Commentary of 1531-1535.* 121-156.

QUANBECK, WARREN A. *Afterword.* 159-165.

LIVES OF LUTHER

ATKINSON, JAMES. *Martin Luther and the Birth of Protestantism.* Baltimore, 1968. xii+331 pages.
Emphasizes the theological struggle.
The Great Light. Luther and Reformation. (The Advance of Christianity through the Centuries series.) Grand Rapids, 1968. 287 pages.
Places Luther in the context of the German, Swiss and English Reformation.

AUDIN, JEAN MARIE VINCENT. *History of the Life, Writings and Doctrines of Luther,* tr. W. B. Turnbull. 2 vols. (Library of translations from select foreign literature III). Ld., 1854.
Catholic polemic.

BAINTON, ROLAND H. *Here I Stand; a Life of Martin Luther.* N.Y., 1950. 386 pages. Available in new paperback editions.
An excellent biography stressing Luther the man.

BEARD, CHARLES. *Martin Luther and the Reformation in Germany until the Close of the Diet of Worms,* ed. J. Frederick Smith. Ld., 1889. xiii+468 pages.
The interest is in intellectual emancipation.

BÖHMER, HEINRICH. *Luther and the Reformation in the Light of Modern Research,* tr. E. S. G. Potter. N.Y., 1930. xi+380 pages.
A sketch of Luther's development and character with par-

ticular reference to controverted points: replies to Grisar, Denifle, Barge.

Martin Luther: Road to Reformation, tr. John W. Doberstein and Theodore G. Tappert. N.Y., 1957. xiii+449 pages.

A classic study of Luther up to the Wartburg period (1521).

COWIE, LEONARD K. *Martin Luther, Leader of the Reformation* (Pathfinder Biographies). N.Y., 1969. vi+122 pages.

A general treatment.

DALLMANN, WILLIAM. *Martin Luther: His Life and His Labor.* St. Louis, 1951. xiv+262 pages.

A dated biography.

DENIFLE, HEINRICH. *Luther and Lutherdom,* tr. Raymond Volz, Vol. 1, pt. 1. Somerset, O., 1917. li+465 pages.

Makes much of Luther's sensuality, rich in citations from late medieval authors. The translation is clumsy.

DICKENS, ARTHUR GEOFFREY. *Martin Luther and the Reformation* (Teach Yourself History Library). London, 1967. viii+184 pages.

A useful introduction.

FEBVRE, LUCIEN. *Martin Luther: A Destiny,* tr. Roberts Tapley. N.Y., 1919. ix+320 pages.

Young Lochinvar succumbs to fatty degeneration.

FIFE, ROBERT HERNDON. *Young Luther . . . to 1518.* N.Y., 1928. 232 pages.

Competent.

The Revolt of Martin Luther. N.Y., 1957. xii+726 pages.

Luther life to 1521; well researched, with an extensive bibliography. New edition, 1970.

FISCHER, ROBERT H. *Luther.* ed. Frank W. Klos. Philadelphia, 1966. 190 pages.

Written for young adults in a Lutheran parish education series.

FOSDICK , HARRY E. *Martin Luther* (World Landmark Books series). N.Y., 1956. 184 pages.

A simple approach, by a famous American preacher.

FREYTAG, GUSTAV. *Doctor Luther,* tr. G. C. L. Riemer. Philadelphia, 1916. 206 pages.

Moves with verve.

FRIEDENTHAL, RICHARD. *Luther; His Life and Times,* tr.

John Nowell. N.Y., 1970. viii+566 pages.
Popular, but lacking historical accuracy.

GAHL, LOIS. *Luther, Young Man of God.* Rock Island, Ill.,
1956. 90 pages.
An introduction for laymen.

GREEN, VIVIAN. *Luther and the Reformation.* N.Y., 1964. 192
pages.
An excellent introduction to Luther.

GRISAR, HARTMAN. *Luther,* tr. E. M. Lamond, ed. Luigi Cappa-
delta. 6 vols. St. Louis, Mo., 1913-1917.
Martin Luther His Life and Work, adapted from the second
German edition by Franz J. Eble, ed. Arthur Preuss. St.
Louis, Mo., 1930. x+609 pages.
The learned Jesuit is scrupulously accurate. He pays tribute
to Luther's courage and piety, but regards him as psyco-
pathic.

JACOBS, HENRY EYSTER. *Martin Luther, the Hero of the Reformation* (Heroes of the Nations). N.Y. and Ld., 1898. xv+
454 pages.
There is a better understanding of Luther's theology than in
the liberal lives.

JØRGENSEN, ALFRED T. *Martin Luther, Reformer of the Church.*
tr. Ronald M. Jenson. Minneapolis, 1953. 225 pages.
A fair biography, containing an evaluation of Luther after
forty years.

KLEINHANS, THEODORE J. *Martin Luther, Saint and Sinner.*
St. Louis, 1956. 144 pages.
Weak.

KOOIMAN, W. J. *By Faith Alone. The Life of Martin Luther.*
London, 1954. 218 pages.
Luther's life to 1525, with closing observations on his im-
pact. A very useful study by a Dutch scholar.

KOPPENHAVER, CARL E. *Martin Luther.* Philadelphia, 1953.
48 pages.
Too sketchy.

KÖSTLIN, JULIUS THEODOR. *Life of Luther.* N.Y., 1883. xvi+
587 pages.
Köstlin, in his day, was the outstanding Protestant authority
on Luther.

LAU, FRANZ. *Luther*, tr. Robert H. Fischer. Philadelphia, 1963.
178 pages. 2d edition, 1966.
A good introduction to Luther by an eminent German
Luther scholar.

LEE, ROBERT E. A. (ED.) *Martin Luther: The Reformation
Years*. Minneapolis, 1967. 96 pages.
With text and pictures from the film.

LEHMANN, HELMUT T. *It Started with Luther* (Faith and Ac-
tion series). Philadelphia, 1955. 96 pages.
Designed for young adults, used in Lutheran parish education.

LILJE, HANNS. *Luther and the Reformation*. tr. Martin O.
Dietrich (An illustrated series, in collaboration with Karl F.
Reinking). Philadelphia, 1967. 223 pages.
Minimal text, but well done, by a German bishop. Contains
reproductions of 16th century woodcuts.

LINDSAY, THOMAS M. *Luther and the German Reformation*,
(Oliphant Smeaton: The World's Epoch Makers xv). N.Y.,
1900. xii+300 pages (reprint Edinburgh, 1908). New edition,
1970.
Popular, contains a charming picture of Luther's home life.

LIPSKY, ABRAM. *Martin Luther, Germany's Angry Man*. N.Y.,
1933. xv+305 pages.
Popular, inadequately informed.

MCGIFFERT, ARTHUR CUSHMAN. *Martin Luther the Man and
His Work*. N.Y., 1917. xi+397 pages.
Popular sketch from the point of view of theological liberal-
ism and social conservatism.

MCNEER, MAY, and LYND, WARD. *Martin Luther*. Nashville,
1953. 96 pages.
Written for Methodist children.

MACKINNON, JAMES. *Luther and the Reformation*. 4 vols. Ld.,
1925-1930.
Abreast of the latest research, staid in treatment.

MARITAIN, JACQUES. *Three Reformers: Luther, Descartes,
Rousseau*. N.Y., 1929. 234 pages.
The Neothomist upbraids Luther for railing against the har-
lot reason.
New edition, Westport, Conn., 1970.

MILLER, BASIL W. *Martin Luther, God's Man of Destiny*. Grand
Rapids, 1942. 149 pages.
An enthusiastic but dated work.
PITTENGER, WILLIAM N. *Martin Luther: the Great Reformer*.
N.Y., 1969. ix+182 pages.
PLASS, EWALD. *This Is Luther. A Character Study*. St. Louis,
1948. xiv+395 pages.
Fair. Based mostly on Luther's letters.
POLACK, WILLIAM G. *The Story of Luther*. St. Louis, 1931.
ix+155 pages.
Not very valuable.
RITTER, GERHARD. *Luther, His Life and Work*, tr. John Riches.
N.Y., 1963. 256 pages.
An excellent introduction to Luther by an eminent German
historian.
SCHWIEBERT, ERNEST G. *Luther and His Times. The Reforma-
tion from a New Perspective*. St. Louis, 1950. xxii+892 pages.
A detailed biography emphasizing the historical background
and the Wittenberg environment.
SHORT, RUTH G. *Meet Martin Luther: His Life and Teachings*.
Grand Rapids, 1959. 194 pages.
The successful attempt of a housewife to understand Luther.
SIMON, EDITH. *Luther Alive. Martin Luther and the Making of
the Reformation* (Crossroads of World History series).
Garden City, N.Y., 1968. xi+371 pages.
Written with journalistic flair by a British novelist and historian.
SMITH, PRESERVED. *The Life and Letters of Martin Luther*.
Boston and N.Y., 1911. xvi+490 pages. New edition 1968.
A humanist biography.
THIEL, RUDOLPH. *Luther*, tr. Gustav K. Wienke. Philadelphia,
1955. xiii+492 pages.
Very sympathetic to the "German" Luther, but lacks
scholarly precision.
THULIN, OSKAR. *A Life of Luther, Told in Pictures and Nar-
rative by the Reformer and Contemporaries*, tr. Martin O.
Dietrich. Philadelphia, 1966. 210 pages.
A fine presentation by the director of the Wittenberg
Lutherhalle.
TODD, JOHN M. *Martin Luther: a Biographical Study*. West-

minster, 1964. xix†290 pages.
A sympathetic biography by a British Roman Catholic lay-
man, emphasizing the "Catholic-Protestant" Luther, and including an interesting appendix on the theory of indulgences.
TOWNSEND, ALLAN W. *A Short Life of Luther*. Philadelphia,
1967. iv+76 pages.
Introduces Luther to a general audience.
VERRES, J. *Luther, an Historical Portrait*. Ld., N.Y., 1884. v+
392 pages.
Catholic polemic, makes much of the inconsistency, coarse-
ness and spitefulness of Luther.

MISCELLANEOUS BIOGRAPHICAL POINTS

ATKINSON, JAMES. *The Trial of Luther* (Historic Trial series).
N.Y., 1971. 212 pages.
Tells the story of Luther from 1518-1521.
BAINTON, ROLAND H. *Luther's Struggle for Faith*. CH XVII 3
(1948), 193-206.
Reprinted in the author's *Studies on the Reformation.
Psychiatry and History: an Examination of Erikson's
"Young Man Luther."* RL XL 4 (1971), 450-478.
BRUEGGEMANN, E. A. *The First Three Bibles that Entered the
Early Life of Martin Luther*. CTM VII 2 (1936), 118-122.
BURR, GEORGE LINCOLN. *New Fragment on Luther's Death
with Other Gleanings from the Age of the Reformation*. AHR
XVI (1911), 723-735.
CARR, DEANNA M. *A Consideration of the Meaning of Prayer
in the Life of Martin Luther*. CTM XLII (1971), 620-629.
CROWE, WILLIAM. *Luther at the Diet of Worms*. BS LXXXV
(1928), 334-346.
DIENER, RONALD. *Brief Studies: the Ninety-Five Theses: Some
Historical and Semantic Aspects*. CTM XXXVIII 9 (1967),
601-606.
DIERKS, THEO. *Luther's Spiritual Martyrdom and Its Appease-
ment*. CTM XII 2 (1941), 102-107.
EBON, MARTIN (ED.) *The Last Days of Luther by Justus Jonas,
Michael Coelius, and Others*. Introduction by Theodore G.
Tappert. Garden City, N.Y., 1970. 120 pages.
The last 31 days of Luther's life, chronicled by friends.

ELDER, MICHAEL. *The Young Martin Luther.* London, 1966.
126 pages.
Illustrated.

ENGELDER, T. *Luther the Reformer.* CTM XVII 1 (1946), 7-31.

ERIKSON, ERIK. *Young Man Luther.* N.Y., 1958. 288 pages.
One-sided, in favor of psychoanalysis.

FAULKNER, JOHN ALFRED. *Luther and Culture.* ASCH 2 S.
VIII (1928), 147-168.

FORD, R. CLYDE. *A Side-Light on Luther.* BS LVI (1899),
114-119.
Translation of Kessler's account of how the Swiss met Luther
in disguise on his way back to Wittenberg.

GRIMM, HAROLD. *Martin Luther as a Preacher.* Columbus, 1929.
136 pages.
Luther's Inner Conflict: a Psychological Interpretation. CH
IV 3 (1935), 173-186.

HAGEN, KENNETH G. *Changes in the Understanding of Luther:
the Development of the Young Luther.* TS XXIX 3 (1968),
472-496.

HILLERBRAND, HANS J. *Martin Luther and the Bull Exsurge
Domine.* TS XXX 1 (1969), 108-112.

HOYER, THEO. *An Anniversary We Forgot.* CTM VI 5 (1935),
349-356.
On the death of Cajetan.
How Dr. Martin Luther Died. CTM XVII 2 (1946), 81-88.

HYMA, ALBERT. *Luther's Theological Development from Erfurt
to Augsburg* (Landmarks in History series). N.Y., 1928.
vi+90 pages. New edition, 1971.
*New Light on Martin Luther; With an Authentic Account of
the Luther Film of 1953.* Grand Rapids, 1957. 287 pages.
Analyzes Luther's career in the light of evidence before 1505
and after 1525. Intended to present facts left out in the film
and in many biographies.

ISERLOH, ERWIN. *The Theses Were Not Posted; Luther Between
Reform and Reformation,* tr. Jared Wicks. Boston, 1968.
xx+116 pages.
A Roman Catholic argument on the 95 theses.

KUIPER, BAREND K. *Martin Luther; the Formative Years.* Grand
Rapids, 1933. 298 pages.

The first 34 years. Dated.

LAU, FRANZ. *The Posting of Luther's Theses—Legend or Fact?* CTM XXXVIII 11 (1967), 691-703.

PAUCK, WILHELM. *Martin Luther's Faith.* RL XVI 1 (1946-47), 3-11.

ROHR, JOHN VON. *The Sources of Luther's Self-Despair in the Monastery.* JBR XIX (1951), 6-11.

RUPP, E. GORDON. *Luther's Progress to the Diet of Worms, 1521.* London, 1951; N.Y., 1964. 109 pages.
A well-written introduction to the young Luther, by an eminent British Methodist scholar.

SAARNIVAARA, UURAS. *Luther Discovers the Gospel: New Light Upon Luther's Way from Medieval Catholicism to Evangelical Faith.* St. Louis, 1951. 146 pages.
The controversial Finnish study tries to show that Luther experienced his real "evangelical breakthrough" in 1519, (not in 1512/13, as must scholars assume).

SCHWIEBERT, E. G. *The Formative Years of Dr. Luther.* CTM XVII 4 (1946), 241-257.

SINGMASTER, J. A. *Luther, the Preacher.* LQ XLVII (1917), 404-412.

STEPHENSON, GEORGE M. *The Conservative Character of Martin Luther.* LCR, XXXV (1916), 129-142. (In book form, Philadelphia, 1921, vii+143 pages.)

TAPPERT, THEODORE G. *Luther Used Rough Language.* CTM XIX 6 (1948), 453-456.

LUTHER IN RELATION TO PREDECESSORS, CONTEMPORARIES AND SUBSEQUENT FIGURES

BAUMAN, HAROLD. *Luther, Descartes and Dehumanization.* D IX 4 (1970), 295-299.

DALLMAN, WILLIAM. *King Henry VIII Attacks Luther.* CTM VI 6 (1935), 419-430.
King Henry VIII Courts Luther. CTM VII 8 (1936), 568-577.
Luther: a Blessing to the English. CTM XIII 2 (1942), 111-120 3 (1942), 207-214; 4 (1942), 273-289; 5 (1942), 330-337; 9 (1942), 662-672; XIV 2 (1943), 110-116; 3 (1943), 191-19 4 (1943), 262-274; 5 (1943), 345-352.
Henry the Eighth's Divorce and Luther. CTM XVIII 2 (1947),

81-93; 3 (1947), 161-170.

DOERNBERG, ERWIN. *Henry VIII and Luther.* Stanford, Calif., 1961. 139 pages.

GRAEBNER, THEODORE. *Reputed Dependence of Luther on Leo the Great.* CTM XV 7 (1944), 485.

HEADLEY, JOHN A. *Thomas More and Luther's Revolt.* ARG LX (1969), 145-159.
Draws attention to More's polemic against Luther.

HILDEBRANDT, FRANZ. *From Luther to Wesley.* London, 1951. 224 pages.
A fine comparison of their theologies, by a Lutheran scholar turned Methodist.

JUNGHANS, HELMAR, *et al.* (ED.) *Vierhundertfünfzig Jahre Lutherische Reformation, 1517-1967. Festschrift für Franz Lau zum 60. Geburtstag.* Göttingen, 1967.
BAINTON, ROLAND H. *Erasmus and Luther and the Dialog Julius Exlusus.* 17-26.

KÄHLER, F. A. *Luther's Last Intercourse with Staupitz* (translation from Köstlin in Theol. Stud. u. Krit. LII, 1879). LCR III (1884), 151-152.

KALLINA, EMANUEL J. *Luther, His Relation to John Huss.* LQ XLV (1915), 501-509.

KEEVER, EDWIN F. *A Man Who Set Luther Thinking, Peter D'Ailly.* LCR, XX (1901), 297-311; XXI (1902), 213-221.

KLEINHANS, ROBERT G. *Luther and Erasmus, Another Perspective.* CH XXXIX 4 (1970), 459-469.

KRODEL, GOTTFRIED G. *Luther, Erasmus and Henry VIII.* ARG LIII (1962), 60-78.
Argues that Erasmus turned away from Luther in 1521 when Henry VIII attacked Luther.
Erasmus-Luther: One Theology, One Method, Two Results. CTM XLI (1970), 648-667.

LEHMANN, M. E. *Justus Jonas—a Collaborator with Luther.* LQ II 2 (1950), 189-200.
Justus Jonas, Loyal Reformer. Minneapolis, 1963. vii+208 pages.

LUEKER, ERWIN L. *Luther and Melanchthon.* CTM XXXI 8 (1960), 476-478.

MEYER, CARL S. *Henry VIII Burns Luther's Books.* JEH IX 2 (1958), 173-187.

Thomas More and the Wittenberg Lutherans. CTM XXXIX (1968), 246-256.

OYER, JOHN S. *The Writings of Luther Against the Anabaptists.* MQR XXVII (1953), 100-110.

PACKER, JAMES I. *Luther Against Erasmus.* CTM XXXVII 4 (1966), 207-221.

PEARCE, E. GEORGE. *Luther and the English Reformation.* CTM XXXI 10 (1960), 597-606.

PELIKAN, JAROSLAV. *Luther's Attitude Toward John Hus.* CTM XIX 10 (1948), 747-763.
Luther's Negotiations with the Hussites. CTM XX 7 (1949), 496-517.
Luther's Endorsement of the "Confessio Bohemica." CTM XX 11 (1949), 829-843.

RICHARDSON, CYRIL C. *Prophet Versus Scholar—Luther and Erasmus.* RL V 2 (1936), 285-294.

RICHTER, FRIEDRICH. *Martin Luther and Ignatius Loyola. Spokesmen for Two Worlds of Belief.* Westminster, 1960. 248 pages.
The author, a convert to Roman Catholicism from Protestantism, regards both men as pioneers of Christian unity.

RUPP, E. GORDON. *Luther in English Theology.* LW II 1 (1955), 12-23.

SCHAFF, DAVID S. *Martin Luther and John Calvin.* PTR XV (1917), 530-552.

SMEND, FRIEDRICH. *Luther and Bach.* LQ I 4 (1949), 399-410.

SIIRALA, AARNE. *Freedom and Authority in Erasmus and Luther* D VII 2 (1968), 108-113.
Divine Humanness. tr. T. A. Kantonen. Philadelphia, 1970. vi+186 pages.
A modern analysis of the anthropological debate between Erasmus and Luther (especially chapt. 2).

SINGMASTER, J. A. *Luther and Calvin.* LQ XXXIX (1909), 566-575.
Luther and the Reformers before the Reformation. LQ XLVII (1917), 457-470.

SPIELER, ROBERT. *Luther and Gregory of Rimini.* LQ V 2 (1953), 155-166.

STAUDT, JOHN JOSEPH. *John Staupitz on God's Gracious Love.*

LQ VIII 3 (1956), 225-244.

STEINMETZ, DAVID C. *Misericordia Dei. The Theology of Johannes von Staupitz in Its Late Medieval Setting* (Studies in Medieval and Reformation Thought series). Leiden, 1968. 198 pages.
An essential study on Luther's prior in Wittenberg, with a detailed bibliography.

STRAND, KENNETH A. (ED.) *The Dawn of Modern Civilization: Studies in Renaissance, Reformation and Other Topics.* Ann Arbor, 1962.
LANDEEN, WILLIAM A. *Martin Luther and the Devotia Moderna in Herford.* 145-164.

TILLMANNS, WALTER G. *The World and Men Around Luther.* Minneapolis, 1959. xv+384 pages.
An excellent handbook tracing Luther's contacts.

TJERNAGEL, NEELAK S. *Henry VIII and the Lutherans. A Study in Anglo-Lutheran Relations from 1521 to 1547.* St. Louis, 1965. xii+326 pages.
Chapters 1, 2 and 5 sketch Luther's involvement with Henry VIII on the papacy and divorce.

TRINTERUD, LJ. *A Reappraisal of William Tyndale's Debt to Martin Luther.* CH XXXI (1962), 24-45.

VERHOEF, PIETER A. *Luther's and Calvin's Exegetical Library.* CTJ III (1968), 5-20.

WANTULA, A. *The Slavonic Luther.* CTM XVII 10 (1946), 728-737.

WATSON, PHILIP. *Erasmus, Luther, and Aquinas.* CTM XL (1969), 747-758.

LUTHER'S VIEW OF HISTORY

DANNENFELDT, KARL H. *Some Observations of Luther on Ancient Pre-Greek History.* ARG XLII (1951), 49-63.

HEADLEY, JOHN M. *Luther's View of Church History.* New Haven, 1963. xvi+301 pages.
Essential.

LUTHER'S TRANSLATION OF THE BIBLE

BLUHM, HEINZ SIEGFRIED. *Martin Luther, Creative Translator.*
St. Louis, 1965. xv+236 pages.
Excellent exposition of Luther's work by a German philologis

CARRUTH, W. H. *Luther on Translation* (translation of his tract,
available also in the Holman edition of his works). OC XXI
(1907), 465-471.

FLORER, WARREN W. *The Language of Luther's Version.* CBQ
XII (1951), 257-267.

GRUBER, L. FRANKLIN. *The Wittenberg Originals of the Luther
Bible.* BSA XII (1918), 1-33.
Reproduces some woodcuts.

KRAUTH, CHARLES P. *Luther's translation of the Holy Scriptures: the New Testament.* MR XVI (1869), 180-200.

KUNSTMANN, JOHN G. *And Yet Again: Wes das Herz voll ist,
des Gehet der Mund Über.* CTM XXIII 7 (1952), 509-527.
On Luther's translation of Matt.12: 34.

LAUER, EDWARD HENRY. *Luther's Translation of the Psalms
in 1523-24.* JEGP XIV (1915), 1-34.

PAINTER, F. V. N. *Luther on the Study and Use of the Ancient
Languages.* CTM VII 1 (1936), 23-27.

RHIEM, EDWARD. *Luther as a Bible Translator,* tr. James F. Mort
BQR VI (1884), 496-521.

STRAND, KENNETH A. *A Reformation Paradox. The Condemned
New Testament of the Rostock Brethren of the Common Life.*
Ann Arbor, 1960. 101 pages.
A critical reappraisal of Luther's condemnation of the Low-
German edition of the Rostock New Testament. Includes re-
prints of the facsimiles.
*The Lutheran New Testament Used by the Rostock Brethren
of the Common Life for Their Catholic Bible Translation.*
ARG LII (1961), 99-100.
On Matthew 5, with comparative texts.
*The Emserian New Testament Used by the Rostock Brethren
of the Common Life for their Low German Translation.* ARG
LV (1964), 216-219.

WENDTE, CHARLES W. *Martin Luther and the German Bible.* UR
XXI (1884), 23-43.

LUTHER AND ART, LITURGY AND MUSIC

Bainton, Roland H. *Speaks on the Martin Luther Motion Picture.*
N.Y., 1954. 22 pages.
Recorded by Lutheran Film Productions.

BUSZIN, WALTER E. *Luther as a Creative Musician.* CTM XV 9
(1944), 625-627.

CHRISTENSEN, CARL C. *Luther's Theology and the Uses of
Religious Art.* LQ XXII (1970), 147-165.

HORN, EDWARD T. *Luther on the Principles and Order of
Christian Worship.* LCR X (1891), 217-256.

*The Hymns of Martin Luther Set to Their Original Melodies with
an English Version, Edited by Leonard Woolsey Bacon Assisted
by Nathan H. Allen.* N.Y., 1883. xxvii+71 pages.

KIEFER, C. J. *Luther and Hymnology.* LQ XLIII (1913), 237-
247.

KIMMEL, WILLIAM. *Martin Luther Musician. HiFi/Stereo Review*
(Dec. 1966), 50-56.
A concise review of Luther's contributions to music.

KLANN, H. RICHARD. *The Relation of the Liturgy to the Word.*
CTM XXIII 5 (1952), 321-341.
On Luther's views.

KLEINHANS, THEODORE. *Printer's Devil from Wittenberg.*
Minneapolis, 1962. 207 pages.
A historical novel, dealing with Luther's life up to his con-
demnation in 1521.

KRÜGER, J. F. *Liturgical Worship in Wittenberg from 1520-1530.*
LCQ IV (1931), 292-303.

LAMBERT, JAMES F. *Luther's Hymns.* Philadelphia, Pa., 1917.
xviii+160 pages.

MACDONALD, GEORGE. *Rampolli . . . Being Translations, New
and Old.* Ld., N.Y., 1897. Luther's Song Book, pp. 117-178.

NETTL, PAUL. *Luther and Music.* tr. Frieda Best and Ralph Wood.
Philadelphia, 1948. New edition, 1967. 174 pages.
A very useful introduction, includes a comparison of Luther
and Bach.

OSBORNE, JOHN. *Luther, a Play.* N.Y., 1961. 102 pages.
Based on Erik Erikson's psychoanalytical interpretation of
Luther, up to 1525.

REESE, RUTH SARA. *Martin Luther, a Rebel Monk; a Play in 3 Acts.* N.Y., 1959. 85 pages.
Deals with Luther's stay at the Wartburg.

REIM, E. *The Liturgical Crisis in Wittenberg, 1524.* CTM XX (1949), 284-292.

RUPP, E. GORDON. *John Osborne and the Historical Luther.* ET LXXIII 5 (1962), 147-151.

SCHOENBOHM, RICHARD. *Music in the Lutheran Church Before and at the Time of J. S. Bach.* CH XII 3 (1943), 195-209.

SESSIONS, KYLE C. *The Sources of Luther's Hymns and the Spread of the Reformation.* LQ XVII (1965), 206-223.

SÖHNGEN, OSKAR. *The Theological Aspect of Music in Luther.* US XVII 1 (1960), 5-12.

SPAETH, A. *Luther's Ordination Service.* LCR IV (1885), 41-48.

STEVENSON, ROBERT. *Luther's Musical Achievement.* LQ III 3 (1951), 255-262.

STRODACH, PAUL ZELLER. *Luther's Hymns.* LCR XIX (1900), 228-234.

VAJTA, VILMOS. *Luther on Worship. An Interpretation.* tr. U.S. Leupold. Philadelphia, 1958. xvv+200 pages.
Essential; contains bibliography.

LUTHER'S THEOLOGY

ALTHAUS, PAUL. *The Theology of Martin Luther.* tr. Robert C. Schultz. Philadelphia, 1966. xv+464 pages.
An excellent compendium of Luther's theology.

BAAR, WILLIAM H. *Luther's Sacramental Thought.* LQ II 4 (1950), 414-425.

BECKER, SIEGBERT W. *Luther's Apologetics.* CTM XXIX 10 (1958), 742-759.

CARLSON, EDGAR M. *The Theology of Luther According to Swedish Research.* JR XXV 4 (1945), 247-260.

COOPER, JOHN C. *Some Radical Elements in Luther's Theology.* LQ XX (1968), 194-201.

DAU, W. H. T. *Luther's Theological Method.* CTM XIII 11 (1942), 834-841.

EBELING, GERHARD. *Luther. An Introduction to His Thought.*

tr. R. A. Wilson. Philadelphia, 1970. 289 pages.
Very good analysis of Luther's dialectic thought, covering
most theological topics.

FEUERBACH, LUDWIG A. *The Essence of Faith According to
Luther* (The Library of Religion and Culture series). tr.
Melvin Cherno. N.Y., 1967. 127 pages.
A commentary on Luther by the famous German agnostic
philosopher.

FISCHER, ROBERT H. *The Place of Reason in Luther's Theology.*
LQ XVI (1964), 41-48.

FOSTER, ROBERT D. *God Hidden or Revealed? Investigations
in Luther's Theology. The Thought of the Reformer Viewed
in the Light of Research and Interpretation.* No pub., 1968.
147 pages.

GERRISH, BRIAN A. *Grace and Reason. A Study in the Theology
of Luther.* Oxford, 1962. 188 pages.
Shows the complexity of Luther's reasoning and rejects the
charge of "irrationalism."

HAEGGLUND, BENGT. *Was Luther a Nominalist?* CTM XXVIII
6 (1957), 441-452.

KÖSTLIN, JULIUS. *The Theology of Luther,* tr. Charles E. Hay,
2 vols. Philadelphia, Pa., 1897.

KRAMM, HANS H. *The Theology of Luther.* London, 1947. 152
pages.
An introduction to Luther for ministers, emphasizing anthropology, soteriology, ecclesiology, eschatology, Scripture and
the question of church and state.

LANDEEN, WILLIAM M. *Martin Luther's Religious Thought.*
Mountain View, Calif., 1971. 218 pages.

LENTZ, HAROLD H. *Reformation Crossroads. A Comparison of
the Theology of Luther and Melanchthon.* Minneapolis, 1958.
92 pages.
An attempt to transcend the differences between Luther and
Melanchthon in terms of the doctrines of atonement and
justification, stressing the Augsburg Confession and the
Formula of Concord.

LOHSE, BERNHARD. *Reason and Revelation in Luther.* SJT XIII
4 (1960), 337-365.

OZMENT, STEVEN E. *HOMO VIATOR: Luther and Late Medieval*

Theology. HTR LXII 3 (1969), 275-288.

PELIKAN, JAROSLAV. *Obedient Rebels. Catholic Substance and Protestant Principle in Luther's Reformation.* N.Y., 1964. 212 pages.
A broad essay on the ecumenical implications of Luther's thought.

PINOMAA, LENNART. *Faith Victorious. An Introduction to Luther's Theology*, tr. Walter Kukkonen. Philadelphia, 1963. xxi+216 pages.
A very useful survey of topics in Luther's thought with bibliography, by an eminent Finnish scholar.

PRENTER, REGIN. *Luther's Theology of the Cross.* LW VI 3 (1959), 222-233. Reprinted Philadelphia, 1971. viii+24 pages.

WARFIELD, BENJAMIN B. *The Ninety-Five Theses in Their Theological Significance.* PTR XV (1917), 501-529.

WATSON, PHILIP S. *Let God Be God!* Philadelphia, 1948. x+203 pages.
A good introduction by a British Methodist scholar influenced by Swedish Luther research. He regards Luther's shift from the anth.opocentric to the theocentric stance as a "Copernican revolution."

Mysticism

HEISEY, PAUL HAROLD. *A Study in the Mysticism of Luther.* LQ XLII (1912), 26-61.

LOOFS, FRIEDRICH. *Solo Verbo: Lutheranism and Mysticism.* ConQ II (1914), 733-754.

MILLER, ARLENE A. *The Theologies of Luther and Boehme in the Light of Their Genesis Commentaries.* HTR LXIII 2 (1970), 261-304.

OZMENT, STEVEN. *Homo Spiritualis. A Comparative Study of the Anthropology of Tauler, Gerson and Luther 1509-16* (Studies in Medieval and Reformation Thought series). Leiden, 1969. vii+226 pages.
A Roman Catholic thesis on Luther's mysticism.
An Aid to Luther's Marginal Comments on Johannes Tauler's Sermons. HTR LXIII 2 (1970), 305-312.

Law and Gospel, Creation and Man

BLUHM, HEINZ. *Luther's View of Man in His First Published Work.* HTR XLI 2 (1948), 103-122.
Luther's View of Man in His Early German Writings. CTM XXXIV 10 (1963), 583-593.

BRAATEN, CARL E. *Reflections on the Lutheran Doctrine of the Law.* LQ XVIII 1 (1966), 72-84.

FORELL, GEORGE W. *Luther's Conception of Natural Orders.* LQ XVIII (1945), 160-177.

GREAVES, R. L. *Luther's Doctrine of Grace.* SJT XVIII 4 (1965), 385-395.

HACKER, PAUL. *The Ego in Faith. Martin Luther and the Origin of Anthropocentric Religion.* Chicago, 1970. xvi+146 pages.
A Franciscan study.

JOHNSON, WAYNE G. *Martin Luther's Law-Gospel Distinction and Paul Tillich's Method of Correlation: a Study in Parallels.* LQ XXIII 3 (1971), 274-288.

KUKKONEN, WALTER J. *The Problem of Sin in the Light of Finnish Luther Research.* AQ XXV (1946), 121-131.

LIEVSAY, JOHN L. (ED.) *Medieval and Renaissance Studies.* Durham, N.C., 1970.
SPITZ, LEWIS W. *Luther's Importance for Anthropological Realism.* 134-175.

LOESCHEN, JOHN. *Promise and Necessity in Luther's De Servo Arbitrio.* LQ XXIII (1971), 257-267.

MCDONOUGH, THOMAS M. *The Law and the Gospel in Luther. A Study of Martin Luther's Confessional Writings.* London, 1963. 180 pages.

MCNEILL, JOHN T. *Natural Law in the Thought of Luther.* CH X 3 (1941), 211-227.

MAYER, F. E. *Human Will in Bondage and Freedom. I, II.* CTM XXII (1951), 719-747; 785-819.
On Luther's doctrine of law and gospel.
The Proper Distinction Between Law and Gospel and the Terminology Visible and Invisible Church. CTM XXV 3 (1954), 177-198.
On Luther's views and Lutheran orthodoxy.

REIMANN, HENRY W. *Luther on Creation.* CTM XXIV 1 (1953), 26-40.

WICKS, JARED. *Luther on the Person Before God.* TS XXX 2 (1969), 289-311.
An extensive review of the book by Wilfried Joest on Luther's ontology.

Eschatology and Demonology

HALL, GEORGE F. *Luther's Eschatology.* AQ XXIII (1944), 13-21.

JACOBS, HENRY E. *A Study in Luther's Eschatology.* LCR IX (1890), 232-239.

MASSON, DAVID. *The Three Devils: Luther's, Milton's, Goethe's.* Ld., 1874. 327 pages.

SECKER, PHILIP J. *Martin Luther's Views on the State of the Dead.* CTM XXXVIII 7 (1967), 422-435.

STANGE, DOUGLAS C. *The Martyrs of Christ—a Sketch of the Thought of Martin Luther on Martyrdom.* CTM XXXVII 10 (1966), 640-644.

Scripture, Canon, Authority, Inspiration, Interpretation

ALAND, KURT. *Luther as Exegete.* ET LXIX 20 (1957), 45-48; 68-70.

BERNET, CARL WALTER. *The Word Principle in Martin Luther.* CTM XIX 1 (1948), 13-33.

BLUHM, H. S. *The Significance of Luther's Earliest Extant Sermon.* HTR XXXVII 2 (1944), 175-184.
The Biblical Quotations in Luther's German Writings. A Preliminary Statistical Report. ARG XLIV (1953), 103-113.

BORNKAMM, HEINRICH. *Luther and the Old Testament*, tr. Eric W. and Ruth C. Gritsch, ed. Victor I. Gruhn. Philadelphia 1969. xii+307 pages.
The best available study on the subject.

BUSZIN, WALTER E. *The Import and Content of Luther's Exegetical Lectures on the Epistle to the Hebrews.* CTM IX 2 (1938), 100-114.

CARTER, DOUGLAS. *Luther as Exegete.* CTM XXXII 9 (1961), 517-525.

CRELL, GEORGE CROFT. *Luther's Lectures on Saint Paul's Epistle to the Romans.* MethR XCIII (1911), 682-693.

A good account of the discovery of the manuscript.

DU BRAU, R. T. *Luther's Monumental Work: Galatians.* CTM VI 12 (1935), 888-892.

The Greatness of Luther's Commentary on Galatians. CTM VII 8 (1936), 577-581.

EBELING, GERHARD. *The New Hermeneutics and the Early Luther.* TT XXI 1 (1964), 34-46.

ETTINGHAUSEN, WALTER. *Luther: Exegesis and Prose Style. German Studies Presented to H. G. Fiedler.* Oxford, 1937. pp. 174-186.

FRANCKE, KUNO. *Luther's Return to the Principle of Authority.* UR XXXIII (1890), 123-134.

FULLERTON, KEMPER. *Luther's Doctrine and Criticism of Scripture.* BS LXIII (1906), 1-34, 284-299.

HAGEN, KENNETH. *The First Translation of Luther's Lectures on Hebrews. A Review Article.* CH XXXIV 2 (1965), 204-213. *The Problem of Testament in Luther's Lectures on Hebrews.* HTR LXIII 1 (1970), 61-90.

HALL, GEORGE F. *Luther and Coverdale: Biblical Glossators.* AQ XIV (1935), 291-303.

Luther's Standards of Canonicity. AQ XV (1936), 299-309.

HEICK, O. W. *Luther's Exposition of Genesis 1-3.* LQ XXI (1948), 61-71.

HOF, OTTO. *Luther's Exegetical Principle of the Analogy of Faith.* CTM XXXVIII 4 (1967), 242-247.

HOWORTH, HENRY H. *The Origin and Authority of the Biblical Canon According to the Continental Reformers.* JTS VIII (1907), 321-365; IX (1908), 188-230.

JOHANSEN, H. H. *Martin Luther on Scripture and Authority and the Church, Ministry and Sacraments.* SJT XV 4 (1962), 350-368.

KOENIG, WALTER H. *Luther as a Student of Hebrew.* CTM XXIV 11 (1953), 845-853.

KOOIMAN, WILLEM JAN. *Luther and the Bible*, tr. John Schmidt. Philadelphia, 1961. 243 pages.

An excellent study by an eminent Dutch scholar.

KUEMMEL, WERNER GEORG. *The Continuing Significance of Luther's Prefaces to the New Testament.* CTM XXXVII 9 (1966), 573-581.

LAWSON, EVALD B. *The Historical Setting of Luther's Commentaries on Galatians.* AQ XV (1936), 310-328.

LOESCHEN, JOHN. *The Function of Promissio in Luther's Commentary on Romans.* HTR LX 4 (1967), 476-482.

LOETSCHER, FREDERICK W. *Luther and the Problem of Authority in Religion.* PTR XV (1917), 553-603; XVI (1918), 497-556.

MARTY, MARTIN E. *Preaching on the Holy Spirit: a Study of Luther's Sermons on the Evangelical Pericopes.* CTM XXVI 6 (1955), 423-441.

MEYER, CARL S. *Scripture, Confession, Justification.* CTM XLII (1971), 199-202.

MOELLERING, H. ARMIN. *Brunner and Luther on Scriptural Authority.* CTM XXI 11 (1950), 801-818.

MUELLER, JOHN THEODORE. *Notes on Luther's Conception of the Word of God as the Means of Grace.* CTM XX 8 (1949), 580-600.
Notes on Luther's Interpretation of John 6:47-58. CTM XX 11 (1949), 802-828.

PELIKAN, JAROSLAV. *Luther the Expositor. Introduction to the Reformer's Exegetical Writings.* Companion volume to *Luther's Works, American Edition.* Philadelphia, 1959. xiii+ 285 pages.
Analysis of Luther's hermeneutic and case studies of his biblical exegesis.

PETERS, PAUL. *Luther's Text—Critical Study of 2 Samuel 23:8.* CTM XVIII 9 (1947), 641-652.

PIEPER, FRANCIS. *Luther's Doctrine of Inspiration.* PRR IV (1893), 249-266.

PILCH, JOHN J. *Luther's Hermeneutical Shift.* HTR LXIII 3 (1970), 445-448.

PREUS, JAMES S. *Old Testament Promissio and Luther's New Hermeneutic.* HTR LX 2 (1967), 145-162.

QUANBECK, WARREN A. *Biblical Interpretation in Luther's Early Studies.* LQ I 3 (1949), 287-293.

REU, JOHANN MICHAEL. *Luther and the Scriptures.* Columbus, O., 1944. 211 pages.
A dated attempt to argue for a theory of verbal inspiration.

SAARNIVAARA, UURAAS. *Written and Spoken Word.*

LQ II 2 (1950), 166-179.
Argues for Luther's position on *Scriptural* authority over
against *doctrinal* authority.
SCHARLEMANN, ROBERT. *The Scriptures and the Church.*
LQ XII 2 (1960), 159-166.
A critical response to Georges H. Tavard's *Holy Writ or Holy
Church,* with reference to his interpretation of Luther.
SIMON, D. W. *The Doctrine of the "Testimonium Spiritus Sancti,"
a Contribution to Its History in the Lutheran Church during
the Sixteenth and Seventeenth Centuries.* BS XLVIII (1891),
27-51.
SPITZ, LEWIS W. *Luther Expounds the Gospels.* CTM XXVIII
1 (1957), 15-27.
Luther's Sola Scriptura. CTM XXXI 12 (1960), 740-745.
SURBURG, RAYMOND F. *The Significance of Luther's Her-
meneutics for the Protestant Reformation.* CTM XXIV 4
(1953), 241-261.
TAVARD, GEORGES H. *Holy Writ or Holy Church. The Crisis
of the Protestant Reformation.* N.Y., 1959, 1960. x+250
pages.
A Roman Catholic reassessment of the doctrines of justifi-
cation and scriptural authority. Luther is especially
criticized.
TRESSLER, V. G. A. *Luther's Attitude toward Scripture.* LQ
XLVII (1917), 355-374 pages.
WEBER, WILLIAM. *Luther and the Decalogue.* LQ XXXVIII
(1908), 490-510.
WOLF, CARL UMHAU. *Luther on the Christmas Prophecy,
Isaiah 9.* LQ V 4 (1953), 388-390.
WOOD, A. SKEVINGTON. *The Theology of Luther's Lectures
on Romans.* SJT III 1 (1950), 1-18; 2 (1950), 113-126.
*Captive to the Word. Martin Luther: Doctor of Sacred Scrip-
ture.* Grand Rapids, 1969. 192 pages.
A full survey of Luther's attitude to the Bible.
ZUCKER, WOLFGANG M. *Linguistic Philosophy and Luther's
Understanding of the Word.* LQ XV (1963), 195-211.

Justification by Faith

DALLMANN, WILLIAM. *Justification in Luther's Theology.*
CTM XVIII 2 (1947), 126-128.

FAULKNER, JOHN ALFRED. *An Eminent Liberal on Luther's
Doctrine of Justification* (Martin Rade) LQ LVI (1926), 191-
199.

Pecca Fortiter. AJT XVIII (1914), 600-604.

FORELL, GEORGE W. *Justification and Eschatology in Luther's
Thought.* CH XXXVIII 2 (1969), 164-174.

Great Dialecticians in Modern Christian Thought. Minneapolis,
1971.

KOENKER, ERNEST B. *Martin Luther on Simul Justus et
Peccator.* 33-52.

HÄGGLUND, BENGT. *The Background of Luther's Doctrine of
Justification in Late Medieval Theology.* LW VIII 1 (1967),
24-47.

HAIKOLA, LAURI. *A Comparison of Melanchthon's and Luther's
Doctrine of Justification.* D II 1 (1963), 32-39.

HUGGENRIK, THEODORE. *God Who Likes Me. Martin Luther's
Search for a Gracious God.* Minneapolis, 1956. 97 pages.

IHMELS, L. *Justification by Faith Alone: Our Bulwark against
Rome.* LQ XXXIV (1904), 477-489.

JOHNSON, JOHN F. *Luther on Justification.* CTM XXXVIII 7
(1967), 411-421.

LOWRIE, WALTER A. *About Justification by Faith Alone.* JR
XXXII 4 (1952), 231-241.

MCGLOTHLIN, W. J. *Luther's Doctrine of Good Works.* AJT XXI
(1917), 529-544.

OBERMAN, HEIKO A. *Iustitia Christi and Iustitia Dei: Luther
and the Scholastic Doctrines of Justification.* HTR LIX 1
(1966), 1-26.

OESCH, W. M. *Luther on Faith.* CTM XXVII 3 (1956), 184-196.

RICHARD, J. W. *The Central Principle of Lutheranism.* LQ XXV
(1895), 162-188.

The Formative Principle of Protestantism. LQ XXXII (1902),
1-32, 228-266, 327-362.

SMITH, PRESERVED. *Luther's Development of the Doctrine of
Justification by Faith Only.* HTR VI (1913), 407-425.

SPITZ, LEWIS W. *Luther's Concept of the Atonement Before*

1517. CTM XXI 3 (1950), 165-180.

WICKS, JARED. *Man Yearning for Grace. Luther's Early Spiritual Teaching* (Veröffentlichung des Instituts für Europäische Geschichte, vol. 56). Wiesbaden, 1969. xviii+438 pages.
A Roman Catholic thesis, associating Luther's evangelical breakthrough with Hebrews rather than Romans.

The Lord's Supper

FAULKNER, JOHN ALFRED. *Luther and the Real Presence.* AJT XXI (1917), 225-239.
Luther and the Lord's Supper in the Critical Years 1517-22. LQ XLV (1915), 202-216.
206; 194-206, 658-670; XIX (1900), 63-73.

FISCHER, ROBERT H. *Luther's Stake in the Lord's Supper Controversy.* D II 1 (1963), 50-59.

FRITSCHEL, GEORGE J. *Luther and Zwingli.* LCR XVIII (1899), 194-206, 658-670; XIX (1900), 63-73.

HEMMETER, H. B. *Luther's Position on the Lord's Supper.* CTM X 10 (1939), 721-742.

KRODEL, GOTTFRIED G. *The Lord's Supper in the Theology of the Young Luther.* LQ XIII 1 (1961), 19-33.

MCCUE, JAMES F. *Luther and Roman Catholicism on the Mass as Sacrifice.* JES II 2 (1965), 205-233.

MILLER, EPHRAIM. *Luther at Marburg.* LQ XIV (1884), 127-145.

MUELLER, JOHN THEODORE. *Miscellanea: Digest of Luther's Brief Confession of the Holy Sacrament Against the Enthusiasts.* CTM XVI 2 (1945), 118-122.

NAGEL, NORMAN. *The Incarnation and the Lord's Supper in Luther.* CTM XXIV 9 (1953), 625-652.
The Presence of Christ's Body and Blood in the Sacrament of the Altar According to Luther. CTM XXXIX (1968), 227-238.

RICHARD, J. W. *The Sacramentarian Controversy.* LQ XVIII (1888), 153-183, 351-376.

SASSE, HERMANN. *This Is My Body, Luther's Contention for the Real Presence in the Sacrament of the Altar.* Minneapolis, 1959. 420 pages.
A conservative approach. Contains bibliography.

SNOOK, LEE E. *Consciousness and Contradiction: Luther's Doctrine of the Real Presence Reconsidered.* D X 1 (1971), 39-48.

YOUNG, JOHN J. *Luther's Attitude at the Marburg Colloquy.* LQ XXVII (1897), 488-500.

Baptism

CAINER, HARRY G. *The Inclusive Nature of Holy Baptism in Luther's Writings.* CTM XXXIII 11 (1962), 645-657.

LAZARETH, WILLIAM H. *Sacraments of the Word in Luther.* LQ XII 4 (1960), 315-330.
On penance, baptism and the Lord's Supper.

The Trinity

ADAMS, FRANK S. *The Doctrine of the Trinity as Held by the Old Lutheran Theologians.* BS XXXIX (1882), 248-269.

ARNDT, W. (TR.) *Discourse of Luther on the Holy Trinity.* CTM XIX 5 (1948), 321-326.
The Wrath of God and the Grace of God in Lutheran Theology. CTM XXIII 8 (1952), 569-582.

BRETSCHER, PAUL M. *Luther's Christ.* CTM XXXI 4 (1960), 212-214.

CARLSON, ARNOLD E. *Luther and the Doctrine of the Holy Spirit.* LQ XI 2 (1959), 135-146.

COATES, THOMAS. *Luther's Picture of Christ on the Basis of the Church Postil Sermons.* CTM XX 4 (1949), 241-267.

DILLENBERGER, JOHN. *God Hidden and Revealed. The Interpretation of Luther's Deus Absconditus and Its Significance for Religious Thought.* Philadelphia, 1953. xxiv+193 pages.
An analysis with implications for modern theology.

GRISLIS, EGIL. *Luther's Understanding of the Wrath of God.* JR XLI 4 (1961), 277-292.

HENDRY, G. S. *Luther's Theology of the Godhead of God,* in *God the Creator.* London, 1937. pp. 87-150.

JOHNSON, DALE A. *Luther's Understanding of God.* LQ XVI (1964), 59-69.

MUELLER, JOHN T. *The Concept of God in Luther and the Lutheran Confessions.* CTM XXVI 1 (1955), 1-16.

PESCH, OTTO H. *The God Question in Thomas Aquinas and
   Martin Luther,* tr. Gottfried G. Krodel. Philadelphia, 1972.
   ix+38 pages.
   The condensed results of an elaborate Roman Catholic
   analysis of the two theologians.
PRENTER, REGIN. *Spiritus Creator,* tr. John M. Jensen. Phila-
   delphia, 1953. xx+311 pages.
   An incisive analysis of Luther's doctrine of the Holy Spirit
   before and during his quarrel with the left wing (*Schwärmer*).
   A Swedish work.
SIGGINS, IAN D. KINGSTON. *Martin Luther's Doctrine of Christ*
   (Yale Publications in Religion series). London, New Haven,
   1970. x+331 pages.
   Attempts to show that Luther's christology (if one can call
   it that) is Johannine rather than Pauline. Includes a bibliography.
TWESTEN, A. D. C. *The Trinity,* tr. H. B. Smith. BS III (1846),
   760-774; IV (1847), 25-68. Discusses Luther and Calvin.

Predestination

FOX, LUTHER A. *Luther and Free Will.* LQ XIX (1809), 453-491.
NELSON, JOHN. *Predestination.* SJT VI 3 (1953), 244-256.
   On the "free will" controversy between Luther and Calvin.
RICHARD, J. W. *The Lutheran Predestination Controversy.* LQ
   XXXIV (1904), 21-66.
   The Old Lutheran Doctrine of Free Will. LQ XXXV (1905),
   153-188, 303-345, 455-500; XXXVII (1907), 195-225, 305-327.

Ethics

ALTHAUS, PAUL. *The Ethics of Martin Luther,* tr. Robert C.
   Schultz. Philadelphia, 1972. XXI+160 pages.
   Companion compendium to the author's *The Theology of
   Martin Luther.*
BERNER, CARL WALTER. *The Social Ethic of Martin Luther.*
   CTM XIV 3 (1943), 161-178.
BLUHM, HEINZ. *Martin Luther and the Idea of Monasticism.*
   CTM XXXIV 10 (1963), 594-603.
   The Idea of Justice in Luther's First Publication. CTM
   XXXVII g (1966), 565-572.

Deals with Luther's *The Seven Penitential Psalms,* 1517.

ENGELDER, THEODORE. *The Right and Wrong of Private Judgment.* CTM XV 5 (1944), 289-314.

FAULKNER, J. A. *Luther and Truth-Telling.* LQ LIV (1924), 349-365.

FISCHER, WALTER F. *Fasting and Bodily Preparation—a Fine Outward Training.* CTM XXX 12 (1959), 887-902.
On Luther's *Small Catechism.*

FORELL, GEORGE W. *Faith Active in Love.* N.Y., 1954. 198 pages.
A useful summary of Luther's ethics.

GRIFFIN, DALE E. *The Christian Answer to the Ethical Problem—a Study of Catechism Question Number 170.* CTM XXX 10 (1959), 733-760.
On Luther's *Small Catechism.*

HEINECKEN, MARTIN J. *Luther and the "Orders of Creation" in Relation to a Doctrine of Work and Vocation.* LQ IV 4 (1952), 393-414.

KEGLEY, CHARLES W. (ED.) *The Philosophy and Theology of Anders Nygren.* London, Amsterdam, Carbondale, Edwardsville, Ill., 1970.
KINDER, ERNST. *Agape in Luther.* 203-219.
More emphasis on Nygren than on Luther.

PFLEIDERER, OTTO. *Luther as Founder of Protestant Morals.* LQ XVIII (1888), 31-53.

PIEPKORN, ARTHUR C. *Did Luther Teach That Christ Committed Adultery?* CTM XXV 6 (1954), 417-432.

RUPPRECHT, O. C. *A Remedy for Modern Chaos—Luther's Concept of Our Calling.* CTM XXI 11 (1951), 820-847.

WATSON, PHILIP S. *Luther's Doctrine of Vocation.* SJT II 4 (1949), 364-377.
Luther and Sanctification. CTM XXX 4 (1959), 243-259.

WINGREN, GUSTAF. *The Christian's Calling According to Luther.* AQ XXI (1942), 3-16.
Luther on Vocation, tr. Carl C. Rasmussen. Philadelphia, 1957. 256 pages.
A Swedish classic.

ZENOS, A. C. *Primitive Lutheran Ethical Theory.* AJT XIII (1909), 302-304.

ZIEMKE, DONALD C. *Love for the Neighbor in Luther's Theology: the Development of His Thought, 1512-1529.* Minneapolis, 1963. 108 pages.
With an extensive bibliography.
ZIMMERMAN, JACQUELYN. *The Christian Life in Luther and Calvin.* LQ XVI (1964), 222-230.

Doctrine of the Two Kingdoms

BERGGRAV, EIVIND. *State and Church—the Lutheran View.* LQ IV 4 (1952), 363-376.
A basic reinterpretation of the doctrine of the Two Kingdoms by a Norwegian bishop.
BORNKAMM, HEINRICH. *Luther's Doctrine of the Two Kingdoms in the Context of His Theology,* tr. Karl H. Hertz. Philadelphia, 1966. v+41 pages.
The best summary of the doctrine.
CARLSON, EDGAR M. *The Two Realms and the Modern World.* LW XII 4 (1965), 373-384.
DAHL, NILS A. *Is There a New Testament Basis for the Doctrine of the Two Kingdoms?* LW XII 4 (1965), 337-354.
ENGELDER, THEODORE. *Ob Man Sich Wider den Kaiser Wehren Moege.* CTM XV 2 (1944), 112-115.
On Luther's view of resistance to the emperor (1530). Partly in German and partly English.
HILLDERDAL, GUNNAR. *Romans 13 and Luther's Doctrine of the Two Kingdoms.* LW X 1 (1963), 10-23.
JEPSEN, ALFRED. *What Can the Old Testament Contribute to the Discussion on the Doctrine of the Two Kingdoms?* LW XII 4 (1965), 325-336.
JOHNSON, WILLIAM A. *Luther's Doctrine of the Two Kingdoms.* LQ XV (1963), 239-249.
LAU, FRANZ. *The Lutheran Doctrine of the Two Kingdoms.* LW XII 4 (1965), 355-372.
LAZARETH, WILLIAM H. *The "Two Kingdom Ethic" Reconsidered.* D I 4 (1962), 30-35.
Luther's Two Kingdoms' Ethic Reconsidered. Christian Social Ethics in a Changing World, ed. John C. Bennet. N.Y., 1966. 119-131.
A defense of Luther's ethic.

SOCIAL AND ECONOMIC

Sex

FAULKNER, JOHN ALFRED. *Luther and the Bigamous Marriage of Philip of Hesse.* AJT XVII (1913), 206-231.

LAZARETH, WILLIAM H. *Luther on the Christian Home. An Application of the Social Ethics of the Reformation.* Philadelphia, 1960. XII+244 pages.
A sympathetic study of Luther's ethics and its theological base in the context of his marriage and the treatises he wrote before 1525.

MATTES, JOHN C. *Luther's Views Concerning Continence.* LCQ IV (1931), 109-423.

SMITH, PRESERVED. *Luther and Henry VIII.* EHR XXV (1910), 656-669.

Social Revolution and Social Service

CRANZ, FERDINAND E. *An Essay on the Development of Luther's Thought on Justice, Law and Society* (Harvard Theological Studies series). Cambridge, 1959. xviii+197 pages.
Based on the writings of the young Luther.

FAULKNER, JOHN ALFRED. *Luther and the Peasants' War.* LQ XXXVIII (1908), 301-314.

GRIMM, HAROLD J. *Luther's Contributions to Sixteenth Century Organization of Poor Relief.* ARG LXI (1970), 222-233.
A systematic evaluation of Luther's sources regarding social welfare.

GRITSCH, ERIC W. *Martin Luther and the Revolutionary Tradition of the West. Gettysburg Seminary Bulletin* LI 1 (1971), 3-19. *Martin Luther and Violence: A Reappraisal of a Neuralgic Theme. SCJ* III 1 (1972), 37-55.

KLANN, H. R. *Luther on War and Revolution.* CTM XXV 5 (1954), 353-366.

MACKENSEN, HEINZ F. *Historical Interpretation and Luther's Role in the Peasant Revolt.* CTM XXXV 4 (1964), 197-209.

MATTES, JOHN C. *Luther's Attitude in the Peasants' Revolt.* LCR XXXV (1916), 110-128.

WALSH, JAMES J. *Luther and Social Service.* CW CIV (1917), 781-791.
Luther's testimony to the hospitals at Florence.

Economic Questions

BEHRINGER, GEORGE F. *Luther's Income and Possessions.*
LQ XXVI (1896), 236-243.

FAULKNER, JOHN ALFRED. *Luther and Economic Questions.*
ASCH 2S II (1910), 133-152. Reprinted in LQ XLI (1911),
387-402.

THE CHURCH: THEORY, POLITY, MINISTRY

BAUGHMAN, HARRY F. *Martin Luther, the Preacher.* LCQ
XXI (1948), 21-49.

BRUCE, G. M. *Luther and Church Government.* LQ V 4 (1953),
370-378.

EASTWOOD, C. CYRIL. *Luther's Conception of the Church.*
SJT XI 1 (1958), 22-36.

EVJEN, JOHN O. *Luther's Ideas Concerning Church Polity.* LCR
XLV (1926), 207-237, 339-373.

FISCHER, ROBERT H. *Another Look at Luther's Doctrine of
the Ministry.* LQ XVIII 3 (1966), 260-271.

FORELL, GEORGE W. *The Reality of the Church as the Com-
munion of Saints.* Wenonah, N.J., 1943. 107 pages.
A useful summary of Luther's ecclesiology.

GERRISH, BRIAN A. *Priesthood and Ministry in the Theology
of Luther.* CH XXXIV 4 (1965), 404-422.

GREEN, LOWELL C. *Change in Luther's Doctrine of the Ministry.*
LQ XVIII 3 (1966), 173-183.

GRIMM, HAROLD J. *The Human Element in Luther's Sermons.*
ARG XLIX (1958), 50-59.
Investigates 194 sermons from 1528-1532.

HÖK, GÄSTA. *Luther's Doctrine of the Ministry.* SJT VII 1
(1954), 16-40.

JACOBS, CHARLES M. *The Genesis of Luther's Doctrine of the
Church.* LCR XXXIV (1915), 141-152.
The Development of Luther's Doctrine of the Church. Ibid.,
202-213.

KASCHADE, ALFRED. *Luther on Missionary Motivation.* LQ
XVII 3 (1965), 224-239.

KIESSLING, ELMER C. *The Early Sermons of Luther and Their
Relation to the Pre-Reformation Sermon.* Grand Rapids,
Mich., 1935. 157 pages.

LINDBECK, GEORGE A. *The Lutheran Doctrine of the Ministry: Catholic and Reformed.* TS XXX 4 (1969), 588-612.

MAYER, F. E. *The Una Sancta in Luther's Theology.* CTM XVIII 11 (1947), 801-815.

PELIKAN, JAROSLAV. *Spirit Versus Structure; Luther and the Institutions of the Church.* N.Y., 1968. x+149 pages.
    Lectures delivered in Czechoslovakia in 1967 on Luther's views of ministry, monasticism, infant baptism, law and sacraments.

Political Consequences of the Reformation: Studies in Sixteenth Century Political Thought. N.Y. 1960.
    MURRAY, ROBERT H. *Luther and the State Church.* 60-79.

PREUS, H. A. *Luther's Doctrine of the Church in His Early Writings.* (Dissertation, Edinburgh, 1928). Not yet published.
    The Communion of Saints. A Study of the Origin and Development of Luther's Doctrine of the Church. Minneapolis, 1948. 172 pages.
    A useful but dated study.

RICHARDSON, CYRIL C. *The Idea of the Church—a Study in Luther.* AQ XV (1936), 291-298.

RUPP, E. GORDON. *Luther and the Doctrine of the Church.* SJT IX (1956), 384-392.

SAARNIVAARA, UURAS. *The Church of Christ According to Luther.* LQ V 2 (1953), 134-154.

SPAETH, A. *Luther's Doctrine of the Church.* LCR VI (1887), 272-286.

SPITZ, LEWIS W. *The Universal Priesthood of Believers with Luther's Comments.* CTM XXIII 1 (1952), 1-15.
    Luther's Ecclesiology and His Concept of the Prince as "Notbischof." CH XXII 2 (1953), 113-141.

WENTZ, FREDERICK K. *The Development of Luther's Views on Church Organization.* LQ VII 3 (1955), 217-232.

WILLIAMS, GEORGE H. *Congregationalist Luther and the Free Churches.* LQ XIX (1967), 283-295.

EDUCATION

BRUCE, GUSTAV MARIUS. *Luther as an Educator.* Minneapolis, 1928. 318 pages.

HORN, EDWARD T. *A Note on Luther's Small Catechism.* LCR

XVI (1897), 630-636.

KRETZMANN, P. E. (COMP.) *Luther on Education in the Christian Home and School.* Burlington, 1940. 116 pages.

PAINTER, FRANKLIN VERZELIUS NEWTON. *Luther on Education.* Philadelphia, 1889. vii+282 pages.
Discussion and translation of two tracts.

SÖLDERGREN, CARL W. *Some Reflections on the Origins of Luther's Catechism.* AQ XXV (1946), 132-141.

REU, M. *The Peculiar Characteristic of Luther's Catechism.* LCR XXIV (1905), 436-451.

SCHMUCKER, BEALE M. *Luther's Small Catechism.* LCR V (1886), 87-113.
Bibliographical notes on translations and explanations prepared for use in America in English and German.

POLITICAL THEORY: SUPPRESSION OF DISSENT
(See also under Reformation and Liberty, Anabaptists)

ALLEN, J. W. *The Political Conceptions of Luther* (Tudor Studies Presented to Albert Frederick Pollard). Ld., 1924, pp. 90-108.

BAINTON, ROLAND HERBERT. *The Development and Consistency of Luther's Attitude to Religious Liberty.* HTR XXII (1929), 107-149.
Reprinted in revised form, as *Luther's Attitudes on Religious Liberty,* in the author's *Studies on the Reformation.*

BERGENDOFF, CONRAD. *Christian Love and Public Policy in Luther.* LQ XIII 3 (1961), 218-228.

CARLSON, EDGAR M. *Luther's Conception of Government.* CH XV 4 (1946), 257-270.

EARLY, J. W. *"Luther and Religious Persecution"* (Discussion of Luther's attitude to the Jews, a reply to Dunlop Moore). LCR XVII (1898), 148-159.

EVANS, AUSTEN P. *An Episode in the Struggle for Religious Freedom,* N.Y., 1924. pp. 98-126.

FAULKNER, JOHN ALFRED. *Luther and Toleration.* ASCH 2S IV (1914), 129-154.

FORELL, GEORGE W. *Luther's View Concerning the Imperial Foreign Policy.* LQ IV 2 (1952), 153-169.

GENSICHEN, HANS W. *We Condemn. How Luther and 16th Century Lutheranism Condemned False Doctrine,* tr. Herbert

J. A. Bouman. St. Louis, 1967. x+213 pages.
A study of Lutheran judgments on heresy from Luther to
the *Book of Concord* (1583).
GREEN, LOWELL C. *Resistance to Authority and Luther.* LQ
VI 4 (1954), 338-348.
GRIMM, HAROLD J. *Luther's Conception of Territorial and
National Loyalty.* CH XVII 2 (1948), 79-94.
HEICK, OTTO W. *Luther on War.* AQ XXVII (1948), 323-335.
HOLMIO, ARMAS K. *Luther and War.* LQ IV 3 (1952), 261-277.
HORSCH, JOHN. *Luther's Attitude to Liberty of Conscience.* AJT
XI (1907), 307-315.
KRAMM, H. H. *Luther's Teaching on Christian Responsibility
in Politics and Public Life.* LQ III 3 (1951), 308-313.
MCGOVERN, WILLIAM M. *From Luther to Hitler. The History
of Fascist-Nazi Political Philosophy.* Boston, N.Y., Chicago,
Dallas, Atlanta, San Francisco, 1941. 683 pages.
Blames Luther and other Germans for the rise of Nazism.
Not factual and quite prejudiced.
MOORE, DUNLOP. *Luther and Religious Persecution.* PRR VIII
(1897), 99-102.
MUELLER, WILLIAM A. *Church and State in Luther and Calvin.*
Nashville, 1954. 183 pages.
A fair survey.
OYER, JOHN S. *Lutheran Reformers Against Anabaptists. Luther,
Melanchthon and Menius and the Anabaptists of Central
Germany.* The Hague, 1964. 269 pages.
A Mennonite analysis of Anabaptist persecution, with an
extensive bibliography.
SCHWIEBERT, ERNEST G. *The Medieval Pattern in Luther's
Views of the State.* CH XII 2 (1943), 98-117.
SIEGEL, WILLIAM. *Luther's Political Philosophy.* AQ (1935),
130-137.
TONKIN, JOHN M. *Luther's Interpretation of Secular Reality.*
JRH VI 2 (1970), 133-150.
WARING, LUTHER HESS. *The Political Theories of Martin Luther.*
N.Y. & Ld., 1910. vi+293 pages.
New edition, Port Washington, Ky., 1968.
WATSON, PHILIP S. *The State as a Servant of God. A Study of
Its Nature and Tasks.* London, 1946. xiv+106 pages.
On Luther's political theory.

OPINIONS ON LUTHER

BAINTON, ROLAND H. *Our Debt to Luther.* CC LXIII (1946), 1276-1278.
> *Luther in a Capsule. Bulletin of the American Congregational Association* III (1952), 1-9.

BAUM, GREGORY (ED.) *Ecumenical Theology Today.* Glen Rock, N.J., 1964.
> QUEDLEY, F. M. *The Changing Image of Luther.* 174-182.

BLUHM, HEINZ. *Nietzsche's Final View of Luther and the Reformation.* CTM XXVII 10 (1956), 765-775.

BOYER, MERLE WILLIAM. *Luther in Protestantism Today.* N.Y., 1958. 188 pages.
> A good summary of Luther's heritage with reference to modern Protestantism.

CARLSON, EDGAR M. *The Interpretation of Luther in Modern Swedish Theology.* Chicago, 1944. ii+246 pages.

CONGAR, YVES. *Church Reform and Luther's Reformation 1517-1967.* LW XIV 4 (1967), 351-359.
> A Roman Catholic opinion.

DALLMANN, WILLIAM. *Catholic Tributes to Luther.* CTM XVI 1 (1945), 24-34.
> *Was Luther Needed?* CTM XVII 3 (1946), 161-181.

DAU, W. H. T. *Luther Examined and Reexamined, a Review of Catholic Criticism and a Plea for Revaluation.* St. Louis, Mo., 1917. 243 pages.

DAVIS, HARRISON, *Luther and Our Hymnbook.* CC LXXIII 43 (1956), 1228-1230.

FAULKNER, JOHN ALFRED. *Luther and His Latest Critic* (Denifle). AJT IX (1905), 359-373.
> *Wesley's Attitude toward Luther.* LQ XXXVI (1906), 155-178.
> *An Interesting Charge against Luther.* LQ LV (1925), 273-282.
> Reply to Denifle.
> *An American Doctor Looks at Luther.* PTR XXVI (1928), 248-264.
> Discussion of the view of John Joseph Mangan, *The Life and Character of Desiderius Erasmus.* 2 vols. N.Y., 1927.

FORELL, GEORGE W. *Luther Today.* AQ XXV (1946), 291-296.

GLEASON, ELIZABETH G. *Sixteenth Century Italian Interpretations of Luther*. ARG LX (1969), 160-173.

GRIMM, KARL JOSEF. *A Roman Catholic View of Luther*
(Denifle's). LQ XXXVI (1906), 234-247, 404-414.

GRITSCH, ERIC W. *Third International Congress for Luther
Research, 1966: a New Ecumenical Luther Image?* US XXIII
4 (1966), 85-87.

HALL, GEORGE F. *Is Luther to Blame?* CC LXI 47 (1944), 1352-
1353.
Defends Luther against English charges making him the father
of Nazism.
You Ask About Luther. 1949. 62 pages.
Questions and answers on Luther's life and on books about
him.

HARVEY, ANDREW EDWARD. *Martin Luther in the Estimate
of Modern Historians*. AJT XXII (1918), 321-348.

HUMPHREY, L. H. *French Estimates of Luther*. LQ XLVIII
(1918), 169-201.

JOELSSON, A. *A Boy Meets Luther,* tr. Ruth Jacobson Ullberg.
Rock Island, 1950. 293 pages.
A Swedish schoolteacher's attempt to make Luther palatable
to children. Based on the *Small Catechism*.

JUNGKUNTZ, THEODORE. *Secularization Theology, Charismatic
Renewal, and Luther's Theology of the Cross*. CTM XLII
(1971), 5-24.

LILJE, HANNS. *Luther Now*. tr. Carl J. Schindler. Philadelphia,
1952. 190 pages.
A biographical survey, and modern defense of Luther, by a
German bishop.

LINDBERG, CARTER. *Martin Luther: Copernican Revolution or
Ecumenical Bridge?* US XXIV 1 (1967), 31-38.

LINDEMANN, HENRY. *Martin Luther Man of God. Selected
Essays*. N.Y., 1955. 102 pages.
An unsuccessful attempt to modernize Luther.

MIGNET, FRANÇOIS A. M. *A Frenchman on Luther at Worms,*
tr. William M. Robbins. LQ XXVI (1896), 394-410.

MONTGOMERY, JOHN W. *Shirer's Re-Hitlerizing of Luther*.
CC LXXIX 50 (1962), 1510-1512.
In Defense of Martin Luther. Milwaukee, 1970. 175 pages.

NEILL, THOMAS P. *Luther and the Modern Mind.* CW (1946), 11-18.

NYGREN, ANDERS. *Martin Luther: a Pertinent Figure.* AQ XXV (1946), 297-305.

In commemoration of the 400th anniversary of his death.

PAUCK, WILHELM. *Luther and the Reformation.* TT III (1946), 314-327.

Criticizes especially Reinhold Niebuhr's position on Luther and the Reformation argued in *The Nature and Destiny of Man* and *The Self and the Dramas of History.*

PETERSON, RUSSELL A. *Luther for Today.* Author's ed., 1948. 50 pages.

A pamphlet on Luther's educational principles, very dated.

PINOMAA, LENNART. *The Meaning of Luther for Our Time.* LQ XIX (1967), 274-282.

RUPP, E. GORDON. *Martin Luther: Hitler's Cause or Cure?* London, 1945. 94 pages.

SCHROEDER, MARTIN. *Luther After Four Centuries.* CC LXIII 7 (1946), 206-208.

SHEERIN, JOHN. *Canonize Martin Luther?* CW CXCVII (1963), 84-87.

Doubts the possibility.

SMITH, PRESERVED. *English Opinion on Luther.* HTR X (1917), 129-158.

SÖDERGREN, C. J. *Luther and Our Times.* AQ XVII (1938), 291-304.

SORMUNEN, EINO. *Luther as a Religious Personality.* AQ XXV (1946), 195-205.

STAUFFER, RICHARD. *Luther as Seen by Catholics,* tr. Mary Parker and T. H. L. Parker. Richmond, 1967. 83 pages.

Reviews Denifle, Grisar, English-speaking critics and the new ecumenical assessment of Luther since World War I in German and Anglo-Saxon Roman Catholicism, with an appendix on France.

SWIHART, ALTMAN K. *Luther and the Lutheran Church—1483-1960.* N.Y., 1960. 703 pages.

Weak on Luther and the Reformation.

TAPPERT, THEODORE G. *On the Translation of Martin Luther's Works.* LQ XIX (1946), 411-417.

WEIDENSCHILLING, J. M. *Living With Luther.* St. Louis, 1945. 47 pages.
For use in schools of the Lutheran Church-Missouri Synod.
World Lutheranism of Today. A Tribute to Anders Nygren. Stockholm and Göttingen, 1950.
FJELLBU, ARNE. *Luther as a Resource of Arms in the Fight of Democracy.* 81-97.
WATSON, PHILIP S. *The Significance of Luther for Christians of Other Communions.* 374-390.
ZEEDEN, ERNST WALKER. *The Legacy of Luther. Martin Luther and the Reformation in the Estimation of the German Lutherans from Luther's Death to the Beginning of the Age of Goethe* tr. Ruth Bethell. London, 1954. 221 pages.
Deals with Luther's self-image and the views of his Lutheran friends and enemies. The major portion covers the post-Reformation period.

MELANCHTHON
(See also Augsburg Confession)

SOURCES

BREEN, QUIRINUS (TR.) *The Subordination of Philosophy to Rhetoric in Melanchthon: a Study of His Reply to G. Pico della Mirandola.* ARG XLIII (1952), 13-27.
HILL, CHARLES H. (TR.) *The Loci Communes of Philip Melanchthon.* Boston, 1944. 274 pages.
The 1521 edition.
Some Theses of Philip Melanchthon. LQ VI 3 (1954), 245-248.
A translation of the *Circular Themes* of 1520.
Melanchthon's Propositions on the Mass. LQ VI 1 (1954), 53-57.
Translation of, and commentary on, the Propositions of 1521.
Melanchthon: Selected Writings, ed. Elmer E. Flack and Lowell J. Satre. Minneapolis, 1962. 190 pages.
Various works between 1519 and 1539, arbitrarily selected to show Melanchthon's theological development.

MACKENSEN, HEINZ (TR.) *The Debate Between Eck and Melanchthon on Original Sin at the Colloquy of Worms.* LQ XI (1959), 42-56.
An abridged version of the colloquy of 1540.

MANSCHRECK, CLYDE L. *Melanchthon on Christian Doctrine: Loci Communes, 1555.* Introduction by Hans Engelland. N.Y., 1965. lvii+356 pages.
The 1555 edition, with an extensive historical introduction.

MOORE, M. A. (TR.) *A Letter of Philipp Melanchthon to the Reader. Isis* I (1959), 145-150.
Preface to the Basel edition of Euclid's Geometry (1537).

BIOGRAPHY

MANSCHRECK, CLYDE L. *Melanchthon: the Quiet Reformer.* N.Y. and Nashville, 1958. 350 pages.
An Apologia of Melanchthon, stressing his thought.

RICHARD, JAMES WILLIAM. *Philip Melanchthon, the Protestant Preceptor of Germany* (Heroes of the Reformation). N.Y., and Ld., 1898. xv+399 pages.

ROGNESS, MICHAEL. *Philip Melanchthon. Reformer Without Honor.* Minneapolis, 1969. viii+165 pages.
Emphasizes the relationship with Luther.

STUPPERICH, ROBERT. *Melanchthon.* tr. Robert H. Fischer. Philadelphia, 1965. 175 pages.
An authoritative biography, with a postscript on research and an English bibliography.

BRIEF SKETCHES

CAEMMERER, RICHARD R. *The Melanchthonian Blight.* CTM XVIII 5 (1947), 321-338.
On the difference from Luther, stressing the shift from the "existential" to the "rational."

COBHAM, J. O. *Melanchthon: Alien or Ally? Church Quarterly Review* LXXI (1946), 23-32.

EDWARDS, B. B. *Life of Philip Melanchthon.* BS III (1846), 301-346.

KELLEY, WILLIAM. *Philip Melanchthon.* LQ XXVII (1897), 12-32.

LAMBERT, W. A. *Melanchthon's Greek Letter to Camerarius.*
LQ XXX (1900), 415-424.
WARFIELD, ETHELBERT D. *Philip Melanchthon.* PRR VIII
(1897), 1-16.

MELANCHTHON'S THOUGHT

BREEN, QUIRINUS. *The Twofold-Truth Theory in Melanchthon.*
RR IX (1945), 115-136.
The Terms "Loci Communes" and "Loci" in Melanchthon.
CH XVI 4 (1947), 197-209.
FAULKNER, JOHN ALFRED. *Melanchthon's Letter on Luther's
Marriage.* LQ XL (1910), 124-126. Translation and discussion.
Melanchthon's Doctrinal Differences from Luther. LQ XLVI,
(1916), 184-195.
*Melanchthon and the Lord's Supper after His Divergence from
Luther.* LQ XLVII (1917), 52-70.
FOSTER, FRANK HUGH. *Melanchthon's "Synergism."* ASCH I
(1888), 185-204.
FRAENKEL, PETER. *Revelation and Tradition. Notes on Some
Aspects of Doctrinal Continuity in the Theology of Philip
Melanchthon. Studia Theologica* XIII (1959), 97-133.
*Testimonia Patrum: the Function of the Patristic Argument
in the Theology of Philip Melanchthon* (Travaux d'Humanisme
et Renaissance series). Geneva, 1961. 382 pages.
A careful work. Contains bibliography.
HAMMER, WILHELM. *Melanchthon, Inspirer of the Study of
Astronomy. With a Translation of His Oration in Praise of
Astronomy (De Orione, 1553). Popular Astronomy, a Review
of Astronomy and Allied Sciences* LIX (1951), 308-319.
MANSCHRECK, CLYDE L. *The Bible in Melanchthon's Philosophy
of Education.* JBR XXIII (1955), 202-207.
Melanchthon and Prayer. ARG LI (1960), 145-157.
MEYER, CARL S. *Melanchthon as Educator.* CTM XXXI 9 (1960),
533-540.
Melanchthon, Theologian of Ecumenism. JEH XVII 2 (1966),
185-207.
PIEPKORN, ARTHUR CARL. *Melanchthon the Confessor.* CTM
XXXI 9 (1960), 541-546.

Melanchthon on Christian Doctrine: a Review Article. CH XXXV 3 (1966), 344-353.

PREUS, ROBERT D. *Melanchthon the Theologian.* CTM XXXI 8 (1960), 469-475.

SCHAFF, PHILIP. *Melanchthon's Theology.* RQR XXXIV (1887), 294-300.

SEEBACH, JULIUS F. *Melanchthon's Doctrine of the Will.* LQ XXX (1900), 190-210.

STUPPERICH, ROBERT. *The Development of Melanchthon's Theological-Philosophical World View.* LW VII 2 (1960), 168-180.

THIELE, GILBERT A. *Melanchthon the Churchman.* CTM XXXI 8 (1960), 479-481.

TOPICS

BREEN, QUIRINUS. *Melanchthon's Sources for a Life of Agricola: the Heidelberg Memories and the Writings.* ARG LII (1961), 49-73.
On Rudolph Agricola, humanist.

DENNIS, GEORGE T. *An Unnoticed Autograph of Philip Melanchthon and of Paul Eber. Medievalia et Humanistica* IX (1955), 102-103.
An interpretation of John 14:23 found in the Jena edition of Luther's works (1557).

HILDEBRANDT, FRANZ. *Melanchthon: Alien or Ally?* Cambridge, 1946. xiii+98 pages.
A comparison with Luther and modern problems.

KOLDE, THEODORE. *Melanchthon's Failure as a Diplomat.* LCR XXVII (1908), 512-538.

MANSCHRECK, CLYDE L. *The Role of Melanchthon in the Adiaphora Controversy.* ARG XLVIII (1957), 165-181.
Discusses the doctrinal quarrel over faith and works of 1548.

OYER, JOHN S. *The Writings of Melanchthon Against the Anabaptists.* MQR XXVI (1952), 259-279.

SALOMON, RICHARD. *The Teuffenbach Copy of Melanchthon's Loci Communes. Renaissance News* VIII 2 (1955), 79-85.

STUPPERICH, ROBERT. *What Does Melanchthon's Genuine Autograph Concerning John 14:23 Look Like? Medievalia et Humanistica* XV (1963), 108-109.

BRENZ

BRENZ JOHANNES. *On the Moderating of the Princes toward the Rebellious Peasants 1525*, tr. C. M. Jacobs. LCQ I (1928), 182-190.

ESTES, JAMES E. *Church Order and the Christian Magistrate According to Johannes Brenz.* ARG LIX (1968), 5-23.
Shows why Brenz differed from Luther when he introduced the Reformation to Swabia and Württemberg.
The Two Kingdoms and the State Church According to Johannes Brenz and an Anonymous Colleague. ARG LXI (1970), 35-49.
Based on a memorandum found in 1530 in Brenz' papers.

HORN, EDWARD T. *Liturgical Work of John BRENZ.* LCR I (1882), 271-291.

WILLS, ELBERT V. *Johann Brenz's Catechism of 1535, a Translation.* AQ XXVI (1947), 291-304.
Johann Brenz's Larger Catechism of 1528. LQ VII 2 (1955), 114-127.

BUCER

BIBLIOGRAPHY

THOMPSON, BARD. *Bucer Study Since 1918.* CH XXV 1 (1956), 63-82.

SOURCES

FUHRMANN, PAUL T. (TR.) *Instruction in Christian Love, 1523.* Richmond, 1951. 68 pages.

WRIGHT, D. F. (ED.) *The Common Places of Martin Bucer.* (Courtenay Library of Reformation Classics, 4). Appleford, Berkshire, England, 1971. Approx. 500 pages.
Contents: summary of *Christian Doctrine* and numerous other sources arranged around theological loci.

BIOGRAPHY AND RELATION TO CONTEMPORARIES

EELLS, HASTINGS. *The Attitude of Martin Bucer toward the Bigamy of Philipp of Hesse* (Yale Historical Publications Miscellany XII). New Haven, 1924. vi+253 pages.
The Correct Date of a Letter to Zwingli (Bucer to Zwingli April 30, 1528). Revue belge de Philologie et d'Histoire. I (1922), 1514-1519.
Martin Bucer and the Conversion of John Calvin. PTR XXII (1924), 402-419.
Martin Bucer, New Haven, 1931. xii+539 pages.
Bucer's Plan for the Jews. CH VI 2 (1937), 127-135.
The Failure of Church Unification Efforts during the German Reformation (In Memoriam Martini Buceri +27. Februar 1551). ARG XLII (1951), 160-173.
Deals with Bucer's efforts to unite Protestants.
HOPF, CONSTANTIN. *Martin Bucer and the English Reformation.* Oxford, 1946. xiv+290 pages.
With a list of 16th Century English translations of Bucer's works and a bibliography.
Martin Bucer and England. ZKG LXXI (1960), 82-109.
PAUCK, WILHELM. *Luther and Butzer.* JR IX (1929), 85-98.
Calvin and Butzer. Ibid., 237-256.
Revised in the author's *The Heritage of the Reformation.*
SMYTH, C. H. *Cranmer and the Reformation under Edward VI.* Cambridge, Eng., 1926. x+315 pages. Includes a chapter on *Cambridge and Bucer.*

TOPICS

EELLS, HASTINGS. *The Genesis of Martin Bucer's Doctrine of the Lord's Supper.* PTR XXIV (1926), 225-251.
The Contribution of Martin Bucer to the Reformation. HTR XXIV (1931), 29-42.
GILBERT, ALLEN H. *Martin Bucer on Education.* JEGP XVIII (1919), 321-345.
LINDSAY, T. M. *Martin Bucer and the Reformation.* QR CCXX (1914), 116-133.
PAUCK, WILHELM. *Martin Bucer's Conception of the Christian State.* PTR XXVI (1928), 80-88.

POLL, G. J. VAN DE. *Martin Bucer's Liturgical Ideas. The Strasburg Reformer and His Connection with the Liturgies of the Sixteenth Century.* Assen, 1954. 179 pages.

STEPHENS, PETER W. *The Holy Spirit in the Theology of Martin Bucer.* London, 1970. ix+291 pages.

TORRANCE, T. F. *Kingdom and Church in the Thought of Martin Butzer.* JEH VI 1 (1955), 48-59.

BUGENHAGEN

Bugenhagen's Order of Services of 1524. LCR X (1891), 288-293.
Translation unsigned.

RUCCIUS, WALTER M. *John Bugenhagen, Pomeranus* (with bibliography of his works). LCR XLII (1923), 119-147, 250-279, 308-337; XLIII (1924), 65-87.

EBERLIN, JOHN VON GÜNZBURG

BELL, SUSAN GROAG. *Johan Eberlin von Günzburg's "Wolfaria": the First Protestant Utopia.* CH XXXVI 2 (1967), 122-139.

COLE, RICHARD G. *Law and Order in the Sixteenth Century: Eberlin von Günzburg and the Problem of Political Authority.* LQ XXIII 3 (1971), 251-256.

DOCTRINAL SETTLEMENTS INCLUDING THE AUGSBURG CONFESSION

BIBLIOGRAPHY

SCHMUCKER, BEALE M. *English Translations of the Augsburg Confession.* LCR VI (1887), 5-38.

TRANSLATIONS

BAUMAN, HERBERT J. *The Sixteenth-Century "Confession of the Fayth of the Germaynes" in Twentieth-Century American English.* CTM XXXI 6 (1960), 363-370.
    On an English edition of the Augsburg Confession.
COCHRANE, ARTHUR C. (ED.) *Reformed Confessions of the 16th Century.* Philadelphia, 1964. 336 pages.
    Contains all Swiss Confessions, the French Confession of 1559 and the Belgic Confession of 1561, and the Heidelberg Catechism of 1563.
BENTE, F. (ED.) *Concordia or Book of Concord. The Symbols of the Evang. Lutheran Church. With Indexes and Historical Introductions. A Reprint of the English Text of the Concordia Triglotta, which Was Published as a Memorial of the Quadricentenary Jubilee of the Reformation A.D. 1917 by Resolution of the Evang. Luth. Church of Missouri, Ohio and Other States.* St. Louis, 1922. 354 pages.
JACOBS, HENRY EYSTER. *The Augsburg Confession,* tr. Richard Taverner, ed. Henry E. Jacobs. Philadelphia, 1888. vi+119 pages.
    The Book of Concord or the Symbolical Books of the Evangelical Lutheran Church. 2 vols. Philadelphia, 1882, 1893 and People's edition in one volume 1912.
    I: *The Confessions.*
    II: *Historical Introductions, Appendices and Indexes.*
REU, JOHANN MICHAEL. *The Augsburg Confession: a Collection of Sources with an Historical Introduction.* Chicago, 1930. xii+258+528 pages.
SCHAFF, PHILIP. *The Creeds of Christendom,* 3 vols. 4th ed. N.Y., 1877.
    I: *History of Creeds.*
    III: *The Evangelical Protestant Creeds with Translations.*
TAPPERT, THEODORE G. (ED.) *The Book of Concord.* Philadelphia, 1959. 717 pages.
    Contains the Augsburg Confession, Apology, Smalcald Articles, Melanchthon's Treatise on the Power and Primacy of the Pope, Luther's two Catechisms, and the Formula of Concord.

HISTORICAL DISCUSSION: GENERAL

RICHARD, JAMES W. *The Confessional History of the Lutheran Church.* Philadelphia, 1909. viii+637 pages.

AUGSBURG DIET AND CONFESSION

ALLBECK, WILLARD D. *The Living Church.* LQ IX 2 (1957), 99-109.
Deals with the Augsburg Confession in the light of modern ecclesiology.

BERGENDOFF, CONRAD J. *The Making and Meaning of the Augsburg Confession.* Rock Island, Ill., 1930. 127 pages.

BOSSERT, G. *Kolde's Discoveries Concerning the Augsburg Confession.* LCR, XXVI (1907), 41-44.

BRETSCHER, PAUL M. *The Unity of the Church.* CTM XXVI 5 (1955), 321-340.
On article 7 of the Augsburg Confession.

EELLS, HASTINGS. *Sacramental Negotiations at the Diet of Augsburg, 1530.* PTR XXIII 2 (1925), pp.?

FLOROVSKY, GEORGES. *The Greek Version of the Augsburg Confession.* LW VI 2 (1959), 153-155.

FORELL, GEORGE W. *The Augsburg Confession. A Contemporary Commentary.* Augsburg, 1968. 112 pages.

FRANZMANN, MARTIN H. *Augustana II: of Original Sin.* CTM XX 12 (1949), 881-893.

HAAS, JOHN A. W. *On the Genesis of the Augsburg Confession.* LCR XVII (1898), 15-29.

HEFELBOWER, S. GRING. *Tschackert's "Unaltered Augsburg Confession."* LQ XXXII (1902), 363-386.

Holman Lectures on the Augsburg Confession.
The first twenty-one were published with the title *Lectures on the Augsburg Confession on the Holman Foundation.* First Series 1866-1886, Philadelphia, 1886, 888 pages. Subsequent lectures will be found in the Lutheran Quarterly. A list is given by Abdel Ross Wentz, *History of the Gettysburg Theological Seminary,* Philadelphia, Pa., 1926, pp. 298-299.
The list is updated in a new edition of Wentz's History, Harrisburg, 1965, p. 480. Since 1967, most lectures are published in the *Bulletin* of the Lutheran Theological

Seminary at Gettysburg, Pa. The Seminary Library will provide further data.

JACOBS, HENRY EYSTER. *The Four Hundred and Four Theses of Dr. John Eck, a Contribution to the History of the Augsburg Confession.* ASCH. 2S II (1910), 21-81.

LACKMANN, MAX. *The Augsburg Confession and Catholic Unity*, tr. Walter R. Bouman. N.Y., 1963. 159 pages.
A German churchman argues for a united church.

MAURER, WILHELM. *Melanchthon as Author of the Augsburg Confession.* LW VII 2 (1960), 153-167.

MAYER, FREDERICK E. *The Voice of Augustana VII on the Church.* CTM XXXIV 3 (1963), 135-146.

MUELLER, JOHN T. *Notes on the "Satis Est" in Article VII of the Augustana.* CTM XVIII 6 (1947), 401-410.

A Question Touching the Augsburg Confession (whether it was submitted to Luther on May 22 and June 2 and received his unqualified approval) Unsigned article in LQ VIII (1878), 161-176.

RICHARD, JAMES W. *The Oldest Redaction of the Augsburg Confession.* LQ XXXVII (1907), 44-68.
The Melanchthon Editions of the Augsburg Confession. LQ XXXVII (1907), 481-507.
Melanchthon and the Augsburg Confession. LQ XXVII (1897) 299-330; XXVIII (1898), 355-395, 545-579.
Luther and the Augsburg Confession. LQ XXIX (1899), 497-527; XXX (1900), 29-61, 359-399, 463-504.

ROLOFF, JÜRGEN. *The Interpretation of Scripture in Article IV of Melanchthon's Apology of the Augsburg Confession.* LW VIII 1 (1961), 47-63.

TAPPERT, THEODORE G. *The Framing of the First Apology of the Augsburg Confession.* LCQ V (1932), 36-56.

BOOK OF CONCORD

ALLBECK, WILLARD D. *Studies in the Lutheran Confessions.* Philadelphia, 1952. xii+305 pages. 2d ed rev., 1968. xi+318 pages.
A historical commentary on the *Book of Concord*, with bibliography.

ARNDT, W. *The Pertinency and Adequacy of the Lutheran Confessions.* CTM XX 9 (1949), 674-700.

BENTE, F. *Historical Introductions to the Book of Concord.* St. Louis, 1965. 266 pages.
Reprint of Historical Introductions contained in *Concordia Or Book of Concord,* edited by the author.

BOMAN, THORLEIF. *The Confessions in Our Preaching.* LW VII 4 (1961), 412-422.

BOUMAN, HERBERT J. *The Doctrine of Justification in the Lutheran Confessions.* CTM XXVI 11 (1955), 801-819.
Some Thoughts on Authentic Lutheranism. CTM XLII 5 (1971), 283-289.
An interpretation of the Formula of Concord.
Some Thoughts on the Church in the Lutheran Symbols. CTM XXXIX (1968), 175-193.

BOUMAN, WALTER R. *The Gospel and the Smalcald Articles.* CTM XL 6&7 (1969), 407-418.

CARLSON, EDGAR M. *The Doctrine of the Ministry in the Confessions.* LQ XV (1963), 118-131.

DAHL, NILS A. *The Lutheran Exegete and the Confessions of His Church.* LW VI 1 (1959), 2-10.

FISCHER, ROBERT H. *The Confessions in Our Congregational Life.* LW VII 4 (1961), 402-411.

GIESCHEN, GERHARD. *The Ecumenicity of the Lutheran Confessions.* LQ VII 4 (1955), 304-319.

GOPPELT, LEONHARD. *The Ministry in the Lutheran Confessions and in the New Testament.* LW XI 4 (1964), 409-426.

HANSON, STIG. *The Confessions—Bridge Between Yesterday and Tomorrow.* LW VII 4 (1961), 379-387.

HOFFMAN, GEORG. *The Confessions of the Church as Gift and Responsibility.* LW II 4 (1955), 334-344.

KRAMER, FRED. *Sacra Scriptura and Verbum Dei in the Lutheran Confessions.* CTM XXVI 2 (1955), 81-95.

LINDBECK, GEORGE A. *The Confessions as Ideology and Witness in the History of Lutheranism.* LW VII 4 (1961), 388-401.

LINSS, WILHELM C. *Biblical Interpretation in the Formula of Concord.* LQ XIV 2 (1962), 165-169.

LITTLE, CARROLL H. *Lutheran Confessional Theology.* A Pre-

sentation of the Doctrines of the Augsburg Confession and the Formula of Concord. St. Louis, 1943. xvi+185 pages.

MAYER, FREDERICK E. *The Formal and Material Principles of Lutheran Confessional Theology.* CTM XXIV 8 (1953), 545-550.

PELIKAN, JAROSLAV. *Doctrine of Man in the Lutheran Confessions.* LQ II 1 (1950), 34-44.

The Relationship of Faith and Knowledge in the Lutheran Confessions. CTM XXI 5 (1950), 321-331.

Church and Church History in the Confessions. CTM XXII 5 (1951), 305-320.

Some Word Studies in the Apology. CTM XXIV 8 (1953), 580-596.

On *Doctrina, evangelium, lex, scriptura* and *verbum.*

The Doctrine of Creation in Lutheran Theology. CTM XXVI 8 (1955), 569-579.

On the Lutheran Confessions.

PIEPKORN, ARTHUR C. *Essays on the Inspiration of Scripture: the Position of the Church and Her Symbols.* CTM XXV 10 (1954), 738-742.

On Lutheran Confessions.

What the Symbols Have to Say About the Church. CTM XXVI 10 (1955), 721-763.

Suggested Principles for a Hermeneutics of the Lutheran Symbols. CTM XXIX 1 (1958), 1-24.

The Sacred Ministry and Holy Ordination in the Symbolical Books of the Lutheran Church. CTM XL (1969), 552-573.

Do the Lutheran Symbolical Books Speak Where the Sacred Scriptures Are Silent? CTM XLIII 1 (1972), 29-35.

PREUS, HERMAN A. *The Written, Spoken, and Signed Word.* CTM XXVI 9 (1955), 641-656.

PREUS, ROBERT D. *The Significance of Luther's Term "Pure Passive" as Quoted in Article II of the Formula of Concord.* CTM XXIX 8 (1958), 561-570.

SCHLINK, EDMUND. *Theology of the Lutheran Confessions,* tr. Paul F. Koehneke and Herbert J. Bouman. Philadelphia, 1961. 353 pages.

A systematic study intended as a prolegomenon to a Lutheran dogmatic.

SINGMASTER, J. A. *The Book of Concord (1580)*. LQ LVI
(1926), 12-37.
SPITZ, LEWIS W. *The Soteriological Aspect of the Doctrine of
the Holy Trinity According to the Lutheran Confessions.*
CTM XXVI 3 (1955), 161-171.

LUTHERANISM

CAMERON, RICHARD M. *The Charges of Lutheranism Brought
Against Jacques Lefevre D'Etaples (1520-1529)*. HTR LXIII
1 (1970), 119-150.
COLACCI, MARIO ET AL. (TR.) *The Doctrine of Man in Classical
Lutheran Theology*. Minneapolis, 1962. 245 pages.
From Chemnitz and Gerhard.
ECHTERNACH, HELMUT. *The Lutheran Doctrine of the "Auto-
pistia" of Holy Scripture*. CTM XXIII 4 (1952), 241-271.
On "inspiration" in Lutheran Orthodoxy.
ELERT, WERNER. *The Structure of Lutheranism,* tr. Walter A.
Hansen. 2 vols. St. Louis, 1962-
Vol. I: xxviii+547 pages. A sympathetic study of major
Lutheran themes from Luther through Lutheran Orthodoxy.
Vol. II not yet available in English.
HEICK, OTTO W. *Let Man be Man*. LQ VI 2 (1954), 143-153.
A critical evaluation of anthropological statements in Luther,
Melanchthon and the Formula of Concord.
HUBER, CURTIS E. *Meaning and the Word in Lutheran Ortho-
doxy*. CTM XXXVI 8 (1965), 561-566.
KORTE, BERTHOLD F. *Early Lutheran Relations with the
Eastern Orthodox*. LQ IX 1 (1957), 53-59.
Analyzes the efforts of Luther, Melanchthon and others.
MACCORMICK, CHALMERS. *The "Antitrinitarianism" of John
Campanus*. CH XXXII 3 (1963), 278-297.
A Lutheran gone astray.
PELIKAN, JAROSLAV. *The Origins of the Object-Subject An-
tithesis in Lutheran Dogmatics: a Study in Terminology*.
CTM XXI 2 (1950), 94-104.
Critical analysis of Lutheran Orthodoxy.
Tradition in Confessional Lutheranism. LW III 3 (1956),
214-222.

PIEPKORN, ARTHUR C. *Philipp Nicolai (1556-1608): Theologian, Mystic, Hymn Writer, Polemicist, and Missiologist: a Biobibliographical Survey.* CTM XXXIX 7 (1968), 432-461.

PREUS, JACOB, A. O. (TR.) *The Two Natures of Christ.* St. Louis, 1971. 542 pages. A translation of Chemnitz.

PREUS, ROBERT D. *The Word of God in the Theology of Lutheran Orthodoxy.* CTM XXXIII 8 (1962), 469-483.

REIMAN, HENRY W. *Vicarious Satisfaction: a Study in Ecclesiastical Terminology.* CTM XXXII 2 (1961), 69-77.
On Luther and Lutheran Orthodoxy.
Matthias Flacius Illyricus. CTM XXXV 2 (1964), 69-93.
Brief sketch of a controversial "orthodoxiast."

SCHARLEMANN, ROBERT. *Thomas Acquinas and John Gerhard* (Yale Publications in Religion series). New Haven, 1964. xi+271 pages.
Theology in Church and University: the Post-Reformation Development. CH XXXIII 1 (1964), 23-33.
Deals with Melanchthon and John Gerhard.

SHERMAN, FRANKLIN. *Christology, Politics, and the Flacian Heresy.* D II 3 (1963), 208-213.

OTHER DIETS AND DOCTRINAL SETTLEMENTS

BAINTON, ROLAND H. *Luther and the Via Media at the Marburg Colloquy.* LQ I 4 (1949), 394-398.

BETO, GEORGE J. *The Marburg Colloquy of 1529: a Textual Study.* CTM XVI 2 (1945), 73-94.

EELLS, HASTINGS. *The Origin of the Regensburg Book.* PTR XXVI (1928), 355-372.

FISHER-GALATI, STEPHEN. *The Turkish Question and the Religious Peace of Augsburg. Südostforschung* XV (1956), 290-311.

HARBOUGH, HENRY. *Reformed Synods.* MR X (1858), 485-520. Begins with Bern 1528.

HOYER, THEO. *The Rise and Fall of the Schmalkaldic League: the Treaty of Passau, 1552.* CTM XXIII 6 (1952), 401-417.
The Religious Peace of Augsburg. CTM XXVI 11 (1955), 820-830.

JACOBS, HENRY EYSTER. *The Strassburg Formula of 1563.*
LCR IV (1885), 49-54.
JEDIN, HUBERT. *The Blind "Doctor Scotus."* JEH I 1 (1950),
76-84.
On the Roman Catholic-Protestant dialogue of 1541 in
Ratisbon and the role of Robert Vauchop.
KRETZMANN, P. E. *Luther, Bucer, and the Wittenberg Con-
cordia.* CTM VII 5 (1936), 340-347.
On the 400th anniversary of the Concordia (1536).
MUELLER, JOHN T. *Notes on the Consensus Tigurinus of 1549.*
CTM XX 12 (1949), 894-909.
NEVE, J. L. *Some New Light Concerning the Schwabach Articles.*
LQ XXXIX (1909), 258-264.
SASSE, HERMANN. *A Lutheran Contribution to the Present
Discussions on the Lord's Supper.* CTM XXX 1 (1959), 18-
40.
VAN HALSEMA, THEA. *Glorious Heretic, the Story of Guido
de Brès, Author of the Belgic Confession.* Grand Rapids,
1961. 38 pages.

THE REFORMATION IN GERMAN SWITZERLAND

OECHSLI, WILHELM. *History of Switzerland 1499-1914,* tr.
Eden & Cedar Paul (Cambridge Historical Series). Cambridge,
Eng., 1922. xiii+480 pages.
RUCHAT, ABRAHAM. *History of the Reformation in Switzer-
land,* abridged from the French by J. Collinson, Ld., 1845.
lxiv+328 pages.

ZWINGLI

BIBLIOGRAPHY

LOCHER, GOTTFRIED. *The Change in the Understanding of
Zwingli in Recent Research.* CH XXXIV 1 (1965), 3-24.

THOMPSON, BARD. *Zwingli Study Since 1918.* CH XIX (1950),
116-128.

WORKS

MEYER, CARL S. (TR.) *Luther and Zwingli's Propositions for
Debate: the Ninety-Five Theses of October 1517 and the
Sixty-Seven Articles of 23 January 1523. Latin and German
texts with a New Translation.* Leiden, 1963. 59 pages.
Selected works of Huldreich Zwingli 1484-1531, translations
edited by Samuel Macauley Jackson. Philadelphia, 1901.
258 pages. Includes: *Visit of the Episcopal Delegation to
Zurich, April, 1522; the Petition of Eleven Priests to be
allowed to marry, July, 1522; The Acts of the First Zurich
Disputation, Jan., 1523; Zurich Marriage Ordinance, 1525;
Refutation of the Tricks of the Catabaptists, 1527.*
*The Latin Works and Correspondence of Huldreich Zwingli to-
gether with Selections from His German works,* ed. Samuel
Macauley Jackson, tr. Henry Preble, Walter Lichtenstein and
Lawrence A. McLouth.
Vol. 1: 1510-1522. N.Y., 1912. xv+292 pages. Includes:
Fable of the Ox (2 versions); *Account by H. Z. of the En-
gagements between the French and the Swiss; The Missing
Dialogues; The Labyrinth; Transcript of the Pauline Epistles;
A Christian Song, 1519; Advice of One Who Desires that Due
Consideration Be Paid Both to the Dignity of the Pope, etc.;
What Z. Said and Preached at This Time (1521) against the
Mercenary Service of the Swiss. Concerning Choice and
Liberty Respecting Food; Letter to Erasmus Fabricius, April,
1522; Solemn Warning . . . to Beware of Foreign Lords; Peti-
tion . . . to the Bishop of Constance . . . to Allow Priests to
Marry; a Friendly Request . . . that no Offense Be Taken if
. . . Preachers were Given Permission to Marry; Defense
Called Archeteles.*
Vol. II: Philadelphia, 1922. xii+295 pages, ed. William John
Hinke, preface by William Walker Rockwell. Includes: *Declara-
tion of H. Z. Regarding Original Sin, Aug. 15, 1526; An Ac-
count of the Faith of H. Z., July 3, 1530; Refutation of the
Articles of Z . . . Made by John Eck, July 17, 1530; Letter of*

H. Z. . . . regarding the Insults of Eck. Aug. 27, 1530. Repro-
duction . . . of a Sermon on the Providence of God, Aug. 20,
1530; A short and clear exposition of the Christian faith,
July 1531.
Vol. III: Philadelphia, 1929. viii+397 pages, ed. Clarence
Nevin Heller, introductions by George Warren Richards,
preface by William Walker Rockwell. Includes: *Commentary*
on true and false Religion; Reply to Emser.

BIOGRAPHY

CLAY, H. ALEXANDER. *Huldreich Zwingli a Man 1484-1531.*
CR CXL (1931), 629-636.
COURVOISIER, JACQUES. *Zwingli, a Reformed Theologian*
(The Annie Kinkead Warfield Lectures, 1961). Richmond,
1963. 101 pages.
Brief expositions on Word of God, Christology, church,
sacraments, and state.
FARNER, OSKAR. *Zwingli the Reformer. His Life and Work,*
tr. D. G. Sear. N.Y., 1952. 135 pages.
A popular biography.
JACKSON, SAMUEL MACAULEY. *Huldreich Zwingli the Re-*
former of German Switzerland (Heroes of the Reformation).
N.Y., Ld., 1901. 519 pages.
New edition, with an historical survey of Switzerland before
the Reformation by John M. Vincent, and a chapter on
Zwingli's theology by Frank H. Foster. N.Y., 1969. xxvi+
519 pages.
RILLIET, JEAN H. *Zwingli, Third Man of the Reformation,* tr.
Harold Knight. Philadelphia, 1964. 320 pages.
A good biography, with a brief bibliography. Contains a
summary of Zwingli's writings.
SIMPSON, SAMUEL. *The Life of Ulrich Zwingli* (Dissertation,
Hartford Theological Seminary) N.Y., 1902. 297 pages.

TOPICS

BIRNBAUM, N. *The Zwinglian Reformation in Zürich, Past and*
Present 15 (1959), 27-47.
The Zwinglian Reformation in Zürich. Archives de Sociologie
des Religions VIII (1959), 15-30.

BOMBERGER, J. H. A. *Zwingli as a Commentator* (translations from his commentaries). MR IV (1852), 55-66, 453-474. *Zwingli at Bern.* MR VI (1854), 223-257.

DIERKS, THEO. *Huldreich Zwingli, the Father of Reformed Theology.* CTM XIV (1943), 335-345; 409-435.

GARSIDE, CHARLES JR. *The Literary Evidence for Zwingli's Musicianship.* ARG XLVIII (1951), 56-74.
Shows that Zwingli was an excellent musician who never gave up playing.
Zwingli and the Arts (Yale Historical Publications series). New Haven, 1966. xiv+190 pages.
Thorough, with a bibliography.

HILLERBRAND, HANS J. *Zwingli's Reformation Turning-Point.* BHR XXXI (1969), 39-46.
Argues against a turning-point in 1523.

HOLLENWEGER, WALTER J. *Zwingli Writes the Gospel Into His World's Agenda.* MQR XLIII (1969), 70-94.
On the evolution of Zwinglian reform.

MÜLLER, G. E. *Zwingli as a Religious Philosopher. The Hibbert Journal* LVIII (1956/60), 164-169.

RICHARDSON, CYRIL C. *Zwingli and Cranmer on the Eucharist.* (M. Dwight Johnson Memorial Lectureship in Church History.) 57 pages.
Demonstrates their basic agreement.

SCHAFF, PHILIP. *The Theology of Zwingli.* RQR XXXVI (1889), 423-431.

WALTON, ROBERT C. *Zwingli's Theocracy.* Toronto, 1967. 258 pages.
Clarifies the relationship between clergy and magistracy, especially before 1523. Contains an extensive bibliography.
Was There a Turning Point in the Zwinglian Reformation? MQR XLII (1968), 45-56.
Argues the negative point of view against John Yoder (MQR 1969).

YODER, JOHN H. *The Turning Point in the Zwinglian Reformation.* MQR XXXII (1958), 128-140.
Argues for a major shift in Zwingli's thought in 1523.
The Evolution of the Zwinglian Reformation. MQR XLIII (1969), 95-122.
On the question of Zwingli's turning point.

SUCCESSORS OF ZWINGLI

Bullinger
The Decades of Henry Bullinger, tr. H. J., edited for the Parker
Society by Thomas Harding. 5 vols. Cambridge, Eng., 1849-
1852.
GOOD, JAMES I. *The Antistes of Zurich.* PRR VI (1895), 593-
613.

THE LEFT WING OR RADICAL REFORMATION

BIBLIOGRAPHY

BENDER, HAROLD S. *Recent Progress in Research in Anabaptist
History.* MQR VIII (1934), 3-17.
*Catalogue of the Mennonite Historical Library in Scottdale,
Pennsylvania.* Scottdale, Pa., 1929. 88 pages.
DOSKER, HENRY ELIAS. *Recent Sources of Information on
the Anabaptists in the Netherlands.* ASCH 2S V (1915), 47-
72.
FRIEDMAN, ROBERT. *Recent Interpretations of Anabaptism.*
CH XXIV 2 (1955), 132-151.
HILLERBRAND, HANS J. (ED.) *A Bibliography of Anabaptism
1520-1630.* Elkhart, Ind., 1962. xv+281 pages.
Includes much of the left wing in general.
KLIEWER, VICTOR D. *A Bibliography of Anabaptist-Mennonite
Historical Works; an Inventory of Works Dealing with
Anabaptist-Mennonite History Located in the Mennonite
Historical Library, Canadian Mennonite Bible College.*
Winnipeg, 1970. 44 pages. Typescript.
KRAHN, CORNELIUS. *Widening the Concept of the Reforma-
tion.* ML (1970), 86-88.
A brief survey of literature on Müntzer, Carlstadt, Münster
and Anabaptism in the Netherlands.
KRAHN, CORNELIUS and GINGERICH, MELVIN. *Mennonite
Research in Progress, 1969.* ML (April 1970), 90-92.
Lists dissertations, lectures and projects.
LOSERTH, JOHANN. *Recent Research in the History of the*

Tyrol-Moravian Anabaptists. MQR II (1928), 5-15.

Mennonite Bibliography. Published in every April issue of ML
since 1949 (except July 1961, July 1963, July 1967, and
July 1968). Contains sections on *Radical Reformation*
(left wing) and *Anabaptism.* English materials are listed in
the pertinent sections.

WHITLEY, W. T. *A Baptist Bibliography.* 2 vols. Vol. I, 1526-
1776. Ld., 1916. vii+238 pages.
Lists early English translations of works against the Anabaptists.

WILLIAMS, GEORGE H. *Studies in the Radical Reformation
(1517-1618): a Bibliographical Survey of Research Since
1939 (Parts I through IV, 4).* CH XXVII 1-2 (1958), 46-69;
124-160.

COLLECTIONS OF SOURCES
(See also individual figures and locations)

BENDER, HAROLD S. *The Discipline Adopted by the Strasburg
Conference of 1568.* MQR I, 1 (1927), 57-66.
The First Edition of the Ausbund (hymnology). MQR III
(1929), 147-150.
*A Hutterite School Discipline of 1578 and Peter Scherer's
Address of 1568 to the Schoolmasters.* MQR V (1931), 231-
244.
*Anabaptist Manuscripts in the Archives at Brno, Czecho-
slovakia.* MQR XXIII (1949), 105-107.
Lists 117 items. *New Discoveries of Important Sixteenth
Century Anabaptist Codices.* MQR XXX (1956), 72-77.

BRAGHT, T. J. VAN. *A Martyrology of the Churches of Christ
Commonly Called Baptists during the Era of the Reformation,*
ed. Edward Bean Underhill for the Hanserd Knollys Society.
2 vols. Ld., 1850-53.

BURRAGE, HENRY SWEESTER. *Baptist Hymn Writers and Their
Hymns.* Portland, Me., 1888. xi+682 pages.

*A Conscientious Objector of 1575. A Controversy between S. B.,
"An English Anabaptist," and William White, Puritan, now
First Printed from the Manuscript in "The Seconde Parte of
a Register," in Dr. William's Library, London, Edited with*

an Introduction and Notes by Albert Peel. BHS VII (1920), 71-128.

CORRELL, ERNST. *The Value of Hymns for Mennonite History.* MQR IV (1930), 215-219.

DYCK, CORNELIUS J. *The First Waterlandian Confession of Faith.* MQR XXXVI (1962), 5-13.
Introduction to and translation of the Dutch Anabaptist confession of 1577.
The Middleburg Confession of Hans de Ries, 1578. MQR XXXVI (1962), 147-154; 161.
Introduction and translation of an imprisoned Dutch Anabaptist's confession.

FAST, HEINOLD. *Peutinger's Manuscript Against the Anabaptists.* MQR XXXIX (1965), 307-308.
A report on Conrad Peutinger's manuscript fragment in Munich.

FRIEDMANN, ROBERT. *The Schleitheim Confession (1527) and Other Doctrinal Writings of the Swiss Brethren in a Hitherto Unknown Edition.* MQR XVI (1942), 82-98.
Discusses five anonymous tracts and a biblical concordance edited together with the Confession.
Reason and Obedience: an Old Anabaptist Letter of Peter Walpot (1571) and Its Meaning. MQR XIX (1945), 27-40.
Includes an English translation of the letter written to Cracow, Poland.
An Example of the Spirit of Early Anabaptism. MQR XXX (1956), 289.
A letter written in 1535 by two Anabaptists who escaped from prison.

GEISER, SAMUEL. *An Ancient Anabaptist Witness for Nonresistance.* MQR XXV (1951), 66-69; 72.
English translation of a document dated April 12, 1529, with comments.

GRATZ, DELBERT. *Manuscript Materials in Europe that Concern the Anabaptists.* MQR XLI (1967), 161-165.

HEIN, GERHARD. *Two Letters by Leupold Scharnschlager.* MQR XVII (1943), 165-168.
In German. On sin, baptism and Holy Scripture.

HILLERBRAND, HANS J. *An Early Anabaptist Treatise on the*

Christian and the State. MQR XXXII (1958), 28-47.
Introduction to and photostatic reproduction of an anony-
mous treatise on nonviolent behavior.
A Sixteenth Century Anabaptist Evangelistic Testimony.
MQR XXXV (1961), 314-317.
Introduction to and translation of a letter dated July 3, 1574
by Hanns Schlegel on gospel and baptism.
KNOX, JOHN. *An Answer to a Great Nomber of Blasphemous
Cauillations Written by an Anabaptist . . . and Confuted by
Iohn Knox, 1560. Works of John Knox,* ed. David Laing,
Edinburgh, 1856, vol. V, 18-468.
LITTELL, FRANKLIN H. *What Butzer Debated with the Ana-
baptists at Marburg: a Document of 1538.* MQR XXXVI
(1962), 256-276.
Introduction to and translation of the secretary's report.
MATTHIJSSEN, JAN P. *The Bern Disputation of 1538.* MQR
XXII (1948), 5-33.
With a translation of the theses.
NEUMANN, GERHARD J. *A Newly Discovered Manuscript of
Melchior Rinck.* MQR XXXV (1961), 197-217.
Edited and transcribed in German, with notes by Harold S.
Bender. On infant baptism and government (with two dif-
ferent titles).
PEACHEY, SHEM AND PAUL. *Answer of Some Who Are Called
(Ana) Baptists. Why They Do Not Attend the Churches: a
Swiss Brethren Tract.* MQR XLV (1971), 5-32.
A translation of an insertion from Heinrich Bullinger's
work *On the Origins of the Anabaptists (1560).*
RAMAKER, A. J. *Hymns and Hymn Writers among the Anabaptists
of the Sixteenth Century.* MQR III (1929), 93-131.
RAUSCHENBUSCH, WALTER. *The Zurich Anabaptists and
Thomas Münzer,* AJT IX (1905), 91-106.
SIPPELL, THEODORE. *The Confession of the Swiss Brethren in
Hesse, 1578.* MQR XXIII (1949), 22-34.
English introduction, German text.
WENGER, JOHN C. *The Schleitheim Confession of Faith,
Translated into English and Edited with an Introduction.*
MQR XIX (1945), 243-253.
Concerning the Satisfaction of Christ. An Anabaptist Tract

on True Christianity. MQR XX (1946), 243-254.
Probably from the works of Michael Sattler.
Two Kinds of Obedience. An Anabaptist Tract on Christian Freedom. MQR XXI (1947), 18-22.
An anonymous tract.
Concerning Divorce. A Swiss Brethren Tract on the Primacy of Loyalty to Christ and the Right to Divorce and Remarriage. MQR XXI (1947), 114-119.
An anonymous tract.
Three Swiss Brethren Tracts. MQR XXI (1947), 275-284.
Two anonymous tracts on church and state, and one written by Melchior Rinck on baptism.

WENGER, JOHN C. *Two Early Anabaptist Tracts.* MQR XXII (1948), 34-42.
An anonymous sermon from 1527 and Eitelhans Langenmantel's exposition of the Lord's Prayer (1527).
Martin Weninger's Vindication of Anabaptism, 1535. MQR XXII (1948), 180-187.
A tract by a leader of the Swiss Brethren.
A Letter from Wilhelm Reublin to Pilgram Marpeck, 1531. MQR XXIII (1949), 67-75.

GENERAL TREATMENT

ARMITAGE, THOMAS. *A History of the Baptists.* N.Y., 1887. xviii+978 pages.
Brief treatment of the continental Anabaptists.

BAINTON, ROLAND H. *The Left Wing of the Reformation.* JR XXI 2 (1941), 124-134.
Reprinted in revised form in the author's *Studies on the Reformation.*

BROWN, DALE. *The Radical Reformation: Then and Now.* MQR XLV (1971), 250-263.

DURNBAUGH, DONALD F. *Theories of Free Church Origins.* MQR XLII (1968), 83-95.
Surveys the literature and suggests an interpretation of the left wing.
The Believers' Church. The History and Character of Radical Protestantism. London, N.Y., 1968. xi+315 pages.
Defines and traces the concept of believers' church through

the left wing. Chapts. 3-4 deal with Anabaptists and English Separatists.

GARRETT, JAMES L. *The Nature of the Church According to the Radical Continental Reformation.* MQR XXXII (1958), 111-127.

JANSSEN, JOHANNES. *History of the German People.* Vol. V. St. Louis, Mo., 1903. Chap. VII, 449-485.
Reign of the Anabaptists at Münster.

KAUTSKY, KARL. *Communism in Central Europe in the Time of the Reformation,* tr. J. L. and E. G. Mulliken. Ld. 1897. 293 pages.
Includes Thomas Münzer and the Anabaptists. The interest is in economic interpretation.
Reissued in N.Y., 1959.

KLAASSEN, WALTER. *Spiritualization in the Reformation.* MQR XXXVII (1963), 67-77.
Emphasizes left wing concepts.

VERDUIN, LEONARD. *The Reformers and Their Stepchildren.* Grand Rapids, 1966. 292 pages.
A survey of left wing groups and their possible relation to the free church tradition in America.

WILLIAMS, GEORGE H. *The Radical Reformation.* Philadelphia, 1962. xxxi+924 pages.
An elaborate attempt to write a typological history of the entire left wing or radical reformation. Indispensable.

ANABAPTISTS

HISTORIOGRAPHY

ARNOLD, EBERHARD. *On the History of the Baptizer Movement in Reformation Times.* MQR XLIII (1969), 213-233. Reprinted Rifton, N.Y., 1970. 24 pages.
Translation of a 1935 German address. Dated.

BAX, E. BELFORT. *The Rise and Fall of the Anabaptists.* Ld. and N.Y., 1903. vi+407 pages.
Socialist, devoted chiefly to the Münster episode.
New edition (Reprints of Economic Classics series) 1970.

BENDER, HAROLD S. *Recent Anabaptist Bibliographies.* MQR
XXIV (1950), 88-91.
*The Zwickau Prophets, Thomas Müntzer, and the Ana-
baptists.* MQR XXVII (1953), 3-16.
Argues for Swiss origins of Anabaptism.
The Historiography of the Anabaptists. MQR XXXI (1957),
88-104.
Covers publications from the 16th century to the 1950s.
BENDER HORSCH, ELIZABETH. *The Portrayal of the Swiss
Anabaptists in Gottfried Keller's Ursula.* MQR XVII (1943),
136-150.
An analysis of a famous German writer's agnostic views.
*The Anabaptist Novelettes of Adolf Stern and Wilhelm
Heinrich Riehl.* MQR XVIII (1944), 174-185.
On two stories of the 19th century.
BURRAGE, HENRY SWEESTER. *The Anabaptists of the Six-
teenth Century.* ASCH III (1890), 145-164.
ESTEP, WILLIAM R. *The Anabaptist Story.* Nashville, 1963.
238 pages.
Well told by a Mennonite historian. Contains bibliography.
FRIEDMANN, ROBERT. *Conception of the Anabaptists.* CH
IX 4 (1940), 341-365.
*The Nicolsburg Articles, a Problem of Early Anabaptist
History.* CH XXXVI 4 (1967), 391-409.
HEATH, RICHARD. *Anabaptism from Its Rise at Zwickau to Its
Fall at Münster 1521-1536.* Ld., 1895. x+194 pages.
Based on the best materials available at the time and not
badly done, except that Anabaptism did not begin at
Zwickau and did not end at Münster.
Early Anabaptism: What It Meant and What We Owe to It.
CR LXVII (1895), 578-591.
HILLERBRAND, HANS J. *Anabaptism and the Reformation:
Another Look.* CH XXIX 4 (1960), 404-423.
*The Origin of Sixteenth Century Anabaptism: Another
Look.* ARG LIII (1962), 152-180.
Argues that Anabaptism is a movement *sui generis.*
Anabaptism and History. MQR XLV (1971), 107-122.
See also Franklin H. Littell's critical "Response to Hans
Hillerbrand," *ibid.,* 377-380.

HORST, IRVIN B. *The Anabaptists in English Literature.* MQR
XXIX (1955), 232-239.
JONES, RUFUS M. *The Anabaptists and Minor Sects in the*
Reformation. HTR XI (1918), 223-246.
The best brief classification and description of the left wing
of the Reformation in English.
LITTELL, FRANKLIN H. *The Importance of Anabaptist Studies.*
ARG LVIII (1967), 15-28.
Surveys issues and reports on the founding of new research
societies.
Anabaptist and Free Church Studies. ML (April 1970), 83-
84.
NEWMAN, ALBERT HENRY. *A History of Anti-Pedobaptism from*
the Rise of Pedobaptism to A.D. 1609. Philadelphia, Pa., 1897.
414 pages.
Covers the whole field of Anabaptist history in the sixteenth
century, abreast of the research of the period.
PIKE, EDWARD CAREY. *The Story of the Anabaptists* (Eras of
Non-conformity, II). Ld., 1904. xi+128 pages.
Popular, depends on Heath.
SMUCKER, DONOVAN E. *Anabaptist Historiography in the*
Scholarship of Today. MQR XXII (1948), 116-127.
WENGER, JOHN C. *Even Unto Death. The Heroic Witness of the*
Sixteenth-Century Anabaptists. Richmond, 1961. 127 pages.
ZUCK, LOWELL H. *Anabaptism: Abortive Counter-Revolt With-*
in the Reformation. CH XXVI 3 (1957), 211-226.

ANABAPTISTS BY GROUPS AND LOCALITIES

Austria

CORRELL, ERNST. *Anabaptism in the Tyrol.* MQR I, 4 (1927),
49-60.
DEDIC, PAUL. *The Social Background of the Austrian Anabap-*
tists. MQR XIII (1939), 5-20.
FOSTER, CLAUDE R. and JEROSCH, WILHELM. *The Reason*
Why God Descended and Became Man in Christ, Through
Whom, and How, He Atoned for and Restored Man's Fall
and Man Himself Through the Messiah Whom He Sent. By

Johannes Bünderlin of Linz. MQR XLII (1968), 260-284.
A translation of the German tract.

FRIEDMANN, ROBERT. *The Oldest Church Discipline of the Anabaptists.* MQR XXIX (1955), 162-166.
A Tyrolian document drafted in 1527.
Leonhard Schiemer and Hans Schlaffer: Two Tyrolean Anabaptist Martyr-Apostles of 1528. MQR XXXIII (1959), 31-41.

LOSERTH, JOHANN. *Anabaptism in Styria in 1528.* MQR VII (1933), 133-141.
The Anabaptists in Carinthia in the Sixteenth Century. MQR XXI (1947), 234-247.
Analyzes Austrian sources.

PEACHEY, PAUL. *Recent Tirolese Anabaptist Research.* MQR XXVII (1953), 76-77.

RISCHAR, KLAUS. *The Martyrdom of the Salzburg Anabaptists in 1527.* MQR XLIII (1969), 322-327.

STEINMETZ, MAX and BRENDLER, GERHARD. *Weltwirkung der Reformation.* 2 vols. East Berlin, 1969.
FOSTER, CLAUDE JR. *Johannes Buenderlein: Radical Reformer of the Reformation.* pp.?
The story of an Austrian Anabaptist leader.

England: Relation of English Baptists to the Continent

FARRER, A. J. D. *The Relation between English Baptists and the Anabaptists of the Continent.* BQ (Ld.) ns II (1924-25), 30-36.

HEATH, RICHARD. *The Anabaptists and Their English Descendents.* CR LIX (1891), 389-406.
The Archetype of the Pilgrim's Progress. CR LXX (1896), 541-558.
The Archetype of the Holy War. CR LXXII (1897), 105-118.

HORST, IRVIN B. *The Radical Brethren: Anabaptism and the English Reformation to 1558.* Nieuwkoop, 1972. pp.?

KLIEVER, LONNIE D. *General Baptist Origins: the Question of Anabaptist Influence.* MQR XXXVI (1962), 291-321.

KRAUS, NORMAN C. *Anabaptist Influence on English Separatism as seen in Robert Browne.* MQR XXXIV (1960), 5-19.
Covers the period 1535-1565.

WHITLEY, W. T. *Continental Anabaptists and the Early English Baptists.* BQ (Ld) ns II (1924-25), 24-30.

Familists

THOMAS, ALLEN C. *The Family of Love, or the Familists.* HCS XI, 4th month (1892), 1-46.

Germany

CLASEN, CLAUS-PETER. *The Sociology of Swabian Anabaptism.* CH XXXII 2 (1963), 150-180.
Nuernberg in the History of Anabaptism. MQR XXXIX (1965), 25-39.
The Anabaptists in Bavaria. MQR XXXIX (1965), 243-261.
The Anabaptists at Lauingen: a Forgotten Congregation. MQR XLII (1968), 144-148.
On Bavarian Anabaptism.
COOKE, PARSONS. *A History of German Anabaptists.* Boston, 1846. xviii+412 pages.
CROUS, ERNST. *Anabaptism in Schleiden-in-the Eifel.* MQR XXXIV (1960), 188-191.
DIRRIM, ALLEN W. *The Hessian Anabaptists: Background and Development to 1540.* MQR XXXVIII (1964), 61-62.
Abstract of a 1962 Indiana University dissertation.
FRIEDMANN, ROBERT. *Anabaptism and Pietism I, II.* MQR XIV (1940), 90-128; 149-169.
Traces contrasts in and beyond the sixteenth century.
HEGE, CHRISTIAN. *The Early Anabaptists in Hesse.* MQR V (1931), 157-78.
HEIN, GERHARD. *Anabaptists in Frankfort on the Main.* MQR XXXIII (1959), 68-72.
Anabaptism in Württemberg. MQR XXXIV (1960), 128-136.
KRAHN, CORNELIUS. *The Emden Disputation of 1578.* MQR XXX (1956), 256-258.
Anabaptism in Westphalia. MQR XXXV (1961), 282-285.
MEIHUIZEN, H. W. *Who Were the "False Brethren" Mentioned in the Schleitheim Confession?* MQR XLI (1967), 200-222.
OYER, JOHN S. *Anabaptism in Central Germany. I. The Rise and Spread of the Movement.* MQR XXXIV (1960), 219-248.

Anabaptism in Central Germany: II Faith and Life. MQR
XXXV (1961), 5-37.

PHILOON, THURMAN E. *Hans Greiffenberger and the Reformation in Nürnberg.* MQR XXXVI (1962), 61-75.

WIEDEMANN, HANS. *The Story of the Anabaptists at Passau,
1527-1535.* MQR XXXIX (1965), 91-103.

YODER, JESSE. *The Frankenthal Debate With the Anabaptists
in 1571: Part I: Purpose, Procedure, Participants. Part II:
Outcome, Issues, Debating Methods.* MQR XXXVI (1962),
14-35; 116-146.

Between the Reformed and the Anabaptists in the Palatinate, under Frederick III.

Hungary

KRISZTINKOVICH, BELA. *Glimpses Into the Early History of
Anabaptism in Hungary.* MQR XLIII (1969), 127-141.

See also the additional comments by Robert Friedmann,
ibid. 327-330.

Hutterian Brethren: Bibliography

FRIEDMANN, ROBERT. *A Comprehensive Review of Research
on the Hutterites, 1880-1950.* MQR XXIV (1950), 353-363.

*Bibliography of Works in the English Language Dealing
With the Hutterite Communities.* MQR XXXII (1958), 237-
238.

Recent Hutterite Studies (1965-1967). MQR XLII (1968),
318-322.

HOSTETLER, JOHN A. *A Bibliography of English Language
Materials on the Hutterian Brethren.* MQR XLIV (1970),
106-113.

Hutterian Brethren: Works

FRIEDMANN, ROBERT. *The Epistle of the Hutterian Brethren
1530-1650. A Study in Anabaptist Literature.* MQR XX
(1946), 147-177.

*Peter Riedemann on Original Sin and the Way of Redemp-
tion.* MQR XXVI (1952), 210-215.

Quotes extensively from the text in English translation.

Claus Felbinger's Confession of 1560. MQR XXIX (1955),
141-161.

A Hutterite document, analyzed and translated.
A Hutterite Book of Medieval Origin. MQR XXX (1956), 65-71.
Shows relation to medieval Franciscans.
Jakob Hutter's Last Epistle to the Church in Moravia, 1535. MQR XXXIV (1960), 37-47.
Introduction to, and translation of the text.
The Oldest Known Hutterite Codex of 1566: a Chapter in Anabaptist Intellectual History. MQR XXXIII (1959), 96-107.
Commentary and German text.
Jakob Hutter's Epistle Concerning the Schism in Moravia in 1533. MQR XXXVIII (1964), 329-343.
Introduction to a translation by the Society of Brothers.
Newly Discovered Hutterite Manuscripts. MQR XLII (1968), 73-74.
Reports on a find of 10 Codices in Czechoslovakia and Hungary.

GROSS, LEONARD. *Newly Discovered Codices of the Hutterites.* MQR XLII (1968), 149-155.
1). A concordance of the New Testament, 1578., and 2) Articles of faith, 1662. With excerpts.
Dialogue Between a Hutterite and a Swiss Brother, 1573. MQR XLIV (1970), 45-58.
Based on correspondence between Paul Glock and Peter Walpot.

HASENBURG, KATHLEEN E. and FRIEDMANN, ROBERT. *A Notable Hutterite Document Concerning True Surrender and Christian Community of Goods.* MQR XXXI (1957), 22-62.
An Introduction to and translation of article III of the *Great Article Book* of Peter Walpot, 1577.

KOOLMAN, DOORNKAAT, J. *The First Edition of Peter Riedemann's "Rechenschaft."* MQR XXXVI (1962), 169-170.
Argues for a Zurich origin.

KRISZTINKOVICH, MARIA H. *Hutterite Codices Rediscovered in Hungary.* MQR XLIV (1970), 114-122.

OYER, JOHN S. *A Newly Discovered Hutterite Codex at Copenhagen.* MQR XLIV (1970), 122-125.
Dates from 1568. Contains 2 confessions, 13 epistles and 11 hymns, most of them published elsewhere.

RIEDEMAN, PETER. *Confession of Faith, Account of Our Religion, Doctrine and Faith . . . Includes: Eberhard Arnold. The Hutterian Brothers; Four Centuries of Common Life and Work.* Rifton, N.Y., 1970. 298 pages.

ZIEGLSCHMID, A. J. F. *Unpublished Sixteenth Century Letters of the Hutterian Brethren, I-II.* MQR XV (1941), 5-25; 118-140.

Edited in German, with an English introduction.

Hutterian Brethren: General Treatments

FRIEDMANN, ROBERT. *Hutterite Studies. Essays,* ed. Harold S. Bender. Goshen, Ind., 1961. 338 pages.

Many of these essays appeared in MQR.

HORSCH, JOHN. *The Hutterian Brethren 1528-1928.* MQR II (1928), 85-110, 176-191; III (1929), 54-89, 254-273.

The Hutterian Brethren 1528-1931 (Studies in Anabaptist and Mennonite History, Mennonite Historical Society), Goshen, Ind., 1931. xxi+168 pages.

LOSERTH, JOHANN. *The Decline and Revival of the Hutterites.* MQR IV (1930), 93-112.

PETERS, VICTOR. *All Things in Common. The Hutterian Way of Life.* Minneapolis, 1965. xiii+233 pages.

Traces the Hutterian Brethren from the 16th century to the present.

Hutterian Brethren: Biography

FRIEDMANN, ROBERT. *Peter Riedemann: Early Anabaptist Leader.* MQR XLIV (1970), 5-44.

GROSS, LEONARD. *Nikolaus Geyersbühler, Hutterite Missionary to Tyrol.* MQR XLIII (1969), 283-292.

Hutterian Brethern: Topics

DEWIND, HENRY A. *Italian Hutterite Martyrs.* MQR XXVIII (1954), 163-185.

FRIEDMANN, ROBERT. *The Christian Communism of the Hutterite Brethren.* ARG XLVI (1955), 196-208.

Economic Aspects of Early Hutterite Life. MQR XXX (1956), 259-266.

Hutterite Worship and Preaching. MQR XL (1966), 5-26.
*Second Generation Anabaptism as Illustrated by the Wal-
pot Era of the Hutterites.* MQR XLIV (1970), 390-393.
HEIMANN, FRANZ. *The Hutterite Doctrines of Church and
Common Life. A Study of Peter Riedemann's Confession
of Faith of 1540, I-II.* MQR XXVI (1952), 22-47; 142-160.
HOLLAND, ROBERT C. *The Hermeneutics of Peter Riedemann
(1506-1556); With Reference to I Cor. 5:9-13 and II Cor.
6:14-7:1.* Basel, 1970. 185 pages.
SOMMER, DONALD. *Peter Ridemann and Menno Simons on
Economics.* MQR XXVIII (1954), 205-223.
SOMMER, JOHN L. *Hutterite Medicine and Physicians in Moravia
in the Sixteenth Century and After.* MQR XXVII (1953),
111-127.
With additional notes by Robert Friedmann, and an appendix
on Paracelsus and the Anabaptists, *ibid.,* 128-136.

Mennonites
(See also the *Mennonite Encyclopedia*)
BAINTON, ROLAND H. *The Church of the Restoration.* ML VIII
(1953), 136-143.
The Menno Simons Lecture of 1952.
DYCK, CORNELIUS J. (ED.) *An Introduction to Mennonite
History. A Popular History of the Anabaptists and the
Mennonites.* Scottdale, Pa., 1967. 324 pages.
A textbook prepared by various Mennonite scholars for young
adults. Chapters 1-8 cover the sixteenth century.
FRIEDMANN, ROBERT. *The Encounter of Anabaptists and Men-
nonites With Anti-Trinitarianism.* MQR XXII (1948), 139-
162.
HORSCH, JOHN. *An Historical Survey of the Position of the Men-
nonite Church on Non-Resistance.* MQR I, 3 (1927), 5-22; I,
4 (1927), 3-20.
*The Principle of Non-Resistance as Held by the Mennonite
Church.* Scottdale, Pa., 1927. 60 pages.
MEIHUIZEN, H. K. *Spiritualistic Tendencies and Movements
Among the Dutch Mennonites of the 16th and 17th Centuries.*
MQR XXVII (1953), 259-304.
SMITH, CHARLES HENRY. *The Mennonites: a Brief History of*

Their Origin and Later Development both in Europe and America. Berne, Ind., 1920. 340 pages.
3d ed. rev. by Cornelius Krahn. Newton, Kan., 1950. x+856 pages.

SMUCKER, DONOVAN E. *The Theological Triumph of the Early Anabaptist Mennonites: the Rediscovery of Biblical Theology in Paradox.* MQR XIX (1945), 5-26.

UNRUH, BENJAMIN H. *Dutch Backgrounds of Mennonite Migration of the 16th Century to Prussia.* MQR X (1936), 173-181.

ZIJPP, N. VAN DER *The Conception of Our Fathers Regarding the Church.* MQR XXVII (1953), 91-99.
On Mennonite origins.

Moravia

FRIEDMANN, ROBERT. *Concerning the True Soldiers of Christ, a Hitherto Unknown Tract of the Philippite Brethren in Moravia.* MQR V (1931), 87-99.
The Philippite Brethren. A Chapter in Anabaptist History. MQR XXXII (1958), 272-297.
The story of a Moravian group led by Philip Plener, known for their hymnody.

NEWMAN, ALBERT H. *The Moravian Baptists.* BQR IX (1887), 41-62. Based on Josef Beck, *Die Geschichtsbücher der Wiedertäufer in Oesterreich-Ungarn.* Wien 1883.

ZEMAN, J. K. *Historical Topography of Moravian Anabaptism.* MQR XL (1966), 266-278; XLI (1967), 40-78; 116-160.
An excellent bibliographical essay.

Muenster

HORSCH, JOHN. *The Rise and Fall of the Anabaptists of Münster.* MQR IX (1935), 92-103; 129-143.

KIRCHHOFF, KARL-HEINZ. *Was There a Peaceful Anabaptist Congregation in Münster in 1534?* MQR XLIV (1970), 357-370.
There was, until the arrival of radicals.

MELLINK, A. F. *The Mutual Relations Between the Münster Anabaptists and the Netherlands.* ARG L (1959), 16-32.

PEARSON, KARL. *The Kingdom of God in Münster.* MdR V (1884), 29-56.

STAYER, JAMES M. *The Münsterite Rationalization of Bernhard Rothmann.* JHI XXVIII 2 (1967), 179-192.
WRAY, FRANK J. *The "Vermahnung" of 1542 and Rothmann's "Bekenntnisse."* ARG XLVII (1956), 243-250.
The relationship between Bernd Rothmann's Muenster Anabaptism and southern German Anabaptism.

Netherlands

DOSKER, HENRY ELIAS. *The Early Dutch Anabaptists.* ASCH 2 S II (1910) 189-200.
The Dutch Anabaptists. Philadelphia, Boston, 1921. 310 pages.
DYCK, CORNELIUS, J. *A Short Confession of Faith by Hans de Ries.* MQR XXXVIII (1964), 5-19.
The Confession is linked with Baptist migration from England to Holland.
HORSCH, JOHN. *Is Dr. Kühler's Conception of Early Dutch Anabaptism Sound?* MQR VII (1936), 48-60, 97-126.
KRAHN, CORNELIUS. *Dutch Anabaptism. Origin, Spread, Life, and Thought (1450-1600).* The Hague, 1968. ix+311 pages.
An authoritative account.
VERDUIN, LEONARD. *The Chambers of Rhetoric and Anabaptist Origins in the Low Countries.* MQR XXXIV (1960), 192-196.
Guido de Bres and the Anabaptists. MQR XXXV (1961), 251-266.
Traces relations between Reformed (the author of the Belgian Confessions of 1561) and Anabaptists.
ZIJPP, N. VAN DER. *The Confessions of Faith of the Dutch Mennonites.* MQR XXIX (1955), 171-187.
Analyzes 9 confessions.

Strassbourg

BAINTON, ROLAND H. *Katherine Zell. Medievalia et Humanistica* I (1970), 3-28.
An account of clerical marriage in Strassbourg.
BENDER, HAROLD S. *An Invitation to an Anabaptist Service in Strasbourg in 1539.* MQR XXXIII (1959), 77.
A translation of a German document.
CHRISMAN, MIRIAM U. *Strasbourg and the Reform: a Study in the Process of Change* (Yale Historical Publications

series). New Haven, 1967. xii+351 pages.
An authoritative study of the period 1480-1568. Contains bibliography.
Women and the Reformation in Strasbourg. ARG LXIII (1972), pp.?
HORSCH, JOHN. *Strasburg. A Swiss Brethren Center.* MQR XIII (1939), 21-27.
KREIDER, ROBERT. *The Anabaptists and the Civil Authorities of Strasbourg, 1525-1555.* CH XXIV 2 (1955), 99-118.

Switzerland

BLANKE, FRITZ. *The First Anabaptist Congregation: Zollikon, 1525.* MQR XXVII (1953), 17-33.
Brothers in Christ. The History of the Oldest Anabaptist Congregation, Zollikon, Near Zurich, Switzerland, tr. Joseph Nordenhaug. Scottdale, Pa., 1961. 78 pages.
A step-by-step account, based on archives.
BURRAGE, HENRY SWEESTER. *A History of the Anabaptists in Switzerland.* Philadelphia, 1882. 231 pages.
FAST, HEINOLD. *The Dependance of the First Anabaptists on Luther, Erasmus, and Zwingli.* MQR XXX (1956), 104-119.
On the Beginnings of Bernese Anabaptism. MQR XXXI (1957), 292-295.
Brief but very helpful research notes.
FRIEDMANN, ROBERT. *The Devotional Literature of the Swiss Brethren.* MQR XVI (1942), 199-220.
Gottesreich Und Menschenreich. Ernst Staebelin zum 80. Geburtstag. 1969.
KLASSEN, PETER J. *Zwingli and the Zurich Anabaptists.* 197-210.
GRATZ, DELBERT. *The Bernese Anabaptists in the Sixteenth Century.* MQR XXV (1951), 147-172.
HORSCH, JOHN. *The Faith of the Swiss Brethren.* MQR IV (1930) 241-266; V (1931), 7-27, 128-147, 245-259.
The Rise and Early History of the Swiss Brethren Church.
I. *The Rise of State Church Protestantism.* MQR VI (1932), 169-191.
II. *The Beginnings in Zürich. Ibid.,* 227-249.
Zwingli and the Swiss Brethren in Zürich. MQR VII (1933), 142-161.

The Swiss Brethren in St. Gall and Appenzell. MQR VII
(1933), 205-226.
*An Inquiry into the Truth of Accusations of Fanaticism and
Crime against the Early Swiss Brethren.* MQR VIII (1934),
18-31.
KAUFMAN, GORDON D. *Some Theological Emphases of the
Early Swiss Anabaptists.* MQR XXV (1951), 75-99.
KLAASSEN, WALTER. *The Bern Debate of 1538: Christ the
Center of Scripture.* MQR XL (1966), 148-156.
The debate between the established church and the Ana-
baptists.
KLÄUI, PAUL. *Hans Landis of Zurich, the Last Swiss Anabap-
tist Martyr.* MQR XXII (1948), 203-211.
MAYOR, LEWIS. *The Anabaptists in Switzerland.* MR II (1850),
213-231.
Seeks to vindicate Zwingli.
PEACHEY, PAUL. *Social Background and Social Philosophy of
the Swiss Anabaptists 1525-1540.* MQR XXVIII (1954),
102-127.
Contains a directory of 150 Anabaptists of the period.
SCHAFF, PHILIP. *The Anabaptists in Switzerland.* BQR XI
(1889), 263-276.
WENGER, JOHN C. *The Doctrinal Position of the Swiss Brethren
in Their Polemical Tracts.* MQR XXIV (1950), 65-72.

ANABAPTIST BIOGRAPHY

Denck

COUTTS, ALFRED. *Hans Denck 1495-1527, Humanist and
Heretic.* Edinburgh, 1927. 262 pages.
EVANS, AUSTIN P. *An Episode in the Struggle for Religious Free-
dom, the Secretaries of Nuremberg 1524-1528.* N.Y., 1924.
xi+235 pages. New edition, 1970.
FARRER, H. J. D. *An Early "Baptist" View of Scripture.* BQ
(Ld) ns I (1922-23), 203-208.
FAST, HEINOLD. *Hans Denck and Thomas Müntzer.* MQR XLV
(1971), 82-83.
An abstract of a Hamburg University dissertation written
by Günther Goldbach in 1969. Argues for the difference be-
tween the two.

FOSTER, CLAUDE R. JR. *Hans Denck and Johannes Buender-lin: a Comparative Study.* MQR XXXIX (1965), 115-124.

HALL, THOR. *Possibilities of Erasmian Influence on Denck and Hubmaier in Their Views on the Freedom of the Will.* MQR XXXV (1961), 149-170.

KELLER, LUDWIG. *An Apostle of the Anabaptists,* tr. Henry S. Burrage (from Preussische Jahrbücher, Sept., 1882). BQR VII (1885), 28-47.

KIWIET, JAN J. *The Life of Hans Denck.* MQR XXXI (1957), 227-259.
The Theology of Hans Denck. MQR XXXII (1958), 3-27.

KLASSEN, WILLIAM. *Was Hans Denck a Universalist?* MQR XXXIX (1965), 152-154.

WEIS, FREDERICK LEWIS. *The Life, Teachings and Works of Johannes Denck 1495-1527.* Strassbourg, 1924. 93 pages.

Grebel

BENDER, HAROLD S. *Conrad Grebel, the First Leader of the Swiss Brethren (Anabaptists). I. Youth and University Years.* MQR X (1936), 5-45.
II. *Grebel's Study in Paris. Ibid.,* 91-137.
III. *The Humanism of Conrad Grebel. Ibid.,* 151-160.
Later published in revised form as a book.
The Theology of Conrad Grebel, I, II. MQR XII (1938), 27-54; 114-134.
Lists and analyzes primary sources.
Conrad Grebel as a Zwinglian 1522-1523. MQR XV (1941), 67-82.
Conrad Grebel, c. 1498-1526. The Founder of the Swiss Brethren Sometimes Called Anabaptists. Goshen, Ind., 1950. xvi+326 pages.
Authoritative biography by the "dean" of Mennonite historical research. Contains a selection of Grebel's writings and a bibliography.

CORRELL, E. H. *Conrad Grebel and the Revival of Geography.* GCI (Review Supplement May-June, 1926), 48-52.

CORRELL, ERNST and BENDER, HAROLD S. *A Letter of Conrad Grebel to Andreas Castelberber, May, 1525.* MQR I, 3 (1927), 41-53.

HORST, IRVIN B. *Conrad Grebel on the Index*. MQR XLIV
(1970), 389-390.
SCHELBERT, LEO. *Jacob Grebel's Trial Revised*. ARG LX
(1969), 32-64.
A reevaluation of Conrad Grebel's father.
WENGER, JOHN C. (ED.) *Conrad Grebel's Programmatic Letters
of 1524, With Facsimilies of the Original German Script of
Grebel's Letters*. Scottdale, Pa., 1970. 71 pages.
Complements works translated by Harold S. Bender.
YODER, EDWARD. *Nine Letters of Conrad Grebel*. MQR II
(1928), 229-259.
Conrad Grebel as a Humanist. MQR III (1929), 132-146.

Haetzer
GARSIDE, CHARLES JR. *Ludwig Haetzer's Pamphlet Against
Images: a Critical Study*. MQR XXXIV (1960), 20-36.
Portions of the text are translated.
GOETERS, GERHARD. *Ludwig Haetzer, a Marginal Anabaptist*.
MQR XXIX (1955), 251-262.
WEIS, FREDERICK LEWIS. *The Life, Teachings and Works of
Ludwig Hetzer 1500-1529* (Dissertation, Strassbourg). Dor-
chester, Mass., 1930. 239 pages.

Hoffmann
STAYER, JAMES M. *Melchior Hoffmann and the Sword*. MQR
XLV (1971), 265-277.
Translates portions of pertinent tracts.

Hubmaier
ESTEP, W. R. JR. *Von Ketzern und Ihren Verbrennern. A Six-
teenth Century Tract on Religious Liberty*. MQR XLIII (1969),
271-282.
A discussion of Hubmaier's 1526 tract.
EVERTS, W. W. JR. *Balthazar Hubmayer*. BR III (1881), 201-222.
Translates part of the dialogue with Zwingli and Oecolampadius.
HOSEK, F. X. *Balthazar Hübmaier*. Brunn, 1867, tr. W. W. Everts,
Jr. from the Bohemian through the German. Texas historical
and biographical magazine, designed to give a complete history
of the Baptists of Texas. 2 vols. 1891-2. (Not seen.)

JOHNSON, JOHN W. *Balthasar Hübmaier and Baptist Historic Commitments.* JR IX (1929), 50-65.

KLAASSEN, WALTER. *Speaking in Simplicity: Balthasar Hubmaier.* MQR XL (1966), 139-147.

STEINMETZ, DAVID C. *Scholasticism and Radical Reform: Nominalist Motifs in the Theology of Balthasar Hubmaier.* MQR XLV (1971), 123-144.

VEDDER, HENRY C. *Balthasar Hübmaier, the Leader of the Anabaptists* (Heroes of the Reformation). N.Y., 1905. 333 pages. New edition, 1971.

YODER, JOHN Y. *Balthasar Hubmaier and the Beginnings of Swiss Anabaptism.* MQR XXXIII (1959), 5-17.

Hut

CLARK, BERTHA W. *An Anabaptist Poet and Dreamer.* CQ IV (1927), 76-83.

KLAASSEN, WALTER. *Hans Hut and Thomas Müntzer.* BQ XIX (1962), 209-227.

KLASSEN, HERBERT. *The Life and Teachings of Hans Hut (Part I and Part II).* MQR XXXIII (1959), 171-205; 267-304.

STAYER, JAMES M. *Hans Hut's Doctrine of the Sword: an Attempted Solution.* MQR XXXIX (1965), 181-191.

John of Leyden

HUNT, ROBERT NIGEL CAREW. *John of Leyden Story of the Rise and Fall of the Anabaptist Kingdom of the New Jerusalem.* ER CCXLIX (1929), 79-92.

Manz

KRAJEWSKY, EKKEHARD. *The Theology of Felix Manz.* MQR XXXVI (1962), 76-87.

Marpeck

BENDER, HAROLD S. *Pilgram Marpeck, Anabaptist Theologian and Civil Engineer.* MQR XXVIII (1964), 231-265.
Contains an extensive bibliography.

BERGSTEN, TORSTEN. *Two Letters By Pilgram Marpeck.* MQR XXXII (1958), 192-210.

English and German texts of a letter dated ca. 1545, and
one dated January 22, 1555, dealing with the "inner church"
and "Christ's humanity."

KLASSEN, WILLIAM. *Pilgram Marpeck in Recent Research.*
MQR XXXII (1958), 211-229.
*Covenant and Community. The Life, Writings and Herme-
neutic of Pilgram Marpeck.* Grand Rapids, 1968. 211 pages.
Very useful; includes bibliography.
Pilgram Marpeck's Two Books of 1531. MQR XXXIII
(1959), 18-30.
Authorship not firmly established.
*The Relation of the Old and New Covenants in Pilgram
Marpeck's Theology.* MQR XL (1966), 97-111.

LITTELL, FRANKLIN H. *Spiritualizers, Anabaptists, and the
Church.* MQR XXIX (1955), 34-43.
Analyzes the literary debate between Schwenckfeld and
Marpeck in the light of contemporary discussion on
"church" and "sect."

QUIRING, HORST. *The Anthropology of Pilgram Marbeck.*
MQR (1935), 154-164.

WENGER, JOHN C. *The Life and Work of Pilgram Marpeck.*
MQR XII (1938), 137-166. With an additional note on a
booklet Marpect wrote in 1531. *Ibid.,* 269-270.
*Pilgram Marpeck's Confession of Faith Composed at
Strassburg, December 1531-January 1532.* MQR XII
(1938), 167-202.
Transcribed and edited in German.
The Theology of Pilgram Marpeck. MQR XII (1938),
205-247.

Menno Simons: Bibliography

HORST, IRVIN B. *A Bibliography of Menno Simons, ca. 1496-
1561. With a Census of Known Copies.* Nieuwkoop, 1962.
157 pages.
Lists all printed works of Menno Simons, with an appendix
listing books and pamphlets about him.

KRAHN, CORNELIUS. *Survey: Menno Simons Research (1910-
1960).* CH XXX (1961), 473-480.

Menno Simons: Works

BENDER, HAROLD S. *Menno Simon's Life and Writings. A Quadr*
  centennial Tribute, 1536-1936. Writings Selected and trans-
  lated by John Horsch. Scottdale, Pa., 1936. viii+110 pages.
KRAHN, CORNELIUS. *Menno Simon's Fundament-Book of*
  1539-1540. MQR XIII (1939), 221-232.
MENNO SIMON. *The Complete Works of.* 2 vols. in one. Elkhart,
  Ind., 1871.
VERDUIN, LEONARD (TR.) *Menno Simons. Complete Writings,*
  ed. John C. Wenger, with a biography by Harold S. Bender.
  Scottdale, Pa., 1956. xi+1092 pages.

Menno Simons: Biography

HILLERBRAND, HANS J. *Menno Simons: Molder of a Tradition.*
  CC LXXVIII 4 (1961), 107-109.
  Menno Simons—Sixteenth Century Reformer. CH XXXI
  (1962), 387-399.
HORSCH, JOHN. *Menno Simons.* Scottdale, Pa., 1916. 324 pages.
KRAHN, CORNELIUS. *The Conversion of Menno Simons: a*
  Quadricentennial Tribute. MQR X (1936), 46-54.

Menno Simons: Topics

BURCKHART, IRVIN E. *Menno Simons on the Incarnation.* MQR
  IV (1930), 113-139, 178-207; VI (1932), 122-123.
DETWEILER, RICHARD C. *The Concept Law & Gospel in the*
  Writings of Menno Simons, Viewed Against the Background
  of Martin Luther's Thought. MQR XLIII (1969), 191-212.
DYCK, CORNELIUS J. (ED.) *A Legacy of Faith. The Heritage*
  of Menno Simons. A Sixtieth Anniversary Tribute to Cornelius
  Krahn. Newton, Kan., 1962. 260 pages.
  Part I deals with 16th century Mennonite history.
  KRAHN, CORNELIUS. *Menno Simon's Concept of the Church*
  17-30.
  POETTCKER, HENRY. *Menno Simons' View of the Bible*
  as Authority. 31-54.
  KEENEY, WILLIAM. *The Incarnation: a Central Theological*
  Concept. 55-68.
  OOSTERBAAN, J. A. *Grace in Dutch Mennonite Theology.*
  69-85.

DYCK, CORNELIUS J. *Sinners and Saints.* 87-102.
DUERKSEN, ROSELLA R. *Dutch Anabaptist Hymnody in the Sixteenth Century.* 103-118.
ZIJPP, N. VAN DER. *The Dutch and the Swiss Mennonites.* 136-158.
GARDNER, RICHARD B. *Menno Simons: a Study in Anabaptist Theological Self-Understanding and Methodology.* MQR XXXIX (1965), 104-114.
HARDING, VINCENT G. *Menno Simons and the Role of Baptism in the Christian Life.* MQR XXXIII (1959), 323-334.
HORSCH, JOHN. *Menno Simon's Attitude Toward the Anabaptists of Muenster.* MQR X (1936), 55-72.
Did Menno Simons Practice Baptism by Immersion? MQR I, 1 (1927), 54-56.
OOSTERBAAN, J. A. *The Theology of Menno Simons.* MQR XXXV (1961), 187-196; 237.
PETERS, FRANK C. *The Ban in the Writings of Menno Simons.* MQR XXIX (1955), 16-33.
POETTCKER, HENRY. *Menno Simons' Encounter With the Bible.* MQR XL (1966), 112-126.
Biblical Controversy on Several Fronts. MQR XL (1966), 127-138.
Describes Menno Simons' controversies with Catholics, Lutherans, Reformed, and radical sects.
STOESZ, WILLIS M. *The New Creature: Menno Simons' Understanding of the Christian Faith.* MQR XXXIX (1965), 5-24.
VERDUIN, LEONARD. *Menno Simons' Theology Reviewed.* MQR XXIV (1950), 53-64.
WEINGART, RICHARD E. *The Meaning of Sin in the Theology of Menno Simons.* MQR XLI (1967), 25-39.

Pastor

NEWMAN, ALBERT HENRY. *Adam Pastor, Antitrinitarian Antipaedobaptist.* ASCH 2S V (1914), 75-99.

Philips, Obbe and Dirck

DYCK, CORNELIUS J. *The Christology of Dirk Philips.* MQR XXXI (1957), 147-155.
KEENEY, WILLIAM. *Dirk Philips' Life.* MQR XXXII (1958), 171-191.

The Writings of Dirk Philips. MQR XXXII (1958), 298-306.
KOOLMAN, DOORNKAAT J. *The First Edition of Dirk Philip's Enchiridion.* MQR XXXVIII (1965), 357-360.
Argues for a date later than 1564.
LIEVESTRO, CHRISTIANO. *Obbe Philips and the Anabaptist Vision.* MQR XLI (1967), 99-115.
PHILIPS, DIRCK, *Enchiridion.* Elkhart, Ind., 1910.
VERDUIN, LEONARD. *An Ancient Version of Obbe Philip's Confession.* MQR XXI (1947), 120-122.

Sattler

BOSSERT, GUSTAV JR. *Michael Sattler's Trial and Martyrdom in 1527.* MQR XXV (1951), 201-218.
WENGER, JOHN C. *Early Anabaptist Tract on Hermeneutics.* MQR XLII (1968), 26-44.
How Scripture Is to Be Discerningly Divided and Explained, attributed to Michael Sattler.

Scharnschlager

HEIN, GERHARD. *Leupold Scharnschlager, +1563, Swiss Mennonite Elder and Hymn Writer.* MQR XVII (1943), 47-52.
KLASSEN, WILLIAM. (TR.) *A Church Order for Members of Christ's Body. Arranged in Seven Articles by Leopold Scharnschlager.* MQR XXXVIII (1964), 354-356; 386.
Tract dating from 1540.
Leupold Scharnschlager's Farewell to the Strassbourg Council. MQR XLII (1968), 211-218.
Address dated 1534.

Spittelmayr

KLASSEN, HERBERT C. *Ambrosius Spittelmayr: His Life and Teachings.* MQR XXXII (1958), 251-271.
A friend of Hut and Denck. Contains a treatise in translation.

ANABAPTIST TEACHINGS
General

BENDER, HAROLD S. *The Anabaptist Vision.* CH XIII 1 (1944), 3-24.
The Anabaptist Theology of Discipleship. MQR XXIV (1950), 25-32.

FRIEDMANN, ROBERT. *The Essence of Anabaptist Faith. An Essay in Interpretation.* MQR XLI (1967), 5-24.
HERSHBERGER, GUY F. (ED.) *The Recovery of the Anabaptist Vision. A Sixtieth Anniversary Tribute to Harold S. Bender.* Scottdale, Pa., 1957. viii+360 pages.
HERSBERGER, GUY F. *Introduction.* 1-10.
CORRELL, ERNEST H. *Harold S. Bender and Anabaptist Research.* 13-28.
BENDER, HAROLD S. *The Anabaptist Vision.* 29-54.
BLANKE, FRITZ. *Anabaptism and the Reformation.* 57-68.
ZIJPP, N. VAN DER. *The Early Dutch Anabaptists.* 69-82.
FRIEDMANN, ROBERT. *The Hutterian Brethren and Community of Goods.* 83-90.
YODER, JOHN H. *The Prophetic Dissent of the Anabaptists.* 93-104.
FRIEDMANN, ROBERT. *The Doctrine of the Two Worlds.* 105-118.
LITTELL, FRANKLIN H. *The Anabaptist Concept of the Church.* 119-134.
BURKHOLDER, J. LAWRENCE. *The Anabaptist Vision of Discipleship.* 135-151.
GRABER, J. D. *Anabaptism Expressed in Missions and Social Service.* 152-166.
WENGER. JOHN C. *The Biblicism of the Anabaptists.* 167-179.
KREIDER, ROBERT. *The Anabaptists and the State.* 180-193.
FRETZ, J. WINFIELD. *Brotherhood and the Economic Ethic of the Anabaptists.* 194-201.
OYER, JOHN S. *The Reformers Oppose the Anabaptist Theology.* 202-218.
KRAHN, CORNELIUS. *Anabaptism and the Culture of the Netherlands.* 219-236.
CROUS, ERNST. *Anabaptism, Pietism, Rationalism, and German Mennonites.* 237-248.
FRANCIS, E. K. *Anabaptism and Colonization.* 248-261.
GINGERICH, MELVIN. *Discipleship Expressed in Alternative Service.* 262-274.

BENDER, MARY ELEANOR. *The Sixteenth Century Anabaptists in Literature.* 275-290.

SMUCKER, DONALD E. *Walter Rauschenbusch and Anabaptist Historiography.* 291-304.

PAYNE, ERNEST A. *The Anabaptist Impact on Western Christendom.* 305-316.

BAINTON, ROLAND H. *The Anabaptist Contribution to History.* 317-326.

PEACHEY, PAUL. *The Modern Recovery of the Anabaptist Vision.* 327-340.

HILLERBRAND, HANS J. *Remarkable Interdependancies Between Certain Anabaptist Doctrinal Writings.* MQR XXXIII (1959), 72-76.

JONES, RUFUS M. *Studies in Mystical Religion.* Ld., 1909. xxxviii+ 518 pages.
Covers the Anabaptists on the continent and in England and the Family of Love.

KRAHN, CORNELIUS. *Prolegomena to an Anabaptist Theology.* MQR XXIV (1950), 5-11.

KREIDER, ROBERT. *Anabaptism and Humanism: an Inquiry into the Relationship of Humanism to the Evangelical Anabaptists.* MQR XXVI (1952), 123-141.

LAWRENSE, LEO. *The Catholicity of the Anabaptists.* MQR XXVIII (1964), 266-279.

SMUCKER, DONOVAN. *Anabaptist Theology in the Light of Modern Theological Trends.* MQR XXIV (1950), 73-87.

STAUFFER, ETHELBERT. *The Anabaptist Theology of Martyrdom.* MQR XIX (1945), 179-214.

Baptism and the Lord's Supper

ARMOUR, ROLLIN S. *Anabaptist Baptism. A Representative Study.* Scottdale, Pa., 1966. 214 pages.
Analyzes the doctrine of Hubmaier, Hut, Hoffmann and Marpeck. Contains bibliography.

NEUMANN, GERHARD J. *The Anabaptist Position on Baptism and the Lord's Supper.* MQR XXXV (1961), 140-148.

Biblical Authority

KLASSEN, WILLIAM. *Anabaptist Hermeneutics: the Letter and the Spirit.* MQR XL (1966), 83-96.

WISWEDEL, WALTER. *The Inner and the Outer Word: a Study in the Anabaptist Doctrine of Scripture.* MQR XXVI (1952), 171-191.

YODER, JOHN H. *The Hermeneutics of the Anabaptists.* MQR XLI (1967), 291-308.

Church and Ministry

HEATH, RICHARD. *Living in Community. A Sketch of Moravian Anabaptism* (Hutterite). CR LXX (1896), 247-261.

HUGHES, RICHARD T. *A Comparison of the Restitution Motifs of the Campbells (1809-1830) and the Anabaptists (1524-1560).* MQR XLV (1971), 312-330.

KIWIET, JOHN J. *The Call to the Ministry Among the Anabaptists.* SWJT XI (1969), 29-42.

KRAHN, CORNELIUS. *The Office of Elder in Anabaptist-Mennonite History.* MQR XXX (1956), 120-127.

LITTELL, FRANKLIN H. *The Anabaptist Theology of Missions.* MQR XXI (1947), 5-17.
The Anabaptist Doctrine of the Restitution of the True Church. MQR XXIV (1950), 33-52.
The Anabaptist View of the Church. 2d ed. rev. Boston, 1958. xviii+229 pages.
Reissued under title *The Origins of Protestant Sectarianism.* N.Y., 1964. Paperback.
An excellent analysis.

MEIHUIZEN, H. W. *The Concept of Restitution in the Anabaptism of Northwestern Europe.* MQR XLIV (1970), 141-158.

PEACHEY, PAUL. *Anabaptism and Church Organization.* MQR XXX (1956), 213-228.

RAMSEYER, ROBERT L. *The Revitalization Theory Applied to Anabaptists.* MQR XLIV (1970), 159-180.

SCHÄUFELE, WOLFGANG. *The Missionary Vision and Activity of the Anabaptist Laity.* MQR XXXVI (1962), 99-115.

WALTNER, ERLAND. *The Anabaptist Conception of the Church.* MQR XXV (1951), 5-16.

WRAY, FRANK J. *The Anabaptist Doctrine of the Restitution of the Church.* MQR XXVIII (1954), 186-196.

Holy Spirit

KLAASSEN, WALTER. *Some Anabaptist Views on the Doctrine of the Holy Spirit.* MQR XXXV (1961), 130-139.

Ethics

BAUMAN, CLARENCE. *The Theology of the Two Kingdoms. A Comparison of Luther and the Anabaptists.* MQR XXXVIII (1964), 37-49.

BENDER, HAROLD S. *The Anabaptists and Religious Liberty in the 16th Century.* ARG XLIV (1953), 32-50. Reprinted in MQR XXIX (1955), 83-100. Published as Facet Book, History series. Philadelphia, 1970. viii+27 pages.
The Pacifism of the Sixteenth Century Anabaptists. CH XXIV (1955), 119-131. Reprinted MQR XXX (1956), 5-18.

DAVIS, KENNETH R. *Evangelical Anabaptism and the Medieval Ascetic Tradition: a Study in Intellectual Origins.* MQR XLV (1971), 380-381.
Abstract of a 1971 Michigan University dissertation.

HILLERBRAND, HANS J. *The Anabaptist View of the State.* MQR XXXII (1958), 83-110.
A summary of the author's German doctoral dissertation on the political ethic of upper-German Anabaptism.

KLASSEN, PETER J. *Mutual Aid Among the Anabaptists: Doctrine and Practice.* MQR XXXVII (1963), 78-95.
Argues the restitution of New Testament Ethics. Based on a 1962 Harvard dissertation entitled *The Economics of Anabaptism, 1525-1560,* abstracted *ibid.,* 131-132.
The Economics of Anabaptism, 1525-1560 (Studies in European History series). London, 1964. 149 pages.
Stresses the separation from the state. Contains appendices of translated sources and a bibliography.

SCHAFF, HAROLD H. *The Anabaptists, the Reformers and Civil Government.* CH I, 1 (1932), 27-46.

STAYER, JAMES M. *The Doctrine of the Sword in the First Decade of Anabaptism.* MQR XLI (1967), 165-166.
Abstract of a 1964 Cornell University dissertation.

Anabaptists and the Sword. MQR XLIV (1970), 371-375.
Anabaptists and the Sword. Lawrence, Kan., 1972. pp.?

Hymnody and Worship

BEACHY, ALVIN J. *The Theology and Practice of Anabaptist Worship.* MQR XL (1966), 163-178.

BENDER, HAROLD S. *The Hymnology of the Anabaptists.* MQR XXXI (1957), 5-10.

DUERKSEN, ROSELLA. *Early German Anabaptist Hymn Books.* ML XII (1957), 61-63; 96.
Doctrinal Implications in Sixteenth Century Anabaptist Hymnody. MQR XXXV (1961), 38-49.

MILLER, PAUL H. *Worship Among the Early Anabaptists.* MQR XXX (1956), 235-246.

Sin and Salvation

AUGSBURGER, MYRON S. *Conversion in Anabaptist Thought.* MQR XXXVI (1962), 243-255.

BEACHY, ALVIN J. *The Concept of Grace in the Radical Reformation.* MQR XXXVI (1962), 91-93.
Abstract of a 1962 Harvard University Ph.D. dissertation.
The Grace of God as Understood by Five Major Anabaptist Writers. MQR XXXVII (1963), 5-33; 52.
On Menno Simons, Dirk Philips, Hoffmann, Denck, Marpeck and Hubmaier.

BENDER, HAROLD S. *Walking in the Resurrection: the Anabaptist Doctrine of Regeneration and Discipleship.* MQR XXXV (1961), 96-119.

FRIEDMANN, ROBERT. *The Doctrine of Original Sin as Held by the Anabaptists.* MQR XXXIII (1959), 206-214.

WENGER, JOHN C. *Grace and Discipleship in Anabaptism.* MQR XXXV (1961), 50-69.

Persecution

BRECHT, MARTIN. *A Statement by Johannes Brenz on the Anabaptists.* MQR XLIV (1970), 192-198.
A hostile statement taken from his sermons on the Gospel of John, dealing with piety.

FISCHER, HANS GEORG. *Lutheranism and the Vindication of*

the Anabaptist Way. MQR XXVIII (1954), 27-38.
A critique of Robert Friedmann's *Anabaptism and Protestantism.*

HORSCH, JOHN. *The Persecution of the Evangelical Anabaptists.*
MQR XII (1938), 2-26.
Based on 16th century evidence.

LINDER, ROBERT D. (ED.) *God and Caesar.* Longview, Tex.,
1970. 140 pages.
ESTEP, WILLIAM R. JR. *Anabaptists Subversives?* pp. 29-43.

WISWEDEL, WILHELM and FRIEDMANN, ROBERT. *The Anabaptists Answer Melanchthon. The Handbuechlein of 1558.*
MQR XXIX (1955), 212-231.

YODER, JOHN H. and FAST, HEINOLD. *How to Deal With
Anabaptists: an Unpublished Letter of Heinrich Bullinger.*
MQR XXXIII (1959), 83-95.
German-English edition, with commentary.

Evaluations

BAGGER, HENRY HORNEMAN. *The Anabaptists—Extinction
or Extension of the Reformation?* LQ IV 3 (1952), 243-260.

BENDER, MARY E. *The Sixteenth-Century Anabaptists as a
Theme in Twentieth-Century German Literature.* MQR XLII
(1968), 226-227.
Abstract of a 1959 Indiana University dissertation.

FRIEDMANN, ROBERT. *Anabaptism and Protestantism.* MQR
XXIV (1950), 12-24.
*Christian Sectarians in Thessalonica and Their Relationship
to the Anabaptists.* MQR XXIX (1955), 54-69.
See also the critical reaction of Henry De Wind, *ibid.,* 71-73.

GISH, ART. *Anabaptism and the New Left. Brethren Life and
Thought.* (1969), 68-86.

KLAASSEN, WALTER. *The Nature of the Anabaptist Protest.*
MQR XLV (1971), 291-311.

LITTELL, FRANKLIN H. *The Anabaptists and Christian Tradition.* JRT IV 2 (1947), 167-181.

NOVAK, MICHAEL. *The Free Churches and the Roman Church.
The Conception of the Church in Anabaptism and in Roman
Catholicism: Past and Present.* JES II 3 (1965), 426-447.

PEACHEY, PAUL. *Today's Counter Culture: the Radical Reformation as Analogue? (Preliminary Abstract).* CH XL 1 (1971), 55-56.
WYNEKEN, KARL H. *Calvin and Anabaptism.* CTM XXXVI 1 (1965), 18-29.

SPIRITUALISTS

HISTORIOGRAPHY

HILLERBRAND, HANS J. *A Fellowship of Discontent.* N.Y., London, 1967. xiv+176 pages.
Contains two essays on Spiritualists:
The Impatient Revolutionary: Thomas Müntzer. 1-30.
The Lonely Individualist: Sebastian Franck. 31-64.
JONES, RUFUS M. *Spiritual Reformers in the Sixteenth and Seventeenth Centuries.* Ld., 1914. li+362 pages.
Includes Denck, Bünderlin, Entfelder, Franck, Schwenckfeld, Castellio, Coornhert, Weigel, etc.
KLAASSEN, WALTER. *Spiritualization in the Reformation.* MQR XXXVII (1963), 67-77.
An attempt to make a theological classification of the left wing.
WILBUR, EARL MORSE. *Our Unitarian Heritage.* Boston, 1925. xiii+495 pages.
The early Anabaptists, pp. 43-52.

CARLSTADT

HILLERBRAND, HANS J. *Andreas Bodenstein of Carlstadt, Prodigal Reformer.* CH XXXV 4 (1966), 379-398.
KRODEL, GOTTFRIED G. *"Figura Prothysteron" and the Lord's Supper.* LQ XII 2 (1960), 152-158.
Analyzes the relationship between Carlstadt and Augustine via Erasmus.
RUPP, E. GORDON. *Andreas Karlstadt and Reformation Puritanism.* JTS X (1959), 308-326.

SIDER, RONALD J. *Karlstadt's Orlamünde Theology: a Theology of Regeneration (Parts I and II).* MQR LXV (1971), 191-218; 352-376.
Karlstadt and Luther's Doctorate. JTS XXII (1971), 168-169.

CASTELLIO

BAINTON, ROLAND H. *Sebastian Castellio and the Toleration Controversy of the Sixteenth Century* in *Persecution and Liberty. Essays in Honor of George Lincoln Burr,* N.Y., 1931, pp. 183-209.
Châteillon, Sebastion. Concerning Heretics. Now First Done Into English (Records of Civilization series). N.Y., 1935. xiv+342 pages.
BAINTON, ROLAND H. ET AL. (EDS.) *Castellioniana: Quatre Études Sur Sébastien Castellion et L'Idée de Tolérance.* Leiden, 1951.
Sebastian Castellio, Champion of Religious Liberty, 1515-1563. 25-79.
Reprinted in revised form in the author's *Studies on the Reformation,* pp. 139-181, with an updated bibliography.
Incorporates previous papers, and a new translated fragment.
JONES, RUFUS M. *A Forgotten Hero of the Reformation.* ConQ I (1913), 412-423.

FRANCK

FRANCKE, KUNO. *The Place of Sebastian Franck and Jakob Böhme in the History of German Literature.* GR I (1926), 4-20.
KINTNER, PHILIP L. *Sebastian Franck. An American Library Finding List.* ARG LV (1964), 48-55.
Excellent bibliographical guide.
PETERS, EUGENE. *Sebastian Franck's Theory of Religious Knowledge.* MQR XXXV (1961), 267-281.
SMITH, J. FREDERICK. *Sebastian Franck, Heretic, Mystic and Reformer of the Reformation.* TR XI (1874), 163-179.
(Based on Carl Alfred Hase, *Sebastian Franck von Wörd,* Leipzig, 1869.)

MÜNTZER

BENDER, HAROLD S. *The Zwickau Prophets, Thomas Müntzer, and the Anabaptists.* MQR XXVII (1953), 3-16.

BURRAGE, HENRY S. *Thomas Münzer.* BQ *(Ph)* XI (1877), 129-147.
Reviews the German literature to date and uses one of Münzer's tracts.

FORELL, GEORGE W. *Thomas Müntzer: Symbol and Reality.* D II (1963), 12-23.

FRIEDMANN, ROBERT. *Thomas Müntzer's Relation to Anabaptism.* MQR XXXI (1957), 75-87.

FRIESEN, ABRAHAM. *Thomas Müntzer in Marxist Thought.* CH XXXIV 3 (1965), 306-327.

GRITSCH, ERIC W. *Thomas Müntzer and the Origins of Protestant Spiritualism.* MQR XXXVII (1963), 172-194.
Reformer Without a Church. The Life and Thought of Thomas Muentzer (1488?-1525). Philadelphia, 1967. xiv+214 pages.
The only biography in English with extensive translations of Müntzer's works and a bibliography.

HILLERBRAND, HANS J. *Thomas Müntzer's Last Tract Against Luther.* MQR XXXVIII (1964), 20-46.
A translation of Müntzer's most polemic work.

IRWIN, JOYCE. *Muentzer's Translation and Liturgical Use of Scripture.* CTM XLIII 1 (1972), 21-28.

JUNGHANS, HELMER ET AL (EDS.) *Vierhundertfünfzig Jahre Lutherische Reformation, 1517-1967. Festschrift für Franz Lau zum 60. Geburtstag.* Göttingen, 1967.
RUPP, E. GORDON. *Programme Notes on the Theme "Müntzer and Luther."* 302-308.

RUPP, E. GORDON. *Thomas Müntzer, Hans Hut and "the Gospel of All Creatures."* BJRL XLIII (1961), 492-519.
An attempt to unearth a lost Müntzer treatise. Reprinted in the author's *Patterns of Reformation.*
Thomas Müntzer: Prophet of Radical Christianity. BJRL XLVIII (1966), pp.?
Müntzer's Writings. JEH XX 2 (1969), 309-311.

STAYER, JAMES M. *Thomas Müntzer's Theology and Revolution in Recent Non-Marxist Interpretation.* MQR XLIII (1969), 142-152.

SCHWENCKFELD

Corpus Schwenckfeldianorum. I. A Study of the Earliest Letters of Caspar Schwenckfeld von Ossig, ed. Chester David Hartranft, Elmer Ellsworth Schultz Johnson, Otto Bernhard Schlutter. Leipzig, 1907. lxxi+661 pages.
This volume alone of the series translates the documents into English.

FURCHA, EDWARD J. *Key Concepts in Caspar von Schwenckfeld's Theological System.* CH XXXVII 2 (1968), 160-173.
Schwenckfeld's Concept of the New Man: a Study in the Anthropology of Caspar von Schwenckfeld as Set Forth in His Major Theological Writings. MQR XLIII (1969), 169-170.
Abstract of a 1966 Hartford Seminary Foundation dissertation.

LOETSCHER, FREDERICK WILLIAM. *Schwenckfeld's Participation in the Eucharistic Controversy of the Sixteenth Century.* (Dissertation, Princeton) Philadelphia, 1906. viii+81 pages.

MAIER, PAUL C. *Caspar Schwenckfeldt on the Person and Work of Christ.* Assen, Kalamazoo, Mich., 1959. 115 pages.
Actually a survey of the theology, with a bibliography.
Caspar Schwenckfeldt—A Quadricentennial Evaluation. ARG LIV (1963), 89-96.

SCHULTZ, SELINA G. *Caspar Schwenckfeld von Ossig. (1489-1561). Spiritual Interpreter of Christianity, Apostle of the Middle Way, Pioneer in Modern Religious Thought.* Norristown, Pa., 1946. 453 pages.
An extremely sympathetic biography by a Schwenckfelder.

SEYPPEL, JOACHIM H. *Schwenckfeld, Knight of Faith.* N.Y., 1961. xvi+185 pages.
Emphasizes eucharist and freedom of the will as the two primary issues in Schwenckfeld's thought.

WACH, JOACHIM. *Caspar Schwenckfeld, a Pupil and a Teacher in the School of Christ.* JR XXVI 1 (1946), 1-29. Republished in the author's *Types of Religious Experience. Christian and Non Christian.* Chicago, 1951.
Regards Schwenckfeld as one of the most attractive figures of the Reformation. A very useful sketch.

WEISER, C. Z. *Caspar Schwenckfeld and the Schwenkfeldians.* MR XVII (1870), 347-373.

THE REFORMATION IN FRENCH SWITZERLAND

BIBLIOGRAPHY

DOWEY, EDWARD A. JR. *Survey—Continental Reformation: Works of General Interest. Studies in Calvin Since 1948.* CH XXIV (1955), 366-367. *Since 1955.* CH XXIX (1960), 196-204.

ERICHSON, ALFRED. *Bibliographia Calviniana.* Berlin, 1900. Reprinted from vol. LIX of the *Calvini Opera.* Works in English are listed and all of the translations of Calvin's works into English. The list must be supplemented, however, from *A Short-Title Catalogue of English Books 1475-1640* compiled by A. W. Pollard & G. R. Redgrave, Ld., 1926. Reprint, Nieuwkoop, 1960.

MCNEILL, JOHN T. *Thirty Years of Calvin Study.* CH XVII 3 (1948), 207-240. *Addendum.* CH XVIII 4 (1949), 241.

NIESEL, WILHELM. *Calvin-Bibliographie, 1901-1959.* Munich, 1961. 120 pages. Lists international works. English titles are listed under pertinent topics.

PARKER, T. H. L. *A Bibliography and Survey of the British Study of Calvin, 1900-1940.* EQ XVIII (1946), 123-131.

WALKER, WILLISTON (ED.) *John Calvin.* 2d ed. N.Y., 1969. MCNEILL, JOHN T. *Fifty Years of Calvin Study.* xvii-lxxvii. Part I (1918-1948) appeared in CH XVII (1948), 207-240 under title *Thirty Years of Calvin Study.* Part II (1948-1968) is new.

SOURCES IN TRANSLATION

ALLEN, JOHN. *Institutes of the Christian Religion by John Calvin.* Ld., 1813, and many subsequent editions as New Haven, 1816, Ld., 1838, Philadelphia 1843, 1844, memorial edition 1909.
New edition. Introduction on the literary history by B. B. Warfield and an account of the American Edition by T. C. Pears. 7th American ed. 2 vols. Philadelphia, 1936. London, 1937; Grand Rapids, Mich., 1949.

BEZA, THEODORE. *A Tragedie of Abraham's Sacrifice Written*

in French by Theodore Beza and Translated into English by Arthur Golding, ed. by Malcolm W. Wallace (University of Toronto Studies, Philological series). Toronto, 1906. lxi+127 pages.

Calvin Translation Society: Commentaries, 45 vols. Edinburgh, 1847-1855. Volume 7 contains at the end an essay by Halle on Calvin as an interpreter, followed by *Opinions and Testimonies Respecting the Writings of John Calvin* and a list of Calvin's Works.

Tracts Relating to the Reformation by John Calvin, tr. Henry Beveridge. 3 vols. Edinburgh 1844, 1849 and 1851. New edition of 45 vols. Grand Rapids, 1948-1950.

On the Prophet Joel, tr. J. Owen. London, 1958. 133 pages.

On the Gospel of John, tr. T. H. C. Parker. Edinburgh, 1959. 2 vols.

On I Corinthians, tr. John W. Fraser. Edinburgh, 1960.

Vol. I: *Life of John Calvin by Theodore Beza; Letter by James Sadolet; Reply by John Calvin; Articles Agreed upon by the Faculty of Sacred Theology of Paris with the Antidote; The Necessity of Reforming the Church; A Paternal Admonition by the Roman Pontiff, Paul III; Remarks on the Letter of Pope Paul III; An Admonition Showing the Advantages which Christendom Might Derive from an Inventory of Relics.*

Vol. II: *Catechism of the Church of Geneva; Forms of Prayer; Form of Administering the Sacraments; Visitation of the Sick; Brief Confession of Faith; Confession of Faith of the Reformed Churches of France; Short Treatise of the Lord's Supper; Mutual Consent as to the Sacraments; Second Defense of the Sacraments; Last Admonition to Joachim Westphal; True Partaking of the Flesh and Blood of Christ; Best Method of Concord of the Sacraments.*

Vol. III. *Canons and Decrees of the Council of Trent, with Antidote; Adultero-German Interim; True Method of Reforming the Church; The Sinfulness of Outward Conformity to Romish Rites; Psychopannychia, or the Soul's Imaginary Sleep between Death and Judgment.*

Institutes of the Christian Religion, tr. Henry Beveridge. 3 vols. Edinburgh, 1845-46.

The translator, in an introductory note, discusses the early

editions. Then follows a list by Robert Pitcairn of the editions and translations up to 1599. The translation is based on the Latin edition of 1559 with the chapter headings of the Amsterdam edition of 1671.
New edition with historical notes and introduction by Thomas F. Torrance. Grand Rapids, 1959; Edinburgh, 1960.

CALVIN

Calvin's First Psalter [1539] Edited with Critical Notes and Modal Harmonies to the Melodies by Sir Richard R. Terry. Ld., 1932. Introduction xiii pages.
Pt. I, The Psalter in facsimile. 63 pages.
Pt. II, The Psalter transcribed into modern notation and type, pp. 67-88.
Pt. III, The Psalter with its melodies (modally) harmonized by R. R. Terry, and an English verse translation by K. W. Simpson, pp. 91-112.
The Catechism of the Church of Geneva by the Rev. John Calvin, tr. Elijah Waterman. Hartford, Conn. 1815. vi+160 pages.
COLE, HENRY (TR.) *Calvin's Calvinism. The Eternal Predestination of God.* Grand Rapids, 1950. 350 pages.
Selections.
DILLENBERGER, JOHN (ED.) *John Calvin. Selections from His Writings.* Garden City, N.Y., 1971. viii+590 pages.
Introduction and selected bibliography. Contains a good cross-section of Calvin's writings: the man, reform, the Genevan church, Institutes, forms of biblical exposition.
Economic Tracts Series of 1880-1881. N.Y., 1882.
IV. *Usury Laws, Opinions of Jeremy Bentham and John Calvin* (translation of his letter to Oecolampadius).
EDWARDS, CHARLES E. (ED.) *Devotions and Prayers of John Calvin.* Grand Rapids, 1954. 120 pages.
FUHRMANN, PAUL T. *Instruction in Faith.* Philadelphia, 1949. 96 pages.
The Genevan Catechism.
FULLER, DAVID O. (ED.) and WILLS, J. P. (TR.) *John Calvin's Instruction in Christianity. An Abbreviated Edition of the*

Institutes. Grand Rapids, 1947. 246 pages.

HIGMAN, FRANCIS M. (ED.) *Three French Treatises* (Athlone Renaissance Library). London, 1970. 171 pages.

HUGHES, PHILIP E. (ED. & TR.) *The Register of the Company of Pastors of Geneva, in the Time of Calvin.* Grand Rapids, 1966. xvi+380 pages.

KERR, HUGH T. *A Compend of the Institutes.* Philadelphia, 1939. x+228 pages.

KROMMINGA, JOHN H. (COMP.) *Thine Is My Heart. Devotional Readings from Calvin's Writings.* Grand Rapids, 1958. pp.?

Letters of John Calvin, Compiled from the Original Manuscripts and Edited with Historical Notes by Dr. Jules Bonnet, tr. David Constable. 2 vols. Edinburgh, 1855-57.
4 vols. Philadelphia 1858, of which the first two were reprinted from the Edinburgh edition and the last two translated by Marcus Robert Gilchrist.

The Life of John Calvin by Theodore Beza, tr. Francis Sibson. Philadelphia, 1836. iv+332 pages.

MCNEILL, JOHN T. (ED.) *On God and Political Duty.* N.Y., 1950. xxv+102 pages.
Selections.
On the Christian Faith. Selections from the Institutes, Commentaries and Tracts. N.Y., 1958. xxxiii+219 pages.

NIXON, LEROY (TR.) *Deity of Christ and Other Sermons.* Grand Rapids, 1950. 302 pages.
The Gospel According to Isaiah. Seven Sermons on Is.53 Concerning the Passion and Death of Christ. Grand Rapids, 1953. 133 pages.
Sermons from Job. Grand Rapids, 1952. xxxvii+300 pages.

OLIN, JOHN C. *A Reformation Debate. Sadoleto's Letter to the Genevans' and Calvin's Reply. With an Appendix on the Justification Controversy.* N.Y., 1966. 136 pages.

PARKER, T. H. L. (TR.) *Sermons on Isaiah's Prophecy of the Death and Passion of Christ.* London, 1956. 161 pages.

A Selection of the Most Celebrated Sermons of John Calvin Philadelphia, 1860. 200 pages.

STRAND, KENNETH A. (ED.) *Reform Essentials of Luther and Calvin: a Source Collection.* Ann Arbor, 1971. pp.?

STROTHMANN, F. W. (ED.) *On God and Man.* N.Y., 1956. 54 pages.

From the Institutes.

WATERMAN, ELIJAH. *Memoirs of the Life and Writings of John Calvin together with a Selection of Letters*. Hartford, Conn. 1813. iv+412 pages.

GENERAL WORKS ON THE GENEVAN REFORMATION

Calvin and Calvinism

(Consult also the general works under German Switzerland.)

BÖHL, EDOUARD. *Separation of the Lutheran Church from the Reformed in the Sixteenth Century*. PRR V (1894), 415-433.

COCHRANE, ARTHUR C. *The Mystery of the Continuity of the Church: a Study in Reformed Symbolics*. JES II 1 (1965), 81-96.

CREMEANS, CHARLES D. *The Reception of Calvinistic Thought in England*. Urbana, Ill., 1949. viii+127 pages.

FOSTER, HERBERT D. *Geneva before Calvin (1387-1536), the Antecedents of a Puritan State*. AHR VIII (1903), 217-240.

GERRISH, B. A. *The Lord's Supper in the Reformed Confessions*. TT XXIII 2 (1966), 224-243.

HAUGARD, WILLIAM P. *John Calvin and the Catechism of Alexander Nowell*. ARG LXI (1970), 50-65.
Shows Calvin's influence on the catechism of 1571 used by Anglican bishops.

LEHMANN, PAUL L. *The Servant Image in Reformed Theology*. TT XV 3 (1958), 333-351.

MERLE D'AUBIGNÉ, JEAN HENRI. *History of the Reformation in Europe in the time of Calvin*. 8 vols. N.Y., 1863-79.
Still useful for citations from sources.

MIGNET, FRANÇOIS AUGUSTE MARIE. *The Genevan Reformation*, tr. Edward T. Fisher. UR VIII (1877), 33-55, 248-261, 408-434, 488-505.

PALM, FRANKLIN CHARLES. *Calvinism and the Religious Wars* (The Berkshire studies in European History). N.Y., 1932. ix+117 pages.
Three lectures for undergraduates, with a bibliography.

REID, J. K. S. *Calvin's Influence in Scotland and England*. CC LXXXI 22 (1964), 699-701.

RICHTER, WERNER. *The Calvinistic Conception of the State*. TT V 2 (1948), 249-269.

ROTONDO, ANTONIO. *Calvin and the Italian Anti-Trinitarians*,

tr. John and Anne Tedeschi. (Reformation Essays and
Studies series.) St. Louis, 1968. 28 pages.
SAVAGE, THEODORE F. *Back to Calvin.* RL XVII 1 (1947-48),
63-69.
SCHMIDT, ALBERT M. *John Calvin and the Calvinistic Tradition,*
tr. Ronald Wallace. (Men of Wisdom series.) N.Y., London,
1960. 122 pages.
An introduction for laymen, with selected texts.
WARFIELD, BENJAMIN BRECKINRIDGE. *Calvin and Calvinism.*
Collected Works, vol. V. N. Y., & Ld., Oxford Press, 1931.
v+428 pages.
Reprints the following articles:
John Calvin: the Man and His Work. MethR XVI (1909),
642-63.
Calvin's Doctrine of the Knowledge of God. PTR VII (1909),
219-325.
Calvin's Doctrine of God. PTR VII (1909), 381-436.
Calvin's Doctrine of the Trinity. PTR VII (1909), 553-652.
Calvin's Doctrine of the Creation. PTR XIII (1915), 190-225.
Calvinism, from the New Schaff-Herzog Encyclopedia.
On the Literary History of Calvin's "Institutes." From the
memorial edition of Allen's translation. I (1909), i-xlvi.
WHITLOCK, GLENN E. *The Call to the Ministry in the Reformed
Tradition.* TT XVII 3 (1960), 311-321.
ZWEMER, SAMUEL M. *Calvinism and the Missionary Enterprise.*
TT VII 2 (1950), 206-216.

The Literature of the Calvin Commemoration in 1909
Much of this literature is listed and discussed by Émile Doumergu
Jean Calvin IV (Lausanne, 1910), 419-485, to whom the material was
supplied by Benjamin Warfield. The Original Secession Magazine I
have not been able to obtain, and one or two of Doumergue's entries
I cannot identify as ever having been in print.
PRESBYTERIAN CHURCH IN THE U.S.A. GENERAL ASSEMBLY.
*Calvin Memorial Addresses, Delivered before the General
Assembly of the Presbyterian Church in the United States
at Savannah, Ga., May, 1909. Richmond, Va., Philadelphia*
[1909]. 286 pages.
REED, RICHARD C. *Calvin's Contribution to the Reformation.*
pp. 15-35.

MINTON, HENRY COLLIN. *Calvin the Theologian.* pp. 37-56.

JOHNSON, THOMAS CARY. *Calvin's Contribution to Church Polity.* pp. 57-88.

ORR, JAMES. *Calvin's Atttitude Towards and Exegesis of the Scriptures.* pp. 89-105.

WEBB, R. A. *Calvin's Doctrine of Infant Salvation.* pp. 107-126.

MORRIS, S. L. *The Relation of Calvin and Calvinism to Missions.* pp. 127-146.

DENNY, GEORGE H. *Calvin's Influence on Educational Progress.* pp. 147-174.

GLASGOW, FRANK T. *Calvin's Influence upon the Political Development of the World.* pp. 175-193.

KING, SAMUEL A. *How Far Has Original Calvinism Been Modified by Time.* pp. 195-221.

WARFIELD, BENJAMIN B. *Present Day Attitude to Calvinism.* pp. 223-239.

FRASER, O. M. *How May the Principles of Calvinism Be Rendered Most Effective under Modern Conditions?* pp. 241-259.

MERLE D'AUBIGNÉ, CHARLES. *John Calvin—the Man and His Times.* pp. 261-286.

With portraits of the contributors at the head of each essay.

Calvin and the Reformation. Four Studies. N.Y., 1909. 260 pages.

DOUMERGUE, ÉMILE. *Epigone or Creator.* pp. 1-55.

LANG, AUGUST. *The Reformation and Natural Law.* pp. 56-98.

BAVINCK, HERMAN. *Calvin and Common Grace.* pp. 99-130.

WARFIELD, BENJAMIN B. *Calvin's Doctrine of the Knowledge of God.* pp. 131-214.

Union Theological Seminary. *Three Addresses Delivered by Professors in Union Theological Seminary at the Service in Commemoration of the Four Hundredth Anniversary of the Birth of John Calvin.*

ROCKWELL, WILLIAM WALKER. *Calvin and the Reformation.* pp. 5-.

BROWN, WILLIAM ADAMS. *Calvin's Influence upon Theology.* pp. 20-.

HALL, THOMAS CUMING. *The Inner Spirit of the Calvinist Puritan State.* pp. 36-47.

Auburn Seminary Record. V, July, 1909.

MOFFAT, JAMES D. *The Influence of Calvin on Religious Thought.* pp. 157-166.

STEVENSON, J. ROSS. *Calvin's Influence on Civic and Social Life.* pp. 167-176.

Bibliotheca Sacra LXVI, No. CCLXIV, Oct., 1909.

CALKINS, WOLCOTT. *John Calvin's Calvinism.* pp. 671-684.

Unsigned. *Calvinism and Darwinism.* pp. 685-691.

Century Illustrated Monthly Magazine. LVI, July, 1909.

LANSDALE, MARYA HORNOR. *The Human Side of Calvin.* pp. 454-464.

BROWN, FRANCIS. *Calvin as a Theologian.* pp. 465-467.

Harvard Theological Review. II, 2, April, 1909; II, 3, July, 1909.

EMERTON, EPHRAIM. *Calvin and Servetus.* pp. 139-160.

FENN, WILLIAM W. *The Marrow of Calvin's Theology.* pp. 323-339.

Hibbert Journal, VIII, Oct., 1909-July, 1910.

TROELTSCH, ERNST. *Calvin and Calvinism.* pp. 102-121.

Homiletic Review. LVIII. July to December, 1909.

Calvin Considered as a Moral Force. pp. 8-13.

The Interior (Chicago) XL, No. 2030. April 22, 1909.

FORD, H. P. *John Calvin—an Outline Biography.* pp. 512 and 521.

WALKER, WILLISTON. *Calvin and Civil Liberty.* pp. 513-515.

ROBERTS, WILLIAM H. *Calvin in Human Relations.* pp. 515-517.

RICHARDS, WILLIAM ROGERS. *Traits of Calvin's Personality.* pp. 517-518.

KNOX, WILLIAM GEORGE. *Intellect of Calvin.* pp. 518-520.

YOUNG, LEIGH. *A Day in the City of Calvin.* pp. 520-521.

North American Review. CXC, Aug. 1909.

MENTON, HENRY C. *John Calvin, Lawyer.* pp. 212-221.

Lutheran Church Review. XXVIII, 1909.

HALL, THOMAS C. *Was Calvin a Reformer or a Reactionary?* pp. 1-15.

Reprinted from HJ VI, Oct. 1907-July 1908. pp. 171-185.

Lutheran Quarterly, XXXIX, 1909.

WOODS, D. W. *John Calvin: His Place in History.* pp. 552-565.

Methodist Review, XCI, 1909. Cf. Warfield's *Calvin and Calvinism.*

STEELE, WILBUR FLETCHER. *Calvin the Heretic.* pp. 551-561.

A frothy arraignment of the doctrine of election.

Presbyterian historical Society, journal of, V, 1909-1910.

BENSON, LOUIS F. *John Calvin and the Psalmody of the Reformed Churches.* pp. 1-21, 55-87, 107-118.

GOOD, JAMES I. *Calvin and the New World.* pp. 179-187.

FREDERIOQ, PAUL. *Self-government and Calvinism.* pp. 270-273.

THOMPSON, ROBERT ELLIS. *The Psalm-Book of the Reformed Churches.* pp. 311-339.

Princeton Theological Review. VII, 1909.

The three articles by Warfield are already listed under his *Calvin and Calvinism,* and one by Bavinck and one by Doumergue under *Four Studies.* This number contains in addition:

DEWITT, JOHN. *John Calvin—the Man.* pp. 369-380.

DOUMERGUE, ÉMILE. *Music in the Work of Calvin.* pp. 529-552.

Reformed Church Review. 4th series. XIII, No. 2, 1909.

KLEIN, H. M. J. *John Calvin, the Man.* pp. 145-164.

HOCH DE LONG, IRWIN. *Calvin as an Interpreter of the Bible.* pp. 165-182.

HERMAN, THEODORE F. *Calvin's Doctrine of Predestination.* pp. 183-208.

WEBER, A. S. *The Doctrine of the Lord's Supper in Calvin's System of Thought.* pp. 209-228.

STAHR, JOHN S. *The Ethics of Calvinism.* pp. 229-244.

BOWMAN, C. *Calvin as a Preacher.* pp. 245-261.

HIESTER, A. V. *Calvin and Civil Liberty.* pp. 262-315.

RICHARDS, GEORGE W. *Calvinism in the Reformed Churches of Germany.* pp. 316-345.

DIPPELL, VICTOR WILLIAM. *Illustrative Anecdotes from the Life of Calvin.* pp. 346-352.

Review and Expositor. VI, 4, Oct., 1909.

EAGER, GEORGE BOARDMAN. *Calvin as a Civic and Social Influence.* pp. 560-561.
NEWMAN, A. H. *The Calvinism of Calvin.* pp. 562-576.
ROBERTSON, A. T. *Calvin as an Interpreter of Scripture.* pp. 577-578.
Union Seminary Magazine (Richmond, Va.) XXI, No. 2. Dec., 1909-Jan., 1910.
JOHNSON, THOMAS CARY. *John Calvin: Who Was He? Of What Sort Was He? What Did He Do for the World?* pp. 108-136.
LINGLE, WALTER L. *The Burning of Servetus.* pp. 96-107.

Collected Essays

DUFFIELD, GERVAISE E. (ED.) *John Calvin.* (Courtney Studies in Reformation Theology series.) Appleford, England, 1966. 240 pages.
Pertinent essays:
HALL, BASIL. *The Calvin Legend.* 1-18.
Calvin Against the Calvinists. 19-37.
BATTLES, FORD L. *The Sources of Calvin's Seneca Commentary.* 39-66.
BENÔIT, JEAN-DANIEL. *Calvin the Letter-Writer.* 67-101.
The History and Development of the Institutio: How Calvin Worked. 102-117.
CADIER, JEAN. *Calvin and the Union of the Churches.* 118-130.
WALKER, G. S. M. *The Lord's Supper in the Theology and Practice of Calvin.* 131-148.
PACKER, J. I. *Calvin the Theologian.* 149-175.
Calvin the Biblical Expositor. 176-189.
PETER, R. *Calvin and Louis Bude's Translation of the Psalms.* 190-209.
CASWELL, R. N. *Calvin's View of Ecclesiastical Discipline.* 210-226.
HOOGSTRA, JACOB T. (ED.) *John Calvin. Contemporary Prophet.* Grand Rapids, 1959. 257 pages.
Pertinent essays:
MARCEL, PIERRE. *The Humility of the Prophet.* 21-37.
ROBINSON, CHILDS W. *The Tolerance of the Prophet.* 39-49.
BENÔIT, JEAN-DANIEL. *Pastoral Care of the Prophet.* 51-67.

HUGHES, P. E. *The Pen of the Prophet.* 71-94.

POLMAN, A. D. R. *Calvin on Inspiration of Scripture.* 97-112.

WURTH, BRILLENBURG G. *Calvin and the Kingdom of God.* 113-126.

STOKER, H. G. *Calvin and Ethics.* 127-147.

KROMMINGA, J. H. *Calvin and Ecumenicity.* 149-165.

BERG, VANDEN J. *Calvin and Missions.* 167-183.

BERKOUWER, G. C. *Calvin and Rome.* 185-196.

COETZEE, J. C. *Calvin and the School.* 197-225.

SINGER, GREGG C. *Calvinism and the Social Order.* 227-241.

REID, STANFORD W. *Calvin and the Political Order.* 243-257.

BIOGRAPHY OF CALVIN

BARR, GLADYS H. *The Master of Seneca. A Novel Based on the Life of John Calvin.* N.Y., 1961. 252 pages.

BRATT, JOHN H. *The Life and Teachings of John Calvin. A Study Manual.* Grand Rapids, 1959. 72 pages.

BREEN, QUIRINIUS. *John Calvin: a Study in French Humanism.* (Dissertation, Chicago) Grand Rapids, Mich., 1931. ix+174 pages.

A careful study of Calvin's early classical studies and of the influence of humanism upon his mature thought. New edition, Hamden, Conn. 1968. xvi+193 pages.

BUNGENER, LAURENCE LOUIS FÉLIX. *Calvin, His Life, His Labors and His Writings.* Edinburgh & Ld., 1863.

I have seen only the French (Paris, 1862). The point of view is apologetic without suppressing any facts.

DAVIES, A. T. *John Calvin and the Influence of Protestantism on National Life and Character.* Worthing, 1946. 46 pages.

John Calvin. Many Sided Genius. N.Y., 1947. 92 pages.

DYER, THOMAS HENRY. *Life of John Calvin.* Ld., 1850. xii+560 pages.

A careful, but too sympathetic an account of Calvin based largely on his letters. Particular attention is devoted to his dealings with the Marian exiles.

GUIZOT, M. *Saint Louis and Calvin.* Macmillan, n.p.n.d. (Guizot's preface. 1868) *Calvin*, pp. 145-362.

"Profound respect and admiration if not affection and sympathy" for Calvin.

HALL, BASIL. *John Calvin, Humanist and Theologian* (Historical Association Publications, General Series). London, 1956. 39 pages.

HARKNESS, GEORGIA E. *John Calvin: the Man and His Ethics.* N.Y., 1931. xiii+266 pages.

Valuable especially for Calvin's economic views.

Reviewed by John T. McNeill JR XII (1932), 124-125. New edition, 1958. Paperback.

HENDERSON, HENRY F. *Calvin in His Letters.* Ld., 1909. vii+ 122 pages+index.

A running sketch illustrated by excerpts from the letters.

HENRY, PAUL. *The Life and Times of John Calvin . . .* tr. from the German by Henry Stebbing, 2 vols. Ld., 1849, N.Y., 1851-2.

A detailed study by an ardent apologist.

HUNT, ROBERT NIGEL CAREW. *Calvin.* Ld., 1933. 335 pages.

Detached, moderately acquainted with recent literature.

IRWIN, CLARKE HUSTON. *John Calvin, the Man and His Work.* Ld., 1909. xiii+208 pages.

Follows Doumergue.

JOHNSON, THOMAS CARY. *John Calvin and the Genevan Reformation: a Sketch.* Richmond, Va., 1900. 97 pages.

Adulatory, based on materials available in English.

MACKINNON, JAMES. *Calvin and the Reformation.* London, N.Y., 1936. xii+302 pages. New Edition, N.Y., 1962.

Scholarly but unsympathetic.

MENZIES, ALLAN. *A Study of Calvin and Other Papers.* Ld., 1918. Includes:

The Career and Personality of Calvin. pp. 127-193.

Calvin's Teaching 1) *Calvin as a Biblical Critic and Interpreter.* pp. 195-210.

2) *Calvin as a Theologian: the "Institutes."* pp. 210-229.

The Influence of Calvin. pp. 230-241.

The Permanent Message of Calvinism. pp. 242-247.

MILES, ROBERT W. *That Frenchman, John Calvin.* N.Y., 1939. 221 pages.

A useful biography.

MOURA, JEAN and LOUVER, PAUL. *Calvin: a Modern Biography,* tr. Ida Zeitlin. Garden City, N.Y., 1932. vi+312 pages.
Racy reading, adorned with imaginative flourishes which will not bear investigation.

PARKER, THOMAS H. *Portrait of John Calvin.* London, 1954, Philadelphia, 1955. 124 pages.
Contains bibliography.

PATTISON, MARK. *Essays by the Late Mark Pattison Collected and Arranged by Henry Nettleship.* 2 vols. Oxford, 1889.
Vol. II, *Calvin at Geneva,* pp. 1-41.
Discusses Calvin's contribution to and sins against liberty.

PENNING, L. *Life and Times of Calvin,* translated from the Dutch by B. S. Berrington. Ld., 1912. vi+392 pages.
Hagiography; paints Servetus in the blackest colors, and palliates the execution as an "error of the age."

REYBURN, HUGH Y. *John Calvin, His Life, Letters and Work.* Ld., N.Y., 1914. viii+376 pages.
Careful, detailed, detached.

ROBBINS, R. D. C. *Life of John Calvin. BS* II (1845), 329-356; 489-527; 710-756.

STEVENSON, RICHARD TAYLOR. *John Calvin: the Statesman* (Men of the Kingdom). Cincinnati, N.Y., 1907. 203 pages.
Acceptable popularization.

STICKELBERGER, EMANUEL. *Calvin. A Life,* tr. David G. Gelzer. Richmond, 1954, London, 1959. 174 pages.
Popular biography.

TULLOCH, JOHN. *Leaders of the Reformation: Luther, Calvin, Latimer, Knox.* Boston, N.Y., 1859. 309 pages.

VAN HALSEMA, THEA B. *This Was John Calvin.* Grand Rapids, 1959. 180 pages.

VOLLMER, PHILIP. *John Calvin.* Philadelphia, 1909. 219 pages.
Slight, apologetic.

WALKER, WILLISTON. *John Calvin* (Heroes of the Reformation). N.Y., Ld., 1906. xviii+456 pages.
Accurate, well balanced, fair.
New edition, 1969.

WILEMAN, WILLIAM. *John Calvin, His Life, His Teaching and His Influence.* Ld., [1909?]. 147 pages.
Popular encomium.

MISCELLANEOUS BIOGRAPHICAL POINTS

BLACKBURN, WILLIAM M. *The College Days of Calvin*. Philadelphia, 1865. 156 pages.

Young Calvin in Paris. Philadelphia, 1865. 166 pages.

Constructs conversations following Merle d'Aubigné.

COLLINS, ROSS W. *Calvin and the Libertines of Geneva*, ed. F. D. Blackly. Toronto, Vancouver, Clark, 1968. ix+210 pages.

DRUMMOND, ROBERT B. *Calvinism*. TR XII (1875), 191-217.

Emphasizes Calvin's tenderness.

HUNTER, MITCHELL A. *Calvin: a Character Sketch*. ET XLIV 11 (1938), 509-513.

The Erudition of John Calvin. EQ XVIII (1946), 199-208.

M'CRIE, THOMAS. *The Early Years of John Calvin, a Fragment, 1509-1536*, ed. William Ferguson. Edinburgh, 1880. 199 pages.

Includes an account of the Reformation at Geneva.

PARKER, T. H. L. *Calvini Opera Sed non Omnia*. SJT XVIII 2 (1965), 194-203.

On the authenticity of Calvin's works.

SCHAFF, PHILIP. *Calvin at Home*. RQR XXXIX (1892), 163-172.

The Friendship of Calvin and Melanchthon. ASCH IV (1891), 143-163.

SMYTH, THOMAS. *Calvin and His Enemies*. Philadelphia, new edition 1856. 180 pages. New edition 1909. 208 pages.

Follows Rilliet on Servetus.

STAUFFER, RICHARD. *The Humanness of John Calvin*, tr. George Shriver. Nashville, N.Y., 1971. 96 pages.

Portrays Calvin as family man, friend, and pastor.

CALVIN'S OPPONENTS: GRUET AND SERVETUS

BAINTON, ROLAND H. *The Present State of Servetus Studies*. JMH IV (1932), 72-92.

Bibliographical.

Servetus and Genevan Libertines. CH V (1936), 141-149.

Michael Servetus and the Pulmonary Transit of the Blood. *Bulletin of the History of Medicine*. XXV (1951), 1-7.

Burned Heretic: Michael Servetus. CC LXX 43 (1953), 1230-1231.

CALVIN 173

Hunted Heretic. The Life and Death of Michael Servetus, 1511-1553. Boston, 1953. xiv+270 pages. Paperback, 1960.
The authoritative biography; contains bibliography.
Documenta Servetiana. ARG XLIV (1953), 223-234; XLV (1954), 99-108.

BECKER, BRUNO (ED.) *Autour de Michel Servet et de Sebastien Castellion; Recuie.* Haarlem, 1953.
BAINTON, ROLAND H. *Michael Servetus and the Trinitarian Speculation of the Middle Ages.* 29-46.

BUCK, COLEMAN G. *Calvin and Servetus. Bibliotheca Sacra* CIV (1947), 236-241.

CONWAY, MONCURE, D. *Jacques Gruet, Calvin's Ethical Victim.* OC X (1896), 5055-5057.

GORDON, ALEXANDER. *Miguel Serveto-y-Revés.* TR XV (1878), 281-307, 408-443.
Michael Servetus, in *Addresses Biographical and Historical.* Ld., 1922, pp. 1-64.
The best brief treatment in English.

NEWMAN, LOUIS ISRAEL. *Michael Servetus the Anti-Trinitarian Judaizer,* in *Jewish Influence on Christian Reform Movements* (Columbia University Oriental studies XXIII). N.Y., 1925. pp. 511-609.
Servetus's Semitic scholarship.

OSLER, SIR WILLIAM. *Michael Servetus.* Oxford, 1909, and JHH, XXI (1910), 1-11.
Servetus' medical contributions.

SCHAFF, PHILIP. *Calvin and Servetus.* RQR XL ns XV (1893), 1-41.
Discriminating, thinks the Libertines tried to make a tool of Servetus.

SHIELDS, CHARLES W. *The Trial of Servetus.* PRR IV (1893), 353-383.
Follows Rilliet.

TWEEDIE, W. K. *Calvin and Servetus.* Edinburgh, 1846. xv+245 pages.
A translation of Rilliet, who makes the trial of Servetus hinge on political offenses.

WILBUR, E. MORSE. *The Two Treatises of Servetus on the Trinity.* HTS XVI (1932), xxxviii+264 pages.
Translation, historical introduction, bibliography, notes.

WILLIS, ROBERT. *Servetus and Calvin.* Ld., 1877. xvi+541 pages.
Antipathy toward without understanding of Calvin.

CALVIN'S THOUGHT

BREEN, QUIRINUS. *John Calvin and the Rhetorical Tradition.*
CH XXVI 1 (1957), 3-21.

BRUGGNIK, DONALD J. *Calvin and Federal Theology.* RfR
XIII 1 (1959), 15-22.

CHANEY, CHARLES. *The Missionary Dynamic in the Theology
of John Calvin.* RfR XVII 2 (1964), 24-38.

HIGMAN, FRANCIS M. *The Style of John Calvin in His French
Polemical Treatises.* (Oxford Modern Language and Litera-
ture Monographs, 42). Oxford, 1967. viii+191 pages.
Contains bibliography.

HUNTER, A. MITCHELL. *The Teaching of Calvin.* Glasgow, 1920.
x+304 pages.
An intelligent summary rather than a penetrating interpretation
The aquaintance with non-English material appears to be slight.
New edition, London, 1970.

LITTLE, LESTER K. *Calvin's Appreciation of Gregory the Great.*
HTR LVI 2 (1963), 145-158.

NIESEL, WILHELM. *The Theology of Calvin,* tr. Harold Knight.
Philadelphia, 1956. 254 pages.
A 1938 German work. Excellent survey of Calvin's thought.

OBERMAN, HEIKO A. *The "Extra" Dimension in the Theology
of Calvin.* JEH XXI 1 (1970), 43-64.
Argues the universality of the "extra."

PARKER, T. H. L. *The Approach to Calvin.* EQ XVI (1944),
165-172.

ROSEN, EDWARD. *Calvin's Attitude Toward Copernicus.* JHI
XXI 3 (1960), 431-441.

VASADY, BELA. *The Main Traits of Calvin's Theology.* Grand
Rapids, 1951. 43 pages.

WARFIELD, BENJAMIN B. *Calvin and Augustine,* ed. Samuel G.
Craig. Philadelphia, 1956. ix+507 pages.
An older work, stressing the theological similarities and
differences.

WEBER, HENRY JACOB. *The Formal Dialectical Rationalism of
Calvin.* ASCH 2S VII (1928), 19-41.

WENDEL, FRANÇOIS. *Calvin: Origins and Development of His Religious Thought.* London, N.Y., 1963. 383 pages.
Based on *The Institutes.* Very useful, with bibliography.

Institutes

GRISLIS, EGIL. *Calvin's Use of Cicero in the Institutes I: 1-5— a Case Study in Theological Method.* ARG LXII (1971), 5-36.

HESSELINK, JOHN. *The Development and Purpose of Calvin's Institutes.* RfR XXIII 3 (1970), 136-142.

MCNEILL, JOHN T. *Books of Faith on Power.* N.Y., 1947. viii+ 183 pages.
Chapter II on *Institutes.*

MUELLER, G. E. *Calvin's Institutes of the Christian Religion as an Illustration of Christian Living.* JHI IV (1943), 287-300.

PAUCK, WILHELM. *Calvin's Institutes of the Christian Religion.* CH XV 1 (1946), 17-27.

The Political Consequences of the Reformation. N.Y., 1960.
MURRAY, ROBERT H. *John Calvin and His Institutes.* 80-128.

WHITNEY, H. J. *Profile of John Calvin and the Institutes.* Brisbane, 1957. 217 pages.
Contains a bibliography.

Doctrine of Scripture

BOYD, DOROTHY. *Calvin's Preface to the French Metrical Psalms.* EQ XXII (1950), 249-254.

CHRISTIE, ALEXANDER. *The Doctrine of Holy Scripture in Calvin and Brunner. Union Seminary Quarterly Review* LII (1940/41), 19-32; 116-127; 325-350.

EDWARDS, CHARLES E. *Calvin on Inerrant Inspiration.* BS LXXXVIII (1931), 465-475.

EENIGENBURG, ELTON M. *The Place of the Covenant in Calvin's Thinking.* RfR X 4 (1957), 1-22.

EMERSON, EVERETT H. *Calvin and Covenant Theology.* CH XXV 2 (1956), 136-144.

FORSTMANN, M. JACKSON. *Word and Spirit: Calvin's Doctrine of Biblical Authority.* Stanford, 1962. viii+178 pages.
Relates the doctrine to contemporary questions.

FUHRMANN, PAUL T. *Calvin. The Exposition of Scripture.* I
  VI (1952), 188-209.
GILBERT, J. H. *The Bible of Calvin.* BW XXVII (1906), 344-347.
HOEKEMA, ANTHONY A. *Calvin's Doctrine of the Covenant
  of Grace.* RfR XV 4 (1962), 1-12.
  The Covenant of Grace in Calvin's Teaching. CTJ II (1967),
  133-161.
LEWIS, A. DAVID (TR.) *Calvin's Saturday Morning Sermon
  on Micah 6: 6-8.* SJT XXIII 2 (1970), 157-165.
MCNEILL, JOHN T. *The Significance of the Word of God for
  Calvin.* CH XXVIII 2 (1959), 131-146.
MOORE, DUNLOP. *Calvin's Doctrine of Holy Scripture.* PRR
  IV (1893), 49-70.
MURRAY, JOHN. *Calvin on Scripture and Divine Sovereignty.*
  Grand Rapids, 1960. 70 pages.
  Three lectures for the Reformed Fellowship.
NIXON, LEROY. *John Calvin. Expository Preacher.* Grand
  Rapids, 1950. 136 pages.
  On Calvin's "theory" and "practice" according to certain
  themes. Contains bibliography.
PARKER, T. H. L. *The Sources of the Text of Calvin's New
  Testament.* ZKG LXXIII (1962), 272-298.
PARKER, THOMAS D. *A Comparison of Calvin and Luther
  on Galatians.* I XVII (1963), 61-75.
PRUST, RICHARD C. *Was Calvin a Biblical Literalist?* STJ XX
  3 (1967), 312-328.
RUSSELL, S. H. *Calvin and the Messianic Interpretation of the
  Psalms.* SJT XXI 1 (1968), 37-47.
SANTMIRE, H. PAUL. *Justification in Calvin's 1540 Romans
  Commentary.* CH XXXIII 3 (1964), 294-313.
WALVOORD, JOHN F. (ED.) *Inspiration and Interpretation.*
  Grand Rapids, 1957.
  KANTZER, KENNETH S. *Calvin and the Holy Scriptures.*
  115-155.

Trinity: God, Christ, Spirit
DOWEY, EDWARD A. *The Knowledge of God in Calvin's
  Theology.* N.Y., 1952. xi+261 pages.
  Deals with the epistemological problem of the *duplex cog-
  nitio Domini,* with references to modern discussions such

as that between Emil Brunner and Karl Barth.

HOOGLAND, MARVIN P. *Calvin's Perspective on the Exaltation of Christ in Comparison With the Post-Reformation Doctrine of the Two States.* Kampen, 1966. x+222 pages.

JANSEN, JOHN F. *Calvin's Doctrine of the Work of Christ.* London, 1956. 120 pages.

MURRAY, JOHN C. *Calvin's Doctrine of Creation. Westminster Theological Journal* XVII (1956), 21-43.

PARKER, T. H. L. *Calvin's Concept of Revelation.* SJT II 1 (1949), 29-47; 4 (1949), 337-351.
Calvin's Doctrine of Justification. EQ XXII (1952), 101-107.
The Doctrine of the Knowledge of God. A Study in the Theology of John Calvin. Edinburgh, London, 1952. Rev. ed., Grand Rapids, 1959. 119 pages. 2d ed. rev., 1959. 128 pages.
An authoritative study.

TORRANCE, THOMAS F. *Calvin and the Knowledge of God.* CC LXXXI 22 (1964), 696-699.

VAN BUREN, PAUL. *Christ in Our Place. The Substitutionary Character of Calvin's Doctrine of Reconciliation.* Edinburgh, 1957. xiii+152 pages.
Excellent on Christology.

WILLIS, EDWARD D. *Calvin's Catholic Christology. The Function of the So-Called Extra Calvinisticum in Calvin's Theology.* Leiden, 1967. ix+171 pages.
Rejects the thesis that Calvin's Christology leads to a natural theology.

Faith

COATES, THOMAS. *Calvin's Doctrine of Justification.* CTM XXXIV 6 (1963), 325-334.

GESSERT, ROBERT A. *The Integrity of Faith: an Inquiry Into the Meaning of Law in the Theology of John Calvin.* SJT XIII 3 (1960), 247-261.

PASTEMA, GERALD J. *Calvin's Alleged Rejection of Natural Theology.* SJT XXIV 4 (1971), 423-434.

STUERMANN, WALTER E. *A Critical Study of Calvin's Concept of Faith.* Tulsa, 1952. xv+397 pages.

THOMAS, JOHN NEWTON. *The Place of Natural Theology in the*

Thought of John Calvin. JRT XV 2 (1958), 107-136.

Predestination

EDWARDS, CHARLES E. *Calvin on Infant Salvation.* BS LXXXVIII (1931), 316-328.

HUNT, LEIGH S. *Predestination in the Institutes of the Christian Religion.* EQ IX (1937), 131-138.

PEYER, ETIENNE DE. *Calvin's Doctrine of Divine Providence.* EQ X (1938), 30-45.

REID, J. K. S. *The Office of Christ in Predestination. I: Calvin.* SJT I (1948), 5-12.

SHIELDS, CHARLES W. *The Doctrine of Calvin Concerning Infant Salvation.* PRR I (1890), 634-651.

WARFIELD, BENJAMIN B. *Predestination in the Reformed Confessions.* PRR XII (1901), 49-128.

Man

BATTENHOUSE, ROY W. *The Doctrine of Man in Calvin and in Renaissance Platonism.* JHI IX 4 (1948), 447-471.

MURRAY, JOHN C. *Calvin's Doctrine of Creation. Westminster Theological Journal* XVII (1954), 21-43.

PELKONEN, J. PETER. *The Teaching of John Calvin on the Nature and Function of the Conscience.* LQ XXI (1969), 74-88.

PRUYSER, PAUL W. *Calvin's View of Man: a Psychological Commentary.* TT XXVI 1 (1969), 51-68.

ROLSTON, HOLMES III. *Responsible Man in Reformed Theology: Calvin versus the Westminster Confession.* SJT XXIII 2 (1970), 129-156.

STUERMANN, WALTER E. and GEOCARIS, K. *The Image of Man. The Perspectives of Calvin and Freud.* I XIV (1960), 28-42.

TORRANCE, T. F. *Calvin's Doctrine of Man.* London, 1949. 183 pages.
Stresses the difference between Calvin and Calvinism.

Education

BROUWER, ARIE R. *Calvin's Doctrine of Children in the Covenant. Foundation for Christian Education.* RfR XVIII 4 (1965), 17-29.

DE JONG, PETER Y. *Calvin's Contributions to Christian Educa-*

tion. CTJ II (1967), 162-201.

HUNTER, MICHELL A. *The Education of Calvin.* EQ (1937),
    pp.?

REID, W. S. *Calvin and the Founding of the Academy of Geneva.*
    Westminster Theological Journal XVIII (1955), 1-33.

Ethics

BIELER, ANDRE. *The Social Humanism of Calvin*, tr. Paul T.
    Fuhrmann. Richmond, 1964. 79 pages.
    On social and financial questions related to our time.

FOSTER, FRANK H. *Calvin's Ethics, an Abstract from the German*
    of P. Lobstein. BS XXXVII (1880), 1-47.

FOSTER, HERBERT D. *Calvin's Programme for a Puritan State*
    in Geneva. HTR I (1908), 391-434.

GRAHAM, FRED W. *The Constructive Revolutionary. John Cal-*
    vin and His Socio-Economic Impact. Richmond, 1971.
    252 pages.
    Ranks Calvin's heritage with Marxism and democracy as a
    third universal force.

HALL, CHARLES. *With the Spirit's Sword. The Drama of Spiritual*
    Warfare in the Theology of John Calvin (Basel Studies of
    Theology). Richmond, 1960. 227 pages.
    A dissertation, includes bibliography.

HIEMSTRA, WILLIAM L. *Calvin's Doctrine of Christian Liberty.*
    RfR XIII 1 (1959), 10-14.

MATHESON, J. G. *Calvin's Doctrine of the Christian Life.* SJT
    II (1949), 48-56.

WALLACE, R. S. *Calvin's Doctrine of the Christian Life.* Edin-
    burgh, 1959. xvi+349 pages.
    An authoritative study.

Church, Ministry and Sacraments

AINSLIE, JAMES L. *The Doctrine of Ministerial Order in the Re-*
    formed Churches of the 16th and 17th Centuries. Edinburgh,
    1940. xiv+251 pages.
    Written by a Scotch Presbyterian stressing the return to apos-
    tolic times.

BARKLAY, JOHN M. *The Meaning of Ordination.* SJT IX (1956),
    150-160.

Calvin's order of Baptism, tr. Thomas C. Porter. MR XI (1859),
    298-303.

CRAWFORD, JOHN R. *Calvin and the Priesthood of All Believers.* SJT XXI 2 (1968), 145-156.

GERRISH, BRIAN A. *John Calvin and the Reformed Doctrine of the Lord's Supper.* US XXV 2 (1968), 27-39.

GRISLIS, EGIL. *Calvin's Doctrine of Baptism.* CH XXXI (1962), 46-65.

HEIDEMAN, EUGENE. *Calvinism and Church Government.* RfR XIII 1 (1959), 1-9.

JANSEN, JOHN F. *Calvin on a Fixed Form of Worship—a Note in Textual Criticism.* SJT XV 3 (1962), 282-287.

MCDONNELL, KILIAN. *The Ecclesiology of John Calvin and Vatican II.* RL XXXVI 4 (1967), 542-556.
John Calvin, the Church and the Eucharist. Princeton, 1967. ix+410 pages.
The doctoral thesis of a Benedictine priest who stresses the pastoral character of Calvin's doctrine of the Eucharist.

MCNEILL, JOHN T. *The Church in Sixteenth Century Reformed Theology.* JR XXII 3 (1942), 251-269.
The Doctrine of the Ministry in Reformed Theology. CH XII 2 (1943), 77-97.

MEYER, BONIFACE. *Calvin's Eucharistic Doctrine: 1536-39.* JES IV 1 (1967), 47-65.

MILNER, BENJAMIN C. JR. *Calvin's Doctrine of the Church.* Leiden, 1970. 210 pages.
A comprehensive survey, with an incomplete bibliography.

PARKER, THOMAS H. *The Oracles of God. An Introduction to the Preaching of John Calvin.* London, 1947. 175 pages.
Also introduces the reader to Calvin's life. Contains risky generalizations.

WALKER, G. S. M. *Calvin and the Church.* SJT XVI 4 (1963), 371-389.

WALLACE, RONALD S. *Calvin's Doctrine of the Word and Sacrament.* Edinburgh, 1953. xii+253 pages.

Church Union

HESSELINK, JOHN. *The Catholic Character of Calvin's Life and Work.* RfR XIX 2 (1965), 13-26.

MCNEILL, JOHN T. *Calvin's Efforts toward the Consolidation of Protestantism.* JR VIII (1928), 411-433.
Unitive Protestantism. N.Y., 1930. 345 pages.

Political Theory

ANDERSON, WILLIAM K. *Luther and Calvin. A Contrast in
    Politics.* RL IX (1940), 256-267.
BARON, HANS. *Calvinist Republicanism and Its Historical Roots.*
    CH VIII (1939), 30-42.
HUDSON, WINTHROP S. *Democratic Freedom and Religious
    Faith in the Reformed Tradition.* CH XV 3 (1946), 177-
    194.
HUIZINGA, A. V. C. P. *The Calvinistic View of Church and State.*
    BS, LXXXIII (1926), 174-189.
HUNT, GEORGE L. (ED.) *Calvinism and the Political Order.*
    Philadelphia, 1965.
    MCNEILL, JOHN T. *John Calvin on Civil Government.*
    22-45.
KINGDON, ROBERT M. *Calvinism and Democracy: Some
    Political Implications of Debates on French Reformed
    Church Government, 1562-1572.* AHR LXIX 2 (1964),
    393-401.
MCNEILL, JOHN T. *The Democratic Elements in Calvin's
    Thought.* CH XVIII 3 (1949), 153-171.
O'SHEA, J. J. *Calvin and the Author of the Prince.* ACQ XXXI
    (1906), 680-694.
    A very unsympathetic treatment provoked by Walker's
    John Calvin.
RICHTER, WARNER. *The Calvinist Conception of the State:
    Its Tradition and Its Secularization.* TT V (1948/49), 249-
    269.

Eschatology

QUISTORP, HEINRICH. *Calvin's Doctrine of the Last Things*,
    tr. H. Knight. London, 1955. 200 pages.
    Excellent.
TORRANCE, T. F. *The Eschatology of Hope: John Calvin. King-
    dom and Church.* Edinburgh, 1956. pp. 90-164.

OPINION ON CALVIN

BRUNETIÈRE, FERDINAND. *Calvin's Literary Work.* PRR XII
    (1901), 392-414.

COCHRANE, ARTHUR C. *John Calvin and Nuclear War.* CC
LXXIX 27 (1962), 837-839.

DAKIN, PRINCIPAL ARTHUR. *Calvin's Age and Ours.* ET LII
10 (1941), 396-397.

FOSTER, HERBERT DARLING. *Brunetière on the Work of
Calvin.* BS LX (1903), 148-157.

KINGDON, ROBERT M. and LINDNER, ROBERT D. *Calvin
and Calvinism: Sources of Democracy?* (Problems in European Civilization series.) Lexington, Mass., 1970. xix+83
pages.
With excerpts from sources and a bibliography.

MCNEILL, JOHN T. *Calvin as an Ecumenical Churchman.* CH
XXXII 4 (1963), 379-391.
Calvin After 400 Years. CC LXXXI 22 (1964), 702-704.

NEILL, THOMAS P. *Calvin and the Modern Mind.* CW CLXIV
(1946), 145-151.

REID, WILLIAM S. *The Present Significance of Calvin's View of
Tradition.* Redhill, 1966. 22 pages.

RENAN, ERNST. *John Calvin,* in *Studies of Religious History and
Criticism,* tr. O. B. Frothingham. N.Y. and Paris, 1864. pp.
285-297.

SCHAFF, PHILIP. *The Calvinistic System in the Light of Reason
and Scripture.* AR XVII (1892), 329-338.

STAUFFER, RICHARD. *The Humanness of John Calvin,* tr.
George H. Shriver. Nashville, Tenn., 1971. 96 pages. Paperback.
A sympathetic attempt to set the record straight on Calvin's
intolerance.

CALVIN'S ASSOCIATES: BEZA, FAREL, VIRET

BAIRD, HENRY MARTYN. *Theodore Beza, the Counsellor of
the French Reformation, 1519-1605* (Heroes of the Reformation). N.Y. and Ld., 1899. xxi+376 pages.

BLACKBURN, W. M. *William Farel and the Story of the Swiss Reform.* Philadelphia, 1865. 357 pages.

KINGDON, ROBERT M. *The First Expression of Theodore Beza's
Political Ideas.* ARG XLVI (1955), 88-99.
The Economic Behavior of Ministers in Geneva in the Middle

of the Sixteenth Century. ARG L (1959), 33-39.
Investigates the years 1550-1570 and argues that the clergy
influenced the growth of capitalism.

FUHRMANN, PAUL T. *Extraordinary Christianity. The Life and
Thought of Alexander Viret.* Philadelphia, 1964. 125 pages.
Very useful introduction; includes a bibliography.

LINDNER, ROBERT D. *The Political Ideas of Pierre Viret.* Geneva,
1964. 217 pages.
Indispensable. Contains detailed bibliography.
*Pierre Viret and the Sixteenth Century French Protestant
Revolutionary Tradition.* JMH XXXVIII (1966), 125-137.
Pierre Viret and the Sixteenth Century English Protestants.
ARG LVIII (1967), 149-170.

LINSE, EUGENE. *Beza and Melanchthon on Political Obligation.*
CTM XLI (1970), 27-35.

RAITT, JILL. *The Eucharistic Theology of Theodore Beza: the
Consolidation of the Reformed Tradition* (AAR Studies in
Religion). Chambersburg, Pa., 1971. pp.?

VAN SCHELVEN, A. A. *Beza's De Iure Magistratuum in Subditos.*
ARG XLV (1954), 62-81.
The fate of a document by Calvin's successor on resistance
to political authority.

GENEVA

BARROIS, GEORGES A. *Calvin and the Genevans.* TT XXI 4
(1965), 458-465.

COLLINS, ROSS W. *Calvin and the Libertines of Geneva,* ed. F.
D. Blackly. Toronto, 1968. ix+210 pages.

COWELL, HENRY J. *The 16th Century English-Speaking Refugee
Churches at Geneva and Frankfort.* HSL XVI (1937-41),
209-230.

KINGDON, ROBERT M. *Social Welfare in Calvin's Geneva.* AHR
LXXVI 1 (1971), 50-69.

Mélanges d'Histoire du XVIe Siècle (Travaux d'Humanisme et
Renaissance series). Geneva, 1970.
KINGDON, ROBERT M. *The Deacons of the Reformed
Church in Calvin's Geneva.* 81-90.

MONTER, WILLIAM E. *Calvin's Geneva* (New Dimensions in
History: Historical Cities series). N.Y., 1967. xv+250 pages.

Excellent analysis of the city, with charts and illustrations.
Witchcraft in Geneva, 1537-1662. JMH XLIII (1971), 179-
204.

REID, WILLIAM S. *Calvin and the Founding of the Academy of
Geneva. Westminster Theological Journal* XVIII (1955), 1-33.

RUSHDOONY, R. J. *Calvin in Geneva: the Sociology of Justificatio
by Faith. Westminster Theological Journal* XV (1952), 11-
39.

CALVINISM IN THE PALATINATE

CLASEN, CLAUS P. *The Palatinate in European History, 1559-
1660.* Oxford, 1963. 48 pages.
An analysis of Heidelberg as a center of German Calvinism.

OLEVIANUS AND URSINUS

GOEBEL, MAX. *Dr. Casper Olevianus.* MR VII (1855), 294-
306.
Dr. Zacharia Ursinus. MR VII (1855), 629-637.

HARBAUGH, HENRY. *The Fathers of the Reformed Church,*
6 vols., 1857-1888.
Volume 1 includes among others Ursinus and Olevianus.

NEVIN, J. W. *Zacharias Ursinus.* MR III (1851), 490-512.

*Sudhoff's Olevianus, a Translation of a Portion of Casper Olevianus,
"Firm Ground of Christian Doctrine in the German Reformed
Church" with the Notes of Dr. Charles Sudhoff, translated
by H. R.* MR VIII (1856), 163-198.

HEIDELBERG CATECHISM

BARTH, KARL. *The Heidelberg Catechism for Today,* tr. Shirley
C. Guthrie, Jr. Richmond, 1964. 141 pages.
A classic exposition.

BRUGGINK, DONALD J. (ED.) *Guilt, Grace, and Gratitude. A*

Commentary on the Heidelberg Catechism, Commemorating Its 400th Anniversary. N.Y., 1963. 226 pages.
Non-scholarly expositions on the various portions of the Catechism by ministers and theologians.

GERHART, E. V. *The Sacramental Theory of the H. C.* MR XIX (1872), 534-563.
The Doctrine of Baptism as Taught in the H. C. MR XX (1873), 537-572.

GOOD, JAMES I. *New Light on the H. C.* (Central Theol. Sem. Inauguration, Tiffin, Ohio, 1907), 3-26.
The H. C. and Its 350th Anniversary. JPHS VII (1913-14), 96-104.

HARBAUGH, HENRY. *The H. C. . . . Its Formation and First Introduction in the Palatinate.* MR XI (1859), 47-62.
The Literature of the H. C. MR XII (1860), 601-625.

The Heidelberg Catechism With Commentary. 400th Anniversary Edition 1563-1963, tr. Allen O. Miller and H. Eugene Osterhaven. Boston, Philadelphia, 1963. 224 pages.
Includes bibliography.

KLOOSTER, FRED H. *Recent Studies on the Heidelberg Catechism.* CTJ 1 (1966), 73-78.
The Heidelberg Catechism and Comparative Symbolics. CTJ I (1966), 205-212.

LEVAN, F. K. *Dalton on the H. C.* MR XX (1873), 573-582.

MASSELINK, EDWARD J. *The Heidelberg Story.* Grand Rapids, 1964. 121 pages.
A popular account of the origins and history of the Heidelberg Catechism and its influence.

MILLER, ALLEN O. and OSTERHAVEN, M. EUGENE. *Heidelberg Catechism 1563-1963.* TT XIX 4 (1963), 536-550.

NEVIN, J. W. *The H. C.* MR IV (1852), 155-190.

PENNINGS, BURRELL. *A Comparison of the Heidelberg Catechism With the Westminster Confession and the Augsburg Confession.* RfR IX (1955), 26-38.

REFORMED CHURCH REVIEW 4 S. XVII, No. 2, April 1913, devoted to the 350th anniversary of the Heidelberg Catechism.
KIEFER, J. SPANGLER, *An Appreciation of the H. C.* 133-151.

HINKE, WILLIAM J. *The Origin of the H. C.* 152-166.
DAHLMANN, A. E. *The Theology of the H. C.* 167-181.
RICHARDS, GEORGE W. *A Comparative Study of the H. C., Luther's Smaller and the Westminster Shorter Catechism.* 193-212.
Symposium on the H. C. 213-249.
SCHAFF, PHILIP, *The H. C.* MR XXIII (1876), 88-119.
SPYKMAN, GORDON J. *Never on Your Own. A Course Study on the Heidelberg Catechism and Compendium.* Grand Rapids, 1969. 202 pages.
For use in Reformed Catechetics.
THELEMANN, OTTO. *An Aid to the H. C.,* tr. M. Peters. Reading, Pa., 1896. xxiv+512 pages.
The text with comments from such men as Ursinus and Olevianus.
THOMPSON, BARD ET AL. *Essays on the Heidelberg Catechism.* Philadelphia, 1963. 192 pages.
Pertinent essays:
THOMPSON, BARD. *Historical Background of the Catechism.* 8-29.
The Reformed Church in the Palatinate. 31-52.
BERKHOF, HENDRIKUS. *The Catechism in Historical Context.* 79-92.
The Catechism as an Expression of Our Faith. 93-122.

THE REFORMATION IN FRANCE

BIBLIOGRAPHY

MORAND, JULIA P. M. *Catalogue or Bibliography of the Library of the Huguenot Society of America.* N.Y., 1920. xi+351 pages.
Covers the older literature extensively.

SOURCES

BOWER, HERBERT M. *The Fourteen of Meaux: an Account of the Earliest "Reformed Church" within France Proper, Organized by Estienne Mangin, and Pierre LeClarc: Who with Twelve Other Persons Suffered Death by Fire in 1546.* Ld.,

1894. 124 pages. Reprint: HSL V (1894-96).

CASTELNAU, MICHEL DE. *Memoirs of the Reigns of Francis II and Charles IX of France . . . Done into English.* Ld., 1724 [tr. George Kelly]. 426 pages.

[LANGUET, HUBERT]. *A Defense of Liberty Against Tyrants; a Translation of the Vindiciae Contra Tyrannos, by Junius Brutus* [pseud.] *with an Historical Introduction by Harold J. Laski . . .* (Classics of social and political science). Ld., 1924. 229 pages. Reprint of the translation of 1689.
On the authorship consult Ernest Barker, CHJ III (1930), 164-181.

[MORNAY, CHARLOTTE ARBALESTE DE.] *A Hugenot Family in the Sixteenth Century. The Memoirs of Philippe de Mornay . . . Written by His Wife,* tr. Lucy Crump. Ld., N.Y. [1926?]. vii+300 pages.

Memoires of Margaret de Valois. Ld., 1895. xxiv+286 pages.

QUICK, JOHN (COMP.) *Synodicon in Gallia Reformata; or, The Acts, Decisions, Decrees, and Canons of Those Famous National Councils of the Reformed Churches in France.* 2 vols. Ld., 1692.

THOMPSON, JAMES W. (ED.) *The Letters and Documents of Armand de Gontaut, Baron de Biron, Marshal of France (1524-1592), Collected by the Late Sidney H. Ehrman.* Berkeley, 1936. 2 vols.

THOU, JACQUES AUGUSTE DE. *The History of the Bloody Massacres of the Protestants in France in the Year of Our Lord, 1572* [tr. Edward Stephens]. Ld., 1694. 196 pages.

WALSH, DORIS V. (COMP.) *Checklist of French Political Pamphlets 1560-1644 in the Newberry Library.* iv+204 pages.

GENERAL TREATMENTS

BROWNING, WILLIAM SHIPTON. *The History of the Huguenots During the Sixteenth Century.* 2 vols. Ld., 1829. New ed. Philadelphia, 1845. xii+452 pages.
Well documented, the sort of book from which one can still glean.

HANNA, WILLIAM. *Wars of the Huguenots.* Edinburgh, 1871. x+314 pages; N.Y., 1882. 344 pages.

Deliberately avoids the "purely religious aspects."

JERVIS, W. H. *A History of the Church of France from the Concordat of Bologna, A. D., 1516 to the Revolution.* 2 vols. Ld., 1872.
Slight on the Reformation.

KELLY, CALEB GUYER. *French Protestantism 1559-1562* (John Hopkins University Studies in history and political science). Baltimore, 1918. 185 pages.
Also published as a dissertation in 1916. Particular attention is given to social and economic forces.

MARTYN, WILLIAM CARLOS. *History of the Hugenots.* N.Y., 1866. 528 pages.
Slight.

PALM, FRANKLIN CHARLES. *Calvinism and the Religious Wars* (Berkshire Studies in European History). N.Y., 1932. ix+117 pages.
The beginner will make no mistake to start here and then go on to Kelly and Thompson.

STONE, DONALD. *France in the Sixteenth Century. A Medieval Society Transformed.* Englewood, 1969. x+180 pages.

THOMPSON, JAMES WESTFALL. *The Wars of Religion in France 1559-1576.* Chicago, 1909. xv+635.
Takes account of the vast amount of new material since Baird and Whitehead. Particular attention is given to the effect of agricultural and weather conditions on the fortunes of the wars.

TILLEY, ARTHUR AUGUSTUS. *The French Wars of Religion* (Helps for the Students of History, No. 8). Ld., 1919. 54 pages.
Brief introduction to the literature.

BRIEF NOTICES

ANONYMOUS. *Protestantism in France.* TR II (1865).
1559-1598, pp. 1-21.
1598-1789, pp. 129-150.
1789-1864, pp. 353-378.

BÖHL, EDOUARD. *Two Phases of the History of the Hugenots,* tr. Dunlop Moore. PRR IX (1898), 83-100.

DUBBS, J. H. *The Hugenots.* RQR XXXVI (1889), 432-453.

SPECIAL PHASES

BLANC, RENÉ. *Lutheranism in France.* LQ VI 2 (1954), 102-
112.
Contains a description of 16th Century beginnings.
CAILLIET, EMILE. *The Reformed Tradition in the Life and
Thought of France.* TT I 3 (1944), 349-360.
ENGLAND, SYLVIA L. *The Massacre at Saint Bartholomew.*
London, 1938. 284 pages.
Contains a good bibliography.
ERLANGER, PHILIPPE. *St. Bartholomew's Night*, tr. Patrick
O'Brian. London, N.Y., 1962. 285 pages.
An authoritative French work, with bibliography.
HEMPSALL, DAVID S. *The Languedoc 1520-1540: a Study of
Pre-Calvinist Heresy in France.* ARG LXII (1972), 225-243.
Describes French reform movements before the appearance
of Calvin's *Institutes.*
JACKSON, SAMUEL MACAULEY. *The Edict of Nantes, Revised
by W. E. Gillette.* N.Y., 1898.
Reprint from the Tercentenary volume of the HSA.
SCHAFF, PHILIP. *History of the Edict of Nantes, Paper Read
March 1, 1889.* HSA II (1888-94), 85-114.
SIMPSON, LESLEY BYRD. *The Struggle for Provence, 1593-
1596* (Univ. Cal. Publ. in History. XVII, 1). Berkeley,
Cal., 1929. 23 pages.
SUTHERLAND, N. M. *Calvinism and the Conspiracy of Amboise.*
H XLVII (1962), 111-138.
TEDESCHI, JOHN A. *Two Italian Translations of Beza and Cal-
vin.* ARG LV (1964), 70-74.
Beza's *Harangues* at the colloquy of Poissy in 1561 between
Calvinists and Roman Catholics, and portions of Calvin's
Institutes.
TILLEY, ARTHUR. *Some Pamphlets of the French Wars of Re-
ligion.* EHR XIV (1899), 450-470.
WHITE, HENRY. *The Massacre of St. Bartholomew.* London,
1868. xviii+505 pages.
Documented.

ECONOMIC QUESTIONS

DAVIS, NATALIE Z. *Strikes and Salvation at Lyons.* ARG LVI (1965), 48-64.
Shows the relationship between religion and economics among the printers of Lyons in the 1560s.

HAUSER, HENRI. *The French Reformation and the French People in the Sixteenth Century.* AHR IV (1899), 217-227.

POLITICAL QUESTIONS

ARMSTRONG, E. *The French Wars of Religion, Their Political Aspects.* Ld., 1892. xi+128 pages.
Political Theory of the Huguenots. EHR IV (1889), 13-40.

BAIRD, HENRY M. *Hotman and the "Franco-Gallia".* AHR I (1896), 609-630.

BEAME, E. M. *The Limits of Toleration in Sixteenth-Century France. Studies in the Renaissance* XIII (1966), 250-265.

CHURCH, WILLIAM F. *Constitutional Thought in Sixteenth-Century France. A Study in the Evolution of Ideas* (Harvard Historical Studies). London, 1941. 360 pages.

FOSTER, HERBERT DARLING. *The Political Theories of Calvinists before the Puritan Exodus to America.* AHR XXI (1915), 481-503.

HAUBEN, PAUL J. *The Salcedos: a Study in Loyalty and Disloyalty in the Wars of Religion.* ARG LX (1963), 174-188.
Illustrates the attitude of French nobility during the wars in France and Holland, through the lives of Pierre (father) and Nicholas (son) Salcedo.

KINGDON, ROBERT M. *Geneva and the Coming of the Wars of Religion in France, 1555-1563.* Geneva, 1956. 163 pages.
Based on the biographies of 88 pastors.
The Political Resistance of the Calvinists in France and the Low Countries. CH XXVII 3 (1958), 220-233.
Some French Reactions to the Council of Trent. CH XXXIII 2 (1964), 149-156.
Geneva and the Consolidation of the French Protestant Movement, 1564-1572. Madison, 1967. 241 pages.
Excellent study on Geneva's involvement in the French wars of religion, and the Calvinist resistance theory.
Contains bibliography.

KOENIGSBERGER, H. G. *Organization of Revolutionary Parties in France and the Netherlands during the Sixteenth Century.* JMH XXVII (1955), 335-351.

PALM, FRANKLIN CHARLES. *Politics and Religion in Sixteenth Century France, a Study of the Career of Henry of Montmorency-Damville.* Boston, N.Y., 1927, xi+299 pages.
Careful work, important for Languedoc.
New edition, Gloucester, 1969.

REYNOLDS, BEATRICE. *Proponents of Limited Monarchy in Sixteenth Century France: Francis Hotman and Jean Bodin* (Studies in history, economics and public law edited by the Faculty of Political Science of Columbia University). N.Y., Ld., 1931. 210 pages.

SALMON, JOHN H. (COMP.) *The French Wars of Religion: How Important Were Religious Factors?* (Problems in European Civilization series.) Boston, 1967. xxii+104 pages.
Contains excerpts from the historiography of the religious wars and a bibliographical essay.

THOMPSON, JAMES W. *The Wars of Religion in France, 1559-1576. The Huguenots, Catherine de Medici, Philip II.* N.Y., 1909.
New edition, 1957. xv+635 pages.

VAN DYKE, PAUL. *The Estates of Pontoise.* EHR XXVIII (1913), 472-495.

BIOGRAPHY

Francis I

HACKETT, FRANCIS. *Francis I.* N.Y., 1935. 448 pages. New edition, Garden City, N.Y., 1970.
A classic biography, provides political background for the French Reformation.

MASSON, GUSTAVE. *Episodes of French History Edited from François Pierre G. Guizot's History of France.*
III. *Francis I and the Sixteenth Century.*
Pt. I. *Francis I and the Emperor Charles.* Ld., 1881. 154 pages.
Pt. II. *Francis I and the Renaissance.* Ld., 1881. viii+108 pages.

TILLEY, ARTHUR. *Humanism under Francis I.* EHR XV (1900), 456-478.

Henry II

ARMSTRONG, E. *The Italian Wars of Henry II.* EHR XXX (1915), 602-612.

BAIRD, HENRY M. *The "Chambre Ardente" under Henry II.* PRR II (1891), 400-411.
Based on Nathaniel Weiss.

WILLIAMS, NOEL H. *Henri II: His Court and Times.* Ld., 1910. xxii+379 pages.
Lumbering style.

Catherine de Medici

HERETIER, JEAN. *Catherine de Medici,* tr. Charlotte Haldance. London, 1941. 480 pages. New edition, 1963.
First work devoted to historical objectivity; contains bibliography.

NEALE, JOHN E. *The Age of Catherine de Medici.* London, 1943. 111 pages.
Four lectures, treating various aspects of the period.

SICHEL, EDITH. *Catherine de' Medici and the French Reformation.* Ld., 1905. xvi+329 pages. New edition, 1969.
The Later Years of Catherine de' Medici. Ld., 1908. viii+446 pages.
Anecdotal.
New edition, 1969.

SUTHERLAND, NICOLA M. *Catherine de Medici and the Ancien Régime.* London, 1966. 36 pages.
A fresh approach based on Catherine's letters.

WATSON, FRANCIS. *The Life and Times of Catherine de Medici.* London, N.Y., 1935. xi+327 pages.

WEBER, BERNARD C. *The Council of Fontainbleau (1560).* ARG XLV (1954), 43-61.
Catherine's attempt to save the throne of Francis II.

Henry IV

HURST, QUENTIN. *Henry of Navarre.* London, N.Y., 1938. 319 pages.
Contains bibliography.

MASSON, GUSTAVE. *Episodes of French History Edited from François Pierre G. Guizot's History of France.* IV. *Henry IV and the End of the Wars of Religion.* Ld., 1881. viii+166 pages.

SEDGWICK, HENRY DWIGHT. *Henry of Navarre,* Indianapolis, 1930. 324 pages.

The "gallant" Henry.

WILLERT, P. F. *Henry of Navarre and the Huguenots in France* (Heroes of the Nations). N.Y., 1893. v+478 pages.

Competent work for the general reader.

Coligny

BERSIER, EUGÈNE ARTHUR FRANÇOIS. *Coligny; the Earlier Life of the Great Huguenot,* tr. Annie Harwood Holmden. Ld., 1884. xxxvi+351 pages.

Has the earmarks of competency.

BLACKBURN, WILLIAM MAXWELL. *Admiral Coligny and the Rise of the Huguenots.* 2 vols. Philadelphia, 1869.

Laudatory, erudition slight.

WHITEHEAD, ARTHUR WHISTON. *Gaspard de Coligny, Admiral of France.* Ld., 1904. ix+387 pages.

Careful workmanship.

The Guises

BROWN, HORATIO. *The Assassination of the Guise as Described by the Venetian Ambassador.* EHR X (1895), 304-32.

Documents in Italian, discussion in English.

EVENNETT, HENRY OUTRAM. *The Cardinal of Lorraine and the Council of Trent.* Cambridge, Eng., 1930. xvii+536 pages.

Competent.

The Cardinal of Lorraine and the Colloquy of Poissy. CHJ, II (1927), 133-150.

JENSEN, DELAMAR. *Diplomacy and Dogmatism: Bernardino de Mendoza and the French Catholics.* Cambridge, 1964. xii+322 pages.

Doctoral thesis. Contains bibliography.

SEDGWICK, HENRY D. *The House of Guise.* Indianapolis, N.Y., 1938. 324 pages.

Portrays the Protestant leadership in the Dutch revolt against Spain; includes bibliography.

Huguenots

BAIRD, HENRY MARTYN. *History of the Rise of the Huguenots of France.* 2 vols. N.Y., 1879.
 The Huguenots and Henry of Navarre. 2 vols. N.Y., 1886.
 The Huguenots and the Revocation of the Edict of Nantes. 2 vols. N.Y., 1895.
 Solid, abreast of the research of the day, strongly Protestant.

COUDY, JULIEN (ED.) *The Huguenot Wars,* tr. Julie Kernan. Philadelphia, 1969. xxi+405 pages.
 Collection of contemporary texts discussing the wars of religion.

DELMAS, LOUIS. *The Huguenots of La Rochelle,* tr. G. L. Catlin. N.Y., 1880. xiv+295 pages.
 About half the book deals with the sixteenth century.

DODGE, G. *The Political Theory of the Huguenots of the Dispersion, With Special Reference to the Thought and Influence of Pierre Jurieu.* N.Y., 1947. ix+287 pages.

GRANT, ARTHUR JAMES. *The Huguenots.* Hamden, Conn., 1969. 255 pages.

MORAND, JULIA P. (COMP.) *Catalogue of Bibliography of the Library of the Huguenot Society of America.* 2d ed. Baltimore, 1971. xi+351 pages.

PINETTE, G. L. *Freedom in Huguenot Doctrine.* ARG L (1959), 200-233.
 Shows the influence of early Huguenot political thought on later developments in France.

ZOFF, OTTO. *The Huguenots,* tr. E. B. Ashton and J. Mayo. N.Y., 1942. vii+340 pages.
 Stimulating work by a Czechoslovakian Catholic.

Marot

MORLEY, HENRY. *Clement Marot and Other Studies.* 2 vols. Ld., 1871.

Postel

BOUWSMA, WILLIAM J. *Concordia Mundi: the Career and Thought of Guillaume Postel (1510-1581)* (Harvard Historical Monographs). Cambridge, 1957. vi+328 pages.
 Doctoral thesis, includes bibliography.

SPECIAL TOPICS

BIETENHOLZ, PETER G. *Basle and France in the 16th Century: the Basle Humanists and Printers in Their Contacts With Francophone Culture* (Travaux d'Humanisme et Renaissance series). Geneva, 1971. pp.?

PRATT, WALDO S. *The Music of the French Psalter of 1562* (Columbia University Studies in Musicology series). N.Y., 1939. x+213 pages.

The melodies are printed in modern notation in the appendix.

ROELKER, NANCY L. *The Appeal of Calvinism to French Noblewomen in the 16th Century: a Study in Psycho-History. The Journal of Interdisciplinary History* II (1971/72), pp.?

THE ITALIAN REFORMERS

BIBLIOGRAPHY

CHIMINELLI, PIERO. *Bibliografia della storia della Riforma religiosa in Italia (Biblioteca di studi religiosi N. 10)*. Rome, 1921. 301+8 pages.

Lists many titles in English.

TEDESCHI, JOHN A. *The Literature of the Italian Reformation: an Exhibition Catalogue.* Chicago, 1971.

SOURCES

COMBA, EMILIO. *Life of Galeazzo Caracciolo from the Italian of Nicolao Balbani 1587 Republished by Professor Emilio Comba Translated by Maria Betts.* Ld., 1907. vii+60 pages.

CURIO, COELIUS SECUNDUS. *A Defense of the True and Old Authority of Christ's Church, an Oration of Coelius, the Second Curio, . . . against Antony Florebell of Mutiny, Translated Out of the Latin into English by Ihon Philpott.* Reprint in *The Examination and Writings of John Philpot* edited for the Parker Society by Robert Eden. Cambridge, Eng., 1842. pp. 319-432.

DUFFIELD, G. E. and MCLELLAND, J. C. (EDS.) *The Life, Early Letters, and Eucharistic Writings of Peter Martyr.* (Courtenay Library of Reformation Classics, 5). Appleford, Abingdon, Berkshire, 1971. pp.?

GIBBINGS, RICHARD. *Records of the Roman Inquisition; Case of a Minorite Friar, Who Was Sentenced by St. Charles Borromeo to Be Walled Up, and Who Having Escaped Was Burned in Effigy, Edited with an English Translation and Notes.* Dublin. 1853. 23 pages.

PLUMPTRE, C. E. *The Tragedy by Bernardino Ochino Reprinted from Bishop Ponet's Translation Out of Ochino's Latin Manuscript in 1549.* Convent Garden, 1899. xxi+255 pages.

The Benefit of Christ's Death: Probably Written by Aonio Paleario: Reprinted in Fac-simile from the Italian Edition of 1543: Together with the French Translation Printed in 1551, to Which Is Added an English Version Made in 1548 by Edward Courtenay with an Introduction by Churchill Babington. Ld., 1855. xciv+[142]+x+188 pages.

VALDÉS, JUÁN DE. Wiffen, Benjamin B. *Life and Writings of Juán de Valdes with a Translation from the Italian of His Hundred and Ten Considerations by John T. Betts.* Ld., 1865. xiii+590 pages.

Alfabeto Christiano from the Italian of 1546 by Benjamin B. Wiffen. Ld., 1861. lxxxii+246 pages.

XVII Opuscules Translated from the Spanish and Italian and Edited by John T. Betts. Ld., 1882. xii+188 pages.

Biblical Commentaries, all edited and translated by John T. Betts, and all four having appended *The Lives of the Twin Brothers, Juán and Alfonso de Valdés by Edward Boehmer,* from the *Bibliotheca Wiffeniana.* In 1 and 4 the pagination is xvi+31, in 2 and 3 xiv+29.

Juán de Valdés' Commentary on the First Book of the Psalms Privately Printed, 1894. xxiii+313 pages.

Juán de Valdés' Commentary upon the Gospel of St. Matthew. Ld., 1882. xi+512 pages.

Juán de Valdés' Commentary upon Our Lord's Sermon on the Mount (reprinted from the commentary on Matthew). Ld., 1882. 1+75 pages.

*Juán de Valdês' Commentary upon St. Paul's First Epistle
to the Church at Corinth.* Ld., 1883. xxv+312 pages.

GENERAL TREATMENTS

BETTS, JOHN T. *A Glance at the Italian Reformation Translated
from the German of Leopold Witte.* Ld., 1885.
I have not seen this. It appears to be a translation of *Das
Evangelium in Italien,* Gotha, 1861.

BROWN, G. K. *Italy and the Reformation to 1550.* Oxford, Eng.,
1933. vii+324 pages.
A competent sketch based on published sources.
Reprint, N.Y., 1971.

CHURCH, FREDERIC C. *The Italian Reformers 1534-64.* N.Y.,
1932. xii+428 pages.
The fruit of research in the archives. More attention is given
to politics than to theology.

HARE, CHRISTOPHER [pseud. of Marian Andrews]. *Men and
Women of the Italian Reformation.* Ld., 1914. xvi+309 pages.
Brief popular survey of the entire movement.

M'CRIE, THOMAS. *The Works of Thomas M'Crie,* a new ed. vol.
III. *The Reformation in Italy, The Reformation in Spain.*
Edinburgh, 1856. xiv+218 pages.
Good work in its day.

MARRIOTT, W. *The Italian Swiss Protestants of the Grisons . . .*
with two introductory prefaces, by the Hon. B. W. Noel and
J. Currie. Ld., [1846].
Work not seen, entry from the British Museum catalog.

STOUGHTON, JOHN. *Footprints of Italian Reformers.* Ld., Preface 1881. vi+308 pages.
Slight.

TRINKAUS, CHARLES E. *In Our Image and Likeness: Humanity
and Divinity in Italian Humanist Thought.* 2 vols. London,
1970. xxxiii+985 pages.
Excellent on the background of Italian Reform movements.
Part IV deals with the Renaissance in Italy. Argues for a
close tie of religious and humanist ideas.

WALSCHE, E. H. *Under the Inquisition, Story of the Reformation
in Italy.* Ld., 1904. Religious Tract Soc. (Work not seen.)

BIOGRAPHY

Carnesecchi

BETTS, JOHN T. *A Glance at the Italian Inquisition, a Sketch of Pietro Carnesecchi Translated from the German of Leopold Witte (Pietro Carnesecchi, ein Bild aus der Italienischen Märtyrergeschichte,* in the series *Der Evangelische Glaube nach dem Zeugnis der Geschichte,* No. 6, Halle, 1883). Ld., 1885. 87 pages.

GIBBINGS, RICHARD. *Report of the Trial and Martyrdom of Pietro Carnesecchi, Sometime Secretary to Pope Clement VII and Apostolic Protonotary, Transcribed from the Original Manuscript.* Ld., 1856.

Caleagnini

BREEN, QUIRINUS. *Celio Caleagnini (1479-1541).* CH XXI 3 (1952), 225-238.
On the relationship of humanism and reformation.

Diodati

BETTS, MARIA. *Life of Giovanni Diodati, Genevese Theologian and Translator of the Italian Bible, 1607.* Ld., 1905. 56 pages.
Not seen, entry from the English Book List.

Gonzaga

HARE, CHRISTOPHER [MARIAN ANDREWS]. *A Princess of the Italian Reformation, Giulia Gonzaga.* N.Y., 1912. xxiv+ 292 pages.
Based on unpublished correspondence.

Manfredi

GIBBINGS, RICHARD. *Were "Heretics" Ever Burned Alive at Rome? A Report of the Proceedings in the Roman Inquisition against Fulgentio Manfredi; Taken from the Original Manuscript Brought from Italy by a French Officer, and Edited, with a Parallel English Version, and Illustrative Additions.* Ld., 1852. 56 pages.

Morata

[SOUTHEY, MRS. CAROLINE ANNE (BOWLES)]. *Olympia Morata*. Ld., 1836. xvi+303+6 pages of ancient psalms with musical notation. Pages 197-303 devoted to translations.

TURNBULL, ROBERT. *Olympia Morata Her Life and Times*. Boston 1836. 234 pages. Slight.

Ochino

BENRATH, KARL. *Bernardino Ochino of Siena*, tr. Helen Zimmern. New York, 1877. xvi+vii+304.
    Thorough work.

CUTHBERT, FATHER *O.S.F.C. The Capuchins*. 2 vols. New York, 1929.
    Valuable for the early days of Ochino.

GORDON, ALEXANDER. *Bernardino Tommasini* (Ochino). TR, XIII (1876), 532-561.

GILBERT, WILLIAM. *The Struggle in Ferrara; a Story of the Reformation in Italy*. Philadelphia, 1871. 145 pages.
    Fiction, deals largely with Ochino.

SMYTH, C. H. *Cranmer and the Reformation under Edward VI*. Cambridge, Eng., 1926. x+315 pages.
    On Ochino in England.

Paleario

BLACKBURN, WILLIAM M. *Aonio Paleario*. Philadelphia, 1866. 112 pages.
    Slight.

YOUNG, M. *The Life and Times of Aonio Paleario*. 2 vols. Ld., 1860.
    A veritable history of the whole movement in Italy.

Pole

HAILE, MARTIN. *Life of Reginald Pole*. 2d ed. Ld., 1911 xi+ 554 pages.

VAN DYKE, PAUL. *The Mission of Cardinal Pole to Enforce the Bull of Deposition against Henry VIII*. EHR, XXXVII (1922), 422-423.
    Reginald Pole and Thomas Cromwell: an Examination of the Apologia ad Carolum Quintum. AHR, IX (1904), 696-724.

ROUTLEDGE, F. J. *Six Letters of Cardinal Pole to the Countess of Huntington.* EHR, XXVIII (1913), 527-531.

Vermigli

MCCLELLAND, JOSEPH C. *The Reformed Doctrine of Predestination.* SJT VIII 3 (1955), 255-271.
On Peter Martyr.
The Visible Words of God: an Exposition of the Sacramental Theology of Peter Martyr Vermigli, A.D. 1500-1562. Grand Rapids, 1957; London, 1957. ix+291 pages.
Stresses the ecumenical aspects of Peter's eucharistic thought.

MCNAIR, PHILIP. *Peter Martyr in Italy: an Anatomy of Apostacy.* Oxford, 1967. xxii+325 pages.
An authoritative biography, lists Peter's works.

PAIST, BENJAMIN F. JR. *Peter Martyr and the Colloquy of Poissy.* PTR XX (1922), 418-447, 616-646.
Scholarly.

SMYTH, C. H. *Cranmer and the Reformation under Edward VI.* Cambridge, Eng., 1926. x+315 pages.
On Peter Martyr in England.

TOPICS

ANDERSON, MARVIN W. *Luther's Sola Fide in Italy: 1542-1551.* CH XXXVIII 1 (1969), 25-42.

DE WIND, HENRY A. *Anabaptism and Italy.* CH XXI 1 (1952), 20-38.

LOGAN, O. M. T. *Grace and Justification: Some Italian Views of the Sixteenth and Early Seventeenth Centuries.* JEH XX 1 (1969), 67-78.

THE SOCINIAN MOVEMENT: ANTI-TRINITARIANS

SOURCES

REES, THOMAS. *The Racovian Catechism, with Notes and Illustrations, Translated from the Latin: to Which Is Prefixed a Sketch of the History of Unitarianism in Poland and Adjacent Countries.* Ld., 1818. cviii+404.

GENERAL TREATMENTS

ALLEN, JOSEPH HENRY and EDDY, RICHARD. *A History of the Unitarians and the Universalists in the United States* (American Church History Series, X). New York, 1894. 506 pages.
Both give a sketch of the European background in the sixteenth century.

KOT, STANISLAW. *Socinianism in Poland. The Social and Political Ideas of the Polish Antitrinitarians in the Sixteenth and Seventeenth Centuries,* tr. Earl M. Wilbur. Boston, 1957. xxvii+226 pages.

RICHARDS, GEORGE W. *Socinianism and Evangelical Protestantism Compared.* RCR, 4S. XIV (1910), 225-236.

ROTONDO, ANTONIO. *Calvin and the Italian Anti-Trinitarians,* tr. John and Anne Tedeschi (Reformation Essays and Studies). St. Louis, 1968. 28 pages.
Shows the evidence of an independent movement after Anti-Trinitarians had to leave Switzerland.

WILBUR, E. MORSE. *Our Unitarian Heritage.* Boston, 1925. xiii+495 pages.
A History of Unitarianism. Cambridge, Mass., 1945. 2 vols.
Vol. I: *Socinianism and Its Antecedents.* xiii+617 pages.
An authoritative account of the history of Anti-Trinitarianism in the continental Reformation.
Vol. II: *In Transylvania, England and America.* 518 pages.
On the Reformation in Transylvania.

BIOGRAPHY

CORY, DAVID MUNROE. *Faustus Socinus.* Boston, 1932. ix+155 pages.
The best treatment, though inadequate.

GORDON, ALEXANDER. *The Sozzini and Their School.* TR XVI (1879), 293-322, 531-571.

HULME, EDWARD M. *Lelio Sozzini's Confession of Faith,* in *Persecution and Liberty, Essays in Honor of George Lincoln Burr.* New York, 1931, pp. 211-225.

WALLACE, ROBERT. *Antitrinitarian Biography, or Sketches of the Lives and Writings of Distinguished Antitrinitarians. . . .* 3 vols. Ld., 1850. Volume II deals with our period.

WILBUR, E. MORSE. *Faustus Socinus: an Estimate of His Life and Influence.* Bull. du Comité international des sciences historiques. Num. 18 (Fév. 1933), 48-60.
Competent survey.

THE REFORMATION IN SPAIN

BOEHMER, EDWARD. *Bibliotheca Wiffeniana Spanish Reformers of Two Centuries from 1520 Their Lives and Writings According to the Late Benjamin B. Wiffen's Plan and with the Use of His Materials.* 3 vols. Strassburg, Ld., 1874, 1883, 1904.
Documents in the original languages, biographies in English. Reprinted, New York, 1963.
HAMILTON, BERNICE. *Political Thought in Sixteenth-Century Spain: a Study of the Political Ideas of Vitoria, De Soto, Suarez, and Molina.* Oxford and New York, 1963. 201 pages.
Contains a bibliography.
HAUBEN, PAUL J. *Three Spanish Heretics and the Reformation: Antonio Del Corro, Cassiodoro De Reina, Cypriano De Valera* (Études de Philologie et d'Histoire 3). Geneva, 1967. xvi+142 pages.
HESS, ANDREW C. *The Moriscos: an Ottoman Fifth Column in Sixteenth-Century Spain.* AHR LXXIV 1 (1968), 1-25.
HIRSCH, ELIZABETH F. *Portugese Humanists and the Inquisition in the Sixteenth Century.* ARG LXVI (1955), 47-67.
LONGHURST, JOHN E. *Erasmus and the Spanish Inquisition: the Case of Juán de Valdés.* Albuquerque, 1950. 114 pages.
An objective study of the relations of the Erasmists.
Luther and the Spanish Inquisition. The Case of Diego de Uceda 1528-1529 (University of New Mexico Publications in History). Albuquerque, 1953. 76 pages.
The Alumbrados of Toledo: Juan del Castillo and the Lucenas. ARG XLV (1954), 233-252.
The story of "Lutheran" martyrs in Spain.
Luther's Ghost in Spain (1517-1546). Lawrence, Kan., 1969. 393 pages.
Investigates the influence of Lutherans, Erasmians, and the

trial of Juan de Vergara. The Appendix sketches all Lutherans
and their influence in Spain; includes bibliography.

M'CRIE, THOMAS. *The Works of Thomas M'Crie*, a new ed. vol.
III. *The Reformation in Italy, The Reformation in Spain.*
Edinburgh, 1856. xiv+218 pages.

PETRIE, CHARLES A. *Philip II of Spain.* New York, 1963. 318
pages.
Focuses on his international activities.

ROTH, CECIL. *The Spanish Inquisition.* London, 1937. xv+320
pages.

RULE, JOHN C. and TEPASKE, JOHN J. (EDS.) *The Character
of Philip II: the Problem of Moral Judgments in History*
(Problems in European Civilization series). Boston, 1963.
Excerpts from 16th century and subsequent historians.
Contains a bibliographical essay.

SELIG, KARL L. *A German Collection of Spanish Books.* BHR
XIX (1957), 51-79.
Describes the Fugger library.

STOUGHTON, JOHN. *The Spanish Reformers, Their Memories
and Dwelling Places.* Ld., Preface 1883. vi+319 pages.
Slight.

WILKENS, C. A. *Spanish Protestants in the Sixteenth Century*,
compiled from the German of C. A. Wilkens by Rachel
Challice. Ld., 1897. xxiv+192 pages.
Solid.

THE REFORMATION IN THE NETHERLANDS

HISTORIOGRAPHY

BROMLEY, J. S. and KOSSMANN, E. H. (EDS.) *Britain and the
Netherlands* (Anglo-Dutch Historical Conference). 2 vols.
London, 1960-1964.
SCHÖFFER, IVO. *Protestantism in Flux During the Revolt
of the Netherlands.* vol. II, pp.?
SMIT, J. W. *The Present Position of Studies Regarding the
Revolt of the Netherlands.* vol. I, pp.?

GENERAL TREATMENTS

AXTERS, STEPHANUS. *The Spirituality of the Low Countries*, tr. Donald Attwater. London, 1954. 88 pages.

BLACK, J. B. *Queen Elizabeth, the Sea Beggars and the Capture of Brille 1572*. EHR XLVI (1931), 30-47.

BRANDT, GERARD. *The History of the Reformation and Other Ecclesiastical Transactions in and about the Low-Countries, from the Beginning of the Eighth Century, down to the Famous Synod of Dort, Inclusive*. 4 folio vols. Ld., 1720-23.
Copious citations from the sources.

CLARK, GEORGE N. *The Birth of the Dutch Republic* (Proceedings of the British Academy 32; the Raleigh Lecture on History). London, 1947. 31 pages.

GEYL, PIETER. *The Revolt of the Netherlands 1555-1609*. London, 1932. 310 pages.
Excellent.
History of the Low Countries, Episodes and Problems. The Trevelyan Lectures 1963 with Four Additional Essays. London, New York, 1964. vii+263 pages.
Contains the history of the Dutch revolt.
Debates With Historians. Cleveland, 1958, 1964. 283 pages.
The National State and the Writers of Netherlands History. 179-197.

GRIFFITHS, GORDON. *The Revolutionary Character of the Revolt of the Netherlands. Comparative Studies in Society and History* II (1960), 462-472.

KAMEN, HENRY A. *The Rise of Toleration*. New York, 1967. 256 pages.
Contains a section on the Dutch revolt and William of Orange's policy of toleration.

MARTYN, CARLOS. *The Dutch Reformation: A History of the Struggle in the Netherlands for Civil and Religious Liberty in the Sixteenth Century*. New York, 1868. 823 pages.
Notes on secondary works.

MERRIMAN, ROGER B. *Six Contemporaneous Revolutions*. (Glasgow University Publications) Glasgow, 1937. 32 pages.
Discussion of the Dutch revolt.

MOTLEY, JOHN LOTHROP. *The Rise of the Dutch Republic*.

3 vols. New York, 1856 and many subsequent editions. Condensed with introduction and notes by William Elliot Griffis, New York 1898.

Detailed, documented, fulsome.

SCHILLER, FRIEDRICH. *The Revolt of the United Netherlands with the Trial of Counts Egmont and Horn, and the Siege of Antwerp: to Which Is Added, The Disturbances in France Preceding the Reign of Henry IV*, tr. A. J. W. Morrison and L. Dora Schmitz (Bohn's Standard Library). Ld., 1897. 452 pages.

VLEKKE, BERNARD M. *Evolution of the Dutch Nation.* New York, 1945. xi+377 pages.

Contains bibliography.

SPECIAL PHASES

CADOUX, CECIL J. *Philip of Spain and the Netherlands. An Essay on Moral Judgements in History.* London, 1947. xv+251 pages.

DE JONG, PETER. *Can Political Factors Account for the Fact That Calvinism Rather than Anabaptism Came to Dominate the Dutch Reformation?* CH XXXIII 4 (1964), 392-417.

GRIFFITHS, GORDON. *William of Hornes, Lord of Heze, and the Revolt of the Netherlands, 1576-1580* (University of California Publications in History). Berkeley, Cal., 1954. 91 pages.

KOENIGSBERGER, H. G. *The Organization of Revolutionary Parties in France and the Netherlands During the Sixteenth Century.* JMH XXVII (1955), 335-351.

ARMINIUS

BANGS, CARL. *Arminius and the Reformation.* CH XXX 2 (1961), 155-170.
Arminius. A Study in the Dutch Reformation. Nashville, 1971. 384 pages.
A biography with a review of Arminius' theology. Contains bibliography.

BRANDT, CASPAR. *The Life of James Arminius*, tr. John Guthrie. Nashville, 1857. xxviii+405 pages.
Originally in Latin. Very dated.

COLIE, ROSALIE L. *Light and Enlightenment: a Study of the Cambridge Platonists and the Dutch Arminians.* Cambridge, New York, 1957. xiii+162 pages.
Chapter 1 deals with Arminian origins.

HAENDERDAAL, G. J. *The Life and Thought of Jacobus Arminius.* RL XXIX 4 (1960), 540-547.

NICHOLS, JAMES and WILLIAM. (TR.) *The Works of James Arminius, D.D.* 3 vols. London, 1825-1875. Photolithographic reprint, Grand Rapids, 1956.
Standard English edition.

TOPICS

DOLAN, JOHN P. *The Influence of Erasmus, Witzel and Cassander in the Church Ordinances and Reform Proposals of the United Dutchees of Cleve, etc.* RST LXXXIII (1957), xv-119.

GRIFFITHS, GORDON. *Democratic Ideas in the Revolt of the Netherlands.* ARG L (1959), 50-63.
Presents evidence from various Dutch sources that Dutch democratic ideas preceded British expressions of them.

ERASMUS
(See also under Luther in Relation to Contemporaries)

BIBLIOGRAPHY

MARGOLIN, JEAN C. *Douze Années de Bibliographie Erasmienne. 1950-1961.* Paris, 1963. 204 pages.
Contains a list of English language publications.

POLLET, J. V. *Erasmiana. Revue des Sciences Religieuses* XVII (1952), pp.?
Contains a list of English publications.

Studies in Philology. North Carolina University, 1906+. Devotes a section to Erasmus in each issue.

STUNT, TIMOTHY F. *Desiderius Erasmus: Some Recent Studies.* EQ XLII (1970), 230-235.
Incomplete bibliography.

THOMSON, D. F. S. *The Quincentenary of Erasmus and Some Recent Books. University of Toronto Quarterly* XXXIX 2 (1970), 181-185.

WORKS

BORN, LESTER K. (TR.) *The Education of a Christian Prince.* (Records of Civilization, Sources and Studies, 27). New York, 1936; 1965. ix+277 pages. Paperback.
With an introduction on Erasmus and on ancient and medieval political thought.
Collected Works of Erasmus, in preparation by the University of Toronto Press.
See progress reports and bibliographies on Erasmus in *Erasmus in English,* a newsletter published by the University of Toronto Press.
DEVEREUX, E. J. *A Checklist of English Translations of Erasmus to 1700* (Oxford Bibliographical Society). Oxford, 1968. viii+40 pages.
The Publication of the English Paraphrases of Erasmus. BJRL LI (1969), 348-367.
DOLAN, JOHN P. (TR.) *The Essential Erasmus.* New York, 1964. 397 pages.
Contains 7 treatises.
HILLERBRAND, HANS J. (ED.) *Erasmus and His Age. Selected Letters of Desiderius Erasmus.* New York, 1970. xxvi+305 pages.
HIMELICK, RAYMOND (TR.) *Erasmus and the Seamless Coat of Jesus.* Lafayette, Ind., 1971. ix+222 pages.
Contains *On Restoring the Unity of the Church.* Duplicates other translations.
HUDSON, HOYT H. *Current English Translations of the Praise of the Folly. Philological Quarterly* XX (1941), 250-265.
HYMA, ALBERT. (ED.) *Erasmus and the Humanists.* New York, 1930. 109 pages.
Selections from major works and from the *Letters of Obscure Men* with an introduction on "transalpine humanism."
NICHOLS, FRANCIS M. (ED. & TR.) *The Epistles of Erasmus.* 3 vols. New York, 1962. Reprint of 1918 edition.

OLIN, JOHN C. (ED.) *Christian Humanism and the Reformation. Selected Writings. With the Life of Erasmus by Beatus Rhenanus.* New York, 1965. ix+201 pages. Paperback. Contains a number of letters and the *Paraclesis.*

PHILLIPS, MARGARET M. (ED.) *The Adages of Erasmus.* Cambridge, 1964. xvi+418 pages. Contains bibliography.

RADICE, BETTY (TR.) *Erasmus: Praise of Folly and Letter to Martin Dorp 1515.* London, 1971. pp.?

REEDIJK, C. (TR.) *The Poems of Desiderius Erasmus.* Leiden, 1956. xii+424 pages. Contains bibliography and a survey of editions and manuscripts.

ROUSCHAUSSE, JEAN. *Erasmus and Fischer: Their Correspondence 1511-1524.* Paris, 1968. pp.?

Studies in Speech and Drama, in Honor of Alexander M. Drummond. Ithaca, 1944.
HUDSON, HOYT H. (TR.) *Compendium Rhetorices by Erasmus. A Translation.* pp. 326-340.

THOMPSON, CRAIG R. *The Translations of Lucian by Erasmus and St. Thomas More.* New York, 1940. 52 pages.
Inquisitio de Fide. A Colloquy by Desiderius Erasmus Roterdamus 1524 (Yale Studies in Religion). New Haven, 1950. vi+131 pages.
Latin text and revised 1725 translation of Nathan Bailey. *The Colloquies of Erasmus.* Chicago, 1965. vol. I, xxxiv+662 pages.
A second volume is projected, to provide a commentary on the Colloquies.

THOMSON, D. F. S. (TR.) *Erasmus and Cambridge: the Cambridge Letters of Erasmus.* Intro., commentary, notes by H. C. Porter. Toronto, 1963. x+233 pages.

COLLECTED ESSAYS

COPPENS, J. (ED.) *Scrinium Erasmianum.* 2 vols. Leiden, 1969. Vol. I, x+444 pages; Vol. II, viii+738 pages.
A collection of essays celebrating the 500th anniversary of Erasmus' birth. English contributions:

PHILLIPS, MARGARET.M. *Erasmus and the Art of Writing.* I, 335-350.

PAYNE, JOHN B. *Toward the Hermeneutics of Erasmus.* II, 13-49.

MCCONICA, J. K. *Erasmus and the Grammar of Consent.* II, 77-99.

VOGEL, E. J. DE. *Erasmus and His Attitude Towards Church Dogma.* II, 101-132.

AUGUSTIJN, C. *The Ecclesiology of Erasmus.* II, 135-155.

HYMA, ALBERT. *The Contributions of Erasmus to Dynamic Christianity.* II, 157-182.

BAINTON, ROLAND H. *Erasmus and the Persecuted.* II, 197-202.

DE MOLEN, RICHARD L. (ED.) *Erasmus of Rotterdam: a Quincentennial Symposium.* New York, 1971. pp.?

DE MOLEN, RICHARD L. *Erasmus of Rotterdam in Profile.*

TRACY, JAMES D. *Erasmus the Humanist.*

SPITZ, LEWIS W. *Erasmus as Reformer.*

OLIN, JOHN C. *Erasmus and His Place in History.*

SCHOECK, RICHARD J. *The Place of Erasmus Today.*

ROPER, MARGARET M. (TR.) *Erasmus' A Devout Treatise Upon the Pater Noster.*

DOREY, T. A. (ED.) *Erasmus* (Studies in Latin Literature and Its Influence). Albuquerque, 1970. x+163 pages.

Essays by Margaret M. Phillips et al. marking the quincentenary of Erasmus' birth (1469). The emphasis is on Erasmus' importance as an interpreter of classics, as a satyrist, biblical scholar and man of letters.

BIOGRAPHY

ALLEN, PERCY S. *The Age of Erasmus. Lectures Delivered in the Universities of Oxford and London.* Oxford, 1914. 303 pages. New edition, New York, 1967.

Contains a valuable chapter on Erasmus and the Bohemian Brethren.

BAINTON, ROLAND H. *Erasmus of Christendom.* New York, 1969. xii+308 pages.

Excellent, with extensive bibliography.

BOUYER, LOUIS. *Erasmus and His Times*, tr. Francis X. Murphy. Westminster, 1959. 220 pages.

Appeared in England under the title *Erasmus and the Humanist Experiment*. London, 1959.

A Roman Catholic portrait by an eminent critic of the Reformation.

DRUMMOND, ROBERT B. *Erasmus. His Life and Character as Shown in His Correspondence and Works*. 2 vols. London, 1873.

Vol. I: 413 pages. Covers the period before Luther's Reformation.

Vol. II: 380 pages. Covers the period after 1517.

ELLIOTT-BINNS, L. E. *Erasmus the Reformer*. London, 1923. 2d ed. 1928. xxii+138 pages.

The Hulsean Cambridge Lectures of 1921-1922. A critical reassessment of Erasmus' significance.

FALUDY, GEORGE. *Erasmus*. New York, 1970. x+297 pages.

A sympathetic biography, not as valuable as Bainton's.

FROUDE, JAMES A. *Life and Letters of Erasmus. Lectures Delivered at Oxford 1893-94.* New York, 1894. 433 pages. New edition, 1971.

A biographical commentary on the letters. Still useful.

HOLLIS, CHRISTOPHER. *Erasmus* (Science and Culture series). Milwaukee, 1933. xi+323 pages.

A straight biography.

HUIZINGA, JOHAN. *Erasmus of Rotterdam*, tr. F. Hopman.

With a selection from the letters of Erasmus tr. by Barbara Flower. London, 1952. New York, 1957. 266 pages. Paperback entitled *Erasmus and the Reformation*.

Excellent.

PHILLIPS, MARGARET M. *Erasmus and the Northern Renaissance* (Teach Yourself History series). London, 1949. xxv+236 pages.

A good introduction to Erasmus.

SMITH, PRESERVED. *Erasmus. A Study of His Life, Ideals and Place in History*. London, New York, 1923. New York, 1962. xiv+479 pages.

A dated but classic biography.

ZWEIG, STEFAN. *Erasmus of Rotterdam*, tr. Eden and Cedar
Paul. New York, 1934. New York, 1956. 247 pages. Paper-
back.
Not always factual, but fascinating in its style.

MISCELLANEOUS BIOGRAPHICAL POINTS

COLA, H. N. *Erasmus and His Diseases. Journal of American
Medical Association* CXLVIII (1952), 529-531.
HYMA, ALBERT. *The Youth of Erasmus*. Ann Arbor, 1930.
xi+350 pages.
Appendix contains 7 poems by Erasmus and William Herman
of Gouda's *Book Against the Barbarians,* 1540.
KOCH, A. C. F. *The Year of Erasmus' Birth, and Other Contribu-
tions to the Chronology of His Life*, tr. E. Franco. Utrecht,
1970. 58 pages.
SOWARDS, JESSE K. *The Two Last Years of Erasmus. Studies
in the Renaissance* IX (1962), 161-186.
Erasmus in England, 1509-1514 (Wichita State University
Studies). Wichita, Kan., 1962. 20 pages.
THOMPSON, CRAIG R. *Erasmus as Internationalist and Cosmo-
politan.* ARG XLVI (1955), 167-195.

RELATION TO PREDECESSORS AND CONTEMPORARIES

BRUCE, ARCHIBALD K. *Erasmus and Holbein.* London, 1936.
x+117 pages. Includes two illustrations.
CAMPBELL, W. E. *Erasmus, Tyndale and More.* London, 1949.
xi+288 pages.
DALLMANN, WILLIAM. *Erasmus on Luther.* CTM IX 9 (1938),
660-674; 735-746.
Erasmus's Pictures of Church Conditions. CTM XI 2 (1940),
100-107; 179-188; 266-280.
HORST, IRVIN B. *Erasmus, the Anabaptists and the Problem of
Religious Unity.* Haarlem, 1967. 32 pages.
HUTTON, JAMES. *Erasmus and France: the Propaganda for
Peace. Studies in the Renaissance* VIII (1961), 103-127.
JONES, ROSEMARY D. *Erasmus and Luther* (Clarendon biog-
raphies). London, 1968. 96 pages.

MANSFIELD, BRUCE E. *Erasmus and the Mediating School.*
JRH IV 4 (1967), 302-316.
Erasmus in the Nineteenth Century. Studies in the Renais-
sance XV (1968), 193-219.
MEYER, CARL S. *Christian Humanism and the Reformation:*
Erasmus and Melanchthon. CTM XLI (1970), 637-647.
MURRAY, ROBERT H. *Erasmus and Luther. Their Attitude to*
Toleration. London, 1920. xxiii+503 pages.
Dated, but valuable on the peasants' war, church reform,
church and state.
MURRAY, W. A. *Erasmus and Paracelsus.* BHR XX (1958), 560-
564.
PETERS, ROBERT. *Erasmus and the Fathers: Their Practical*
Value. CH XXXVI 3 (1967), 254-261.
REYNOLDS, ERNEST E. *Thomas More and Erasmus.* New York,
1965. x+260 pages.
Covers Erasmus' activities in England.
SCHENCK, W. *Erasmus and Melanchthon. Heythrop Journal*
VIII (1967), 249-259.

ERASMUS' THOUGHT

ALLEN, PERCY S. *Erasmus. Lectures and Wayfaring Sketches.*
Oxford, 1934. xii+216 pages.
An assessment by a classic Erasmus scholar.
FERGUSON, W. K. *Renaissance Tendencies in the Religious Thought*
of Erasmus. JHI XV (1954), 499-508.
RICE, EUGENE F. *Erasmus and the Religious Tradition.* JHI XI
4 (1950), 387-411.
SCHENK, W. *The Erasmian Idea. The Hibbert Journal.* XLVIII
(1950), 257-265.

Biblical Interpretation
ALDRIDGE, JOHN W. *The Hermeneutic of Erasmus* (Basel Studies
of Theology). Richmond, 1966. 134 pages.
Stresses the impact of Erasmus on modern hermeneutics.
ANDERSON, MARVIN. *Erasmus the Exegete.* CTM XL (1969),
722-733.
BAINTON, ROLAND H. *The Querela Pacis of Erasmus, Classical*
and Christian Sources. ARG XLII (1951), 32-48.

The Paraphrases of Erasmus. ARG LVII (1966), 67-75.
Shows the specific characteristic of Erasmus' biblical exegesis.
JARROTT, C. A. L. *Erasmus' Biblical Humanism. Studies in the Renaissance.* XVII (1970), 119-152.
Cambridge History of the Bible. Vol. II. *West from the Fathers to the Reformation,* edited by G. W. H. Lampe. Cambridge, 1969.
BOYER, LOUIS. *Erasmus in Relation to the Medieval Biblical Tradition.* 492-505.
MEYER, CARL S. *Erasmus on the Study of Scriptures.* CTM XL (1969), 734-746.
RABIL, ALBERT, JR. *Erasmus and the New Testament: the Mind of a Christian Humanist.* San Antonio, 1972. pp.?
TARELLI, C. C. *Erasmus' Manuscripts of the Gospels.* JTS XLIV (1942), 155-162.

Church and Sacraments

HYMA, ALBERT. *Erasmus and the Sacrament of Matrimony.* ARG XLVIII (1957), 145-164.
PAYNE, JOHN B. *Erasmus: His Theology of the Sacraments.* Richmond, 1970. 341 pages.
Excellent.

Education

WOODWARD, W. H. *Desiderius Erasmus Concerning the Aim and Method of Education* (Classics in Education series). New York, 1904. xxx+244 pages. New edition, New York, 1964. With a foreword by Craig R. Thompson.
Part II contains translations from Erasmus' educational treatises, and a brief bibliography.

History

BIETENHOLZ, PETER G. *History and Biography in the Work of Erasmus of Rotterdam.* Geneva, 1966. 110 pages.
Henry S. Hughes Essays in Honour of Laurence B. Packard. New York, 1954.
GILMORE, MYRON P. *Fides et Eruditio. Erasmus and the Study of History.* 9-27.

Social and Political Questions

ADAMS, ROBERT P. *Designs by More and Erasmus for a New Social Order. Studies in Philology.* XLII (1945), 131-145.
Erasmus' Ideas of His Role as a Social Critic ca. 1480-1500. Renaissance News. XI (1958), 11-16.
The Better Part of Valor. More, Erasmus, Colet and Viret on Humanism, War and Peace, 1496-1535. Seattle, 1962. 363 pages.
Stresses the pacifist movement in the English Renaissance.

CASPARI, F. *Erasmus on the Social Functions of Christian Humanism.* JHI VIII (1947), 78-106.

SALMON, ALBERT. *Democracy and Religion in the World of Erasmus.* RR XIV (1950), 227-249.

SCRIBNER, R. W. *The Social Thought of Erasmus.* JRH VI 1 (1970), 3-26.

SOUTHGATE, W. M. *Erasmus, Christian Humanism and Political Theory.* H XL (1955), 240-254.

OTHER TOPICS

APPELT, THEDOR C. *Studies in the Contents and Sources of Erasmus' Adagia, with Particular Reference to the First Edition, 1500, and the Edition of 1526.* Chicago, 1942. iv+ 155 pages.
Lithoprint of a thesis. Contains an appendix on American editions and a bibliography.

CHRISTIAN, LYND G. *The Metamorphoses of Erasmus' Folly.* JHI XXXII (1971), 289-294.

GAVIN, AUSTIN J. and WALSH, THOMAS M. *The Praise of Folly in Context. The Commentary of Girardus Listrius. Renaissance Quarterly.* XXIV 2 (1971), 193-209.

GIESE, RACHEL. *Erasmus in Effigy.* SAQ XLIV (1945), 195-201.

KAISER, WALTER J. *Praises of Folly: Erasmus, Rabelais, Shakespeare* (Harvard Studies in Comparative Literature). Cambridge, 1963. viii+318 pages.

KRISTELLER, PAUL O. *Erasmus from an Italian Perspective. Renaissance Quarterly.* XXIII (1970), 1-14.

PHILLIPS, MARGARET M. *Erasmus and Propaganda. A Study*

of the Translations of Erasmus in English and French. Modern Language Review. XXXVII (1942), 1-17.

REDEKER, HANS. *Man Not Citizen. Erasmus in Our Time,* tr. H. Romeijn. Amsterdam, 1969. 64 pages.

SCREECH, M. A. *An Approach to Erasmus. The Heythrop Journal* XII 2 (1971), 150-163.
A review of Bainton's *Erasmus of Christendom.*

SOWARDS, JESSE K. *Erasmus and the Apologetic Textbook. A Study of the De Duplici Copia Verborum ac Rerum. Studies in Philology* LV (1958), 122-135.
Erasmus and the Making of Julius Exclusus (Wichita State University Studies). Wichita, Kan., 1964. 16 pages.

TEUTLER, T. N. *Forgiveness and Consolation in the Religious Thought of Erasmus. Studies in the Renaissance.* XII (1965), 110-133.

WILLIAM THE SILENT

HARRISON, FREDERICK. *William the Silent* (Great Hollanders II). New York, 1897. vi+260 pages; New York, 1924. x+294 pages.
Good summary.

LEHMANN, LEO H. *The Drama of William of Orange.* New York, 1937. 118 pages.
Contains English translations of Philip II's *Proscription* against William, William's *Apology* response, and several letters. Originally published in London in 1707, with a historical summary by Oscar M. Voorhees.

PFANSTIEHL, A. A. *William the Silent and His Times.* RQR, XLII, ns XVII (1895), 103-121.

PUTNAM, RUTH. *William the Silent, Prince of Orange, the Moderate Man of the Sixteenth Century.* 2 vols. 2d ed. New York, Ld., 1898.
Detailed, documented.

WEDGEWOOD, CECILY V. *William the Silent, William of Nassau, Prince of Orange, 1533-1584.* New Haven, London, 1944. 256 pages.
Excellent.

THE REFORMATION IN DENMARK

DANSTRUP, JOHN. *A History of Denmark*, tr. Verner Lindberg. Copenhagen, 1948. 195 pages. 2d ed., 1949. 190 pages.
Touches on the Reformation.

DUNKLEY, E. H. *The Reformation in Denmark*. London, 1949. 192 pages.
Useful survey, with appendices and a brief bibliography.

THE REFORMATION IN NORWAY AND SWEDEN

NORWAY

DERRY, THOMAS K. *A Short History of Norway*. London, 1957. 281 pages.
Touches on the Reformation; contains a bibliography.

GARSTEIN, O. *The Reformation in Norway. The Month*. N.S. XXI (London, 1959), 95-103.

GJERSET, KNUT. *History of the Norwegian People*. 2 vols. in one, New York, 1932.
Brief treatment of the Reformation in Norway and Iceland.

LARSEN, KAREN. *A History of Norway*. Princeton, 1968. x+591 pages. 2d ed. 1950.
Chapter 11 deals with the Reformation. Emphasizes political history.

QUAM, JOHN E. *Jørgen Erikssøn: a Study in the Norwegian Reformation, 1571-1604*. New Haven, 1968. xii+272 pages.

WILLSON, THOMAS BENJAMIN. *History of Church and State in Norway from the Tenth to the Sixteenth Century*. Westminster, 1903. xii+382 pages.
The last chapter reaches the Reformation.

SWEDEN

ANJOU, LARS ANTON. *History of the Reformation in Sweden*, translated from the Swedish by Henry M. Mason. New York, 1859. x+668 pages.

Wordsworth says that this translation is "sometimes unintelligible and sometimes misleading."

BUTLER, CLEMENT MOORE. *The Reformation in Sweden.*
New York, 1883. 259 pages.
Textbook style.

ERLING, BERNHARD. *The Confessions in the Church of Sweden.*
LQ XIII 3 (1961), 255-261.

HAMMARSTRÖM, I. *The Price Revolution of the XVIth Century,
Some Swedish Evidence. The Scandinavian Economic
History Review* V (Uppsala, 1957), 118-154.

International Congress of Historical Sciences in Stockholm,
edited by Institute for History of the Polish Academy of
Sciences. Warsaw, 1960.
LEPSKY, K. *The Union of the Crowns Between Poland and
Sweden in 1587.* 155-178.
HERBST, S. *Swedish Immigrants in Poland at the Turn of
the XVIth and XVIIth Centuries.* 205-216.

ROBERTS, MICHAEL. *The Early Vasas: a History of Sweden
1523-1611.* London, Cambridge, 1968. xiv+509 pages.
Excellent, with an extensive bibliography.

STOMBERG, ANDREW A. *A History of Sweden.* Ld., 1932. xiv+
823 pages.
A chapter on the Reformation.

WATSON, PAUL BARRON. *The Swedish Revolution under
Gustavus Vasa.* Boston, 1889. xvi+310 pages.
A chapter on the church, wide use of Swedish and Latin sources.

WORDSWORTH, JOHN. *The National Church of Sweden* (Hale
Lectures 1910). Ld., and Milwaukee, 1911. xix+459 pages.
Chapter on the Reformation. Thorough use of sources.

YELVERTON, ERIC E. (ED. & TR.) *The Mass in Sweden. Its Development from the Latin Rite from 1531-1917* (Henry
Bradshaw Society Publications). London, 1920. xv+189
pages.
Translations of Swedish originals: medieval mass, the masses
of Olavus and Laurentius Petri and the latter's Trinity Collects.
*An Archbishop of the Reformation, Laurentius Petri Nericus,
Archbishop of Uppsala, 1531-1573.* London, 1958. 153 pages.
With appendices containing translations of Petri's liturgical
writings and ecclesiastical ordinances.

Olavus Petri

BERGENDOFF, CONRAD JOHANN IMMANUEL. *Olavus Petri and the Ecclesiastical Transformation in Sweden (1521-1552); a Study of the Swedish Reformation.* New York, 1928. 264 pages.
   Competent.

FORSANDER, N. *Olavus Petri.* CCR XIII (1894), 262-270.

YELVERTON, ERIC E. (ED. & TR.) *The Manual of Olavus Petri 1529.* London, 1953. ix+136 pages.
   The *Swedish Book of Common Prayer.*

THE REFORMATION IN THE BALTIC LANDS

FORD, GORDON B. JR. (ED.) *The Lithuanian Catechism of Baltramiejus Vilentas, 1579.* Louisville, Ky., 1964. 77 pages. *The Old Lithuanian Catechism of Baltramiejus Vilentas* (1579). *A Phonological, Morphological and Syntactical Investigation.* The Hague, 1969, 1970. 347 pages.

LAANTEE, KARL. *The Beginning of the Reformation in Estonia.* CH XXII 4 (1953), 269-278.

THE REFORMATION IN BOHEMIA AND MORAVIA

DE WIND, HENRY A. *A Sixteenth Century Description of Religious Sects in Austerlitz, Moravia.* MQR XXIX (1955), 44-53.
   An Italian description compared with two others from the same period.

HEYMANN, FREDERICK G. *The Hussite-Utraquist Church in the Fifteenth and Sixteenth Centuries.* ARG LII (1961), 1-15.
   Develops a typology, emphasizing the relation to Luther rather than the left wing.

ODLOŽILÍK, OTAKAR. *Bohemian Protestants and the Calvinistic Churches.* CH VIII (1939), 342-355.

THOMSON, HARRISON S. *Luther and Bohemia.* ARG XLIV (1953), 160-180.
Shows the influence of the Bohemian Brethren on Luther.

UNITY OF THE CZECH BRETHREN (UNITAS FRATRUM)

BROCK, PETER. *The Political and Social Doctrines of the Unity of the Czech Brethren in the Fifteenth and Sixteenth Centuries* (Slavistic Printings and Reprintings). 'S-Gravenhage, 1957. 302 pages.
Comprehensive and well researched; includes a bibliography.
FOUSEK, MARIANKA S. *The Perfectionism of the Early Unitas Fratrum.* CH XXX 4 (1961), 396-413.
Spiritual Direction and Discipline: a Key to the Flowering and Decay of the 16th Century Unitas Fratrum. ARG LXII (1972), 207-224.
HEYMANN, FREDERICK. *John Rokycana—Church Reformer Between Hus and Luther.* CH XXVIII 3 (1959), 240-280.
ODLOŽILÍK, OTAKAR. *Two Reformation Leaders of the Unitas Fratrum.* CH IX 3 (1940), 253-263.
On Peter Chelcický and John Augusta.
SPINKA, MATTHEW. *Peter Chelcický, Spiritual Father of the UNITAS FRATRUM.* CH XII 4 (1943), 271-291.
STRUPL, MILOS. *The Confessional Theology of the Unitas Fratrum.* CH XXXIII 3 (1964), 279-293.

THE REFORMATION IN HUNGARY AND POLAND

HUNGARY

History of the Protestant Church in Hungary, from the Beginning of the Reformation to 1850 with Special Reference to Transylvania, tr. J. Craig ... with an introduction by J. H. Merle d'Aubigné. Boston, 1854. xxix+559 pages.

REVESZ, IMRE. *History of the Hungarian Reformed Church.* (Hungarica Americana). tr. George A. Knight. Washington, 1956. 163 pages.

TOTH, WILLIAM. *Highlights of the Hungarian Reformation.* CH IX 2 (1940), 141-156.
Trinitarianism and Antitrinitarianism in the Hungarian Reformation. CH XIII 4 (1944), 255-267.
Stephan Kis of Szeged: Hungarian Reformer. ARG XLIV (1953), 86-102.
Lists his literary works.

POLAND

BONET-MAURY, GASTON. *John à Lasko and the Reformation in Poland 1499-1560.* AJT IV (1900), 314-327.

The Cambridge History of Poland, edited by W. F. Redaway *et al.* 2 vols. Cambridge, 1941-.
Vol. I (1950), chapter 14, covers the Reformation in Poland.

DALTON, HERMANN. *John à Lasco,* tr. Maurice J. Evans. Ld., 1886. viii+382 pages.

FOX, PAUL. *The Reformation in Poland, Some Social and Economic Aspects.* Baltimore, 1924. 153 pages.
New edition (Johns Hopkins University Studies in Historical and Political Science series). New York, 1971.

GERHART, E. V. *The Reformer, John de Lasky.* MR IX (1857), 446-466.

KRASINSKI, VALÉRIAN. *Historical Sketch of the Rise, Progress and Decline of the Reformation in Poland.* 2 vols. Ld., 1838-40.
Appears to be solid work.

KROPF, LEWIS.L. *John à Lasco's Church Preferments,* EHR XI (1896), 103-112.

PELIKAN, JAROSLAV. *The Consensus of Sandomierz: a Chapter from the Polish Reformation.* CTM XVIII 11 (1947), 825-837.